Mission Yu

Mission Yugoslavia

*The OSS and the Chetnik and
Partisan Resistance Movements,
1943–1945*

BLAŽ TORKAR

Foreword by BOŽO REPE

McFarland & Company, Inc., Publishers
Jefferson, North Carolina

LIBRARY OF CONGRESS CATALOGUING-IN-PUBLICATION DATA

Names: Torkar, Blaž, 1981– author. |
Repe, Božo, writer of foreword.
Title: Mission Yugoslavia : the OSS and the
Chetnik partisan resistance movements,
1943-1945 / Blaž Torka ; foreword by Božo Repe.
Other titles: OSS and the Chetnik partisan
resistance movements, 1943-1945
Description: Jefferson, North Carolina :
McFarland & Company, Inc., Publishers, 2020 |
Includes bibliographical references and index.
Identifiers: LCCN 2020020595 | ISBN 9781476682396
(paperback : acid free paper) ∞
ISBN 9781476640631 (ebook)
Subjects: LCSH: World War, 1939-1945—
Underground movements—Yugoslavia. |
World War, 1939-1945—Secret service—United States. |
United States. Office of Strategic Services—History. |
Yugoslavia—History—Axis occupation, 1941-1945. |
World War, 1939-1945—Social aspects—Yugoslavia.
Classification: LCC D802.Y8 T63 2020 | DDC 940.53/497—dc23
LC record available at https://lccn.loc.gov/2020020595

BRITISH LIBRARY CATALOGUING DATA ARE AVAILABLE

ISBN (print) 978-1-4766-8239-6
ISBN (ebook) 978-1-4766-4063-1

Front cover images: Partisan doctor helping wounded
Captain James Goodwin, photo © John Phillips 1981, 1984,
Obalne galerije Piran/Gallerie costiere Pirano;
Allied aircraft dropping military aid for the Partisans
(photograph National Museum of Contemporary History)

Printed in the United States of America

*McFarland & Company, Inc., Publishers
Box 611, Jefferson, North Carolina 28640
www.mcfarlandpub.com*

Table of Contents

Table of Contents

Foreword
by Božo Repe

This book presents the operations of the American intelligence agency the Office of Strategic Services in Yugoslavia, its structure, the changes it underwent during the war, and its activities, ranging from training agents to field operations. It places the intelligence aspect within the broader context of American policy toward Yugoslavia during the Second World War. This policy shifted from supporting the Chetniks, who were initially acknowledged as the only resistance movement, to gradual predominant support for the Yugoslav Partisans. OSS operations in Yugoslavia were key to shaping American policy toward the developments in this region (even though they were not the only source of information; intelligence was also available from other Allied missions and the activities of Slovenian immigrants in the United States) because OSS provided the United States government with the most relevant information for making decisions regarding relations with Yugoslavia.

The book presents in detail the operation of OSS bases in North Africa and (after the successful invasion of Italy) in southern Italy, from which agents and strategically important aid were sent to Yugoslavia. It discusses various segments of OSS operations, followed by an analytical overview of OSS attitude toward Yugoslav resistance movements (Chetniks and Partisans), and the postwar Yugoslav borders. The author outlines the main characteristics of missions in Yugoslavia and describes in detail the composition and activities of OSS missions in Slovenia, from the Littoral region through central Slovenia to Styria. In addition, he discusses OSS's intent to expand its operations from Yugoslavia to Austria in order to establish separate intelligence operations there that would not be directly connected with the Slovenian resistance movement. Because of this as well as other reasons (e.g., mistrust of American policy), the Yugoslav

Foreword by Božo Repe

Department of National Security kept close watch on OSS agents. Within this context, the book raises an interesting research question that calls for further examination: what view did OSS and the United States in general take on the issue of the Yugoslav postwar borders?

The author in the end concludes that the Partisan authorities and military commanders cooperated well with OSS agents and that they deemed their activity important within the context of the alliance against the Axis powers. However, at the same time they tried to limit them to the units they operated in or to Partisan-controlled territory. They were especially mistrustful of their attempts at operating independently in Austria. This assessment also proves accurate when taking into account the broader international situation and the Allied policy toward Yugoslavia, whereby the unreliability of the intelligence sources should also be considered.

Blaž Torkar's book provides the most detailed overview of OSS operations in Yugoslavia to date. It is based on data obtained from American archives (i.e., the National Archives and Records Administration in Washington) and British archives (i.e., the National Archives in London), as well as on Slovenian material held by the Archives of the Republic of Slovenia in Ljubljana. Some of the material was obtained from collections already published, such as United States foreign policy documents (*Foreign Relations of the United States*). In addition, the book also takes into account relevant older literature (especially contributions by Dušan Biber, who for a long time was the only one studying this issue) and relevant Yugoslav and international literature.

By using primary archival sources, as well as some oral sources that could still be collected, and published literature, Torkar sought to present this somewhat mysterious issue as comprehensively as possible. These efforts have resulted in a book with a solid expert and research foundation, and that reads well at the same time, and so it will not only attract attention among the expert community but will also appeal to the general public.

Božo Repe

Božo Repe is a full professor of contemporary history at the Faculty of Arts in Ljubljana. His research areas include contemporary Slovene, Southern Slavic and Central European history.

Preface

The Second World War started in Yugoslavia with the attack by the Axis powers on April 6, 1941. Patriots in the annexed and divided territory decided to resist the Axis forces, who viewed the subsequent conflict in terms of a guerrilla war against bands of nationalists, communists, or simply outlaw brigands. The Yugoslav Army in Fatherland (the Chetniks) led by General Dragoljub "Draža" Mihailović and the communist Partisans led by Josip Broz (nom de guerre Tito) saw this war as a civil war between themselves and a guerrilla war against the Axis forces. After the Axis powers took control of Yugoslavia, the first news of the resistance movements in Yugoslavia favored the Chetniks because there was a lack of information about the other movement, the Partisans, or such information was tailored and suppressed by the Yugoslav government in exile. Gradually more precise information about the resistance movements was gathered as the number of various channels for information from the Yugoslavia increased.

The Anglo-American Allies were initially convinced that the true resistance in Yugoslavia was the Chetniks. Therefore they sent missions and agents to the Chetniks in order to verify the true nature of the resistance. Soon they realized that it was the Partisans that were organizing military activities against the Axis forces and that the Chetniks were quite passive in the military sense. The liberation movement launched in Yugoslavia in July 1941 by the Communist Party under Tito's leadership was explicitly oriented toward immediate struggle against the Axis forces, which gave it a special place and role in the European resistance.

Thus the British and the Americans obtained a clear picture of the goals and actual activities of both resistance movements. Initially, the Anglo-American Allies supported the Chetniks, later both movements, and after the Teheran Conference, held from November 28 to December 1, 1943, only the Partisans. The Anglo-American Allies supported the Partisans less for political reasons than for clear military ones. It was a case of pragmatism because especially the British and the Americans disagreed with or even opposed the Partisans, but nevertheless saw them as valuable military allies. After spending more than a year in Yugoslav territory, the Allies realized that it was the Partisans carrying out the majority of the campaign in the struggle against the Axis units; therefore they decided to call on them in the common fight. Until then the Partisans had fought alone because none of the Allies, not even the Soviet Union, provided them with any material assistance or recognized them as combatting the common enemy. Only after direct connections were established through missions, which had various purposes or tasks, did joint military operations of the Partisans and the Allies begin in Yugoslav territory.

This book concentrates on the wartime activities of the American intelligence agency known as the Office of Strategic Services (OSS) and its military missions to Axis-controlled Yugoslavia during the Second World War. It presents the American policy toward Yugoslavia at the beginning of the Second World War and plans for sending aid and agents to Axis-controlled Yugoslavia. The book presents how OSS established the first bases for training agents in North Africa and in the Mediterranean, and for the first time catalogues all OSS missions with the Chetniks and Partisans in Yugoslavia to date. It specially analyzes reports of OSS missions and their field operations in relation to the Chetnik and Partisan leadership. In addition, it describes OSS views on Yugoslav border claims against Italy and Austria, supervision and suspicions of OSS missions by the Yugoslav Department of National Security (OZNA), the OSS view of Slovenia in postwar Yugoslavia, and the role of Yugoslavs cooperating with OSS, with the main emphasis on the operation of Slovenians in OSS.

Although Yugoslavia was within the British and Soviet spheres of influence, no independent OSS missions were active in Yugoslav territory until mid–1944. OSS had prepared a plan for dispatching aid and its first missions to the Chetniks and Partisans as early as 1942. OSS also expanded its operations to include northern Africa and southern Italy, where it established military bases with the aid of the British. OSS formed a Yugoslav Section, which operated at these bases; its main objective was to train agents and send them to Yugoslavia. In addition, at Bari OSS established an effective system of dispatching aid to the Yugoslav Partisans on the Dalmatian islands and developed a system of operational groups that performed acts of sabotage on the Dalmatian islands. OSS also developed a propaganda activity plan for Yugoslavia and a proposal for destroying the Yugoslav railway network—which, however, was never carried out in practice. After the Teheran Conference and the Allies' decision to support Tito's National Liberation Movement in Yugoslavia, the head of OSS, General William J. Donovan, was prepared to follow this decision and increase the quantity of aid sent to Tito. However, he was not prepared to call off all of his liaison officers stationed with Draža Mihailović because they were an excellent source of intelligence and helped evacuate American airmen. In this way, the United States developed a different policy toward Yugoslavia than the British, which, after the Tito–Šubašić Agreement in June 1944 and the dispatch of the Ranger mission in August 1944 to the Chetniks, only further aggravated the already tense relations between the Allies and made it more difficult to supervise the Anglo-American missions in Yugoslavia. OSS became actively involved in addressing the issue of postwar Yugoslavia and its borders, and it produced a number of intelligence analyses and reports concerning the military and political situation in Yugoslavia.

The book focuses specifically on OSS missions that were sent to the Slovenian Partisans operating in the northern part of Yugoslavia (i.e., Slovenia). This region was strategically the most important at the end of the war because of Yugoslav border issues with Italy and Austria, as well as for providing escape routes to German and quisling units leaving the Balkans through Slovenian territory to enter Italy and Austria. At the beginning, all Anglo-American missions at Partisan headquarters operated under joint British command; specifically, the command of the joint Anglo-American officer at the Tito's Supreme Headquarters of the Yugoslav National Liberation Army, British Brigadier Fitzroy Maclean. In addition, joint Anglo-American missions had been under his command until October 1944, when they were finally divided into separate British and American missions. It is only from that point onward that one can speak of independent American missions operating separately from the British. OSS missions played an important role because it was through them that the United States and other Allies received important information about the military power and deployment of the Axis powers, the Partisan resistance movement, and weather conditions in the Balkans. The Anglo-American Allies sent significant amounts of material and strategic aid to the Yugoslav Partisan movement through the communications maintained by OSS.

In addition, OSS missions for infiltration into Austria are also very important. These had no intention of operating among the Partisans.

Preface

Their goal was to penetrate Austria with the aid of the Partisans and stimulate the Austrian resistance movements inside the Third Reich. Some OSS missions that had been dispatched to the Italian Partisans also came in contact with the Yugoslav Partisans when these assisted in their evacuation. The Partisans did not allow the American and British members of these missions to carry out any independent actions to gather intelligence or to interrogate prisoners, deserters, and other persons that had come from areas held by the Germans.

OSS analysts examined every intelligence report sent from Yugoslavia and tried to assess the authenticity of its content. It was most often proven in practice that all OSS liaison officers favored and supported the movement they were involved in; some officers preserved a certain degree of criticism, whereas others acted under the influence of the movement. One must not forget that they also wrote a considerable number of critiques concerning the Chetnik movement and Partisan National Liberation Movement. OSS officers were especially critical of the Partisan movement at the end of the war and after it, when they operated in the areas under Allied administration as members of OSS or diplomatic personnel. However, the Allied liaison officers' intelligence reports were not key to the Allies' decision to support the Partisan National Liberation Movement in Yugoslavia. The key role in this regard was played by the German reports from the Balkans that the British intercepted using the Ultra decoding system.

The Yugoslav-born OSS agents entered OSS voluntarily, and their only wish was the liberation of their homeland. OSS recruited Yugoslavs into its ranks based on prior consent by the Yugoslav government in exile and, later on, the Partisan authorities. After OSS selected and trained Yugoslavs to become their agents, they were normally sent to Yugoslav resistance movements; that is, Partisan and Chetnik movements. Some of the Yugoslav-born agents who joined the Partisans and worked for the British or American intelligence services suffered a tragic fate after the war as a result of distrust and intrigues of the Yugoslav Communist Party and the Yugoslav intelligence services.

The fundamental archival sources dealing with OSS and its operations in Yugoslavia during the Second World War are housed in the United States National Archives and Records Administration (NARA). The archives have units across the entire country, but the majority of archival sources on OSS are located at NARA II in College Park, Maryland. The records about Yugoslavia during the war are kept in numerous collections, and so this book will only list the collections concerning the relevant research topic. Archival sources collected under Record Group 226 (RG 226) are especially abundant. A large part of the archival sources are in the form of written documents, and some of them have been preserved on microfilm and microfiche. Donovan's estate (Washington Director's Office), stored in the collections marked M1642, is particularly generous, consisting of 136 microfilm reels, which total over ten thousand images. RG 266 is one of the many collections concerning wartime events in Yugoslavia. To a lesser extent, the book references documents of the State Department, collected under RG 59, and in RG 331, which comprise documents of the Allied Force Headquarters (AFHQ).

The book also uses British archival sources connected with relations between the British Special Operations Executive (SOE) and OSS regarding British policy toward Yugoslavia. These are sources of Special Operations Executive (HS), the British Foreign Office (FO), and the British War Cabinet (CAB), and the sources Prime Minister's Office (PREM) and the British War Office (WO), which are held in the National Archives (TNA) in London.

Several documents relating to the operations of Allied missions among the Partisans in Yugoslavia and Slovenia comprise the archival sources housed in the Archives of the Republic of Slovenia (AS); namely discrete units II and III. In discrete unit III, I examined documents of the Yugoslav Department of National Security (OZNA) in the collection AS 1931, which concerns an American and British mission at the Slovenian Partisan headquarters, the Fourth Operational Zone, and the Ninth Corps. In discrete unit II, I examined the collection of the Slovenian Partisan headquarters AS 1851. I also found some sources in the collection on the Ninth Corps, marked AS 1848, and the Fourth Operational Zone, marked AS 1859.

Some historical reconstructions and studies on OSS operations during the Second World War have proven useful, but mostly they merely touch upon OSS activities in Yugoslavia. The number of books published about OSS kept growing from one year to the next after the Second World War, especially during the 1970s and 1980s, when the first OSS archival documents were opened. The production of books dealing with OSS doubled in the 1970s compared to the production in the 1960s. The majority of the literature published on OSS is concerned with areas that were of great strategic importance to the United States. Yugoslavia was not one of them during the Second World War, and this is why until now there has been no book about the role of OSS in Yugoslavia. One of the most prominent authors examining OSS activities in Yugoslav territory is Kirk Ford, Jr.,[1] who wrote a book in 1992, in which his findings challenge the view of Mihailović as collaborator and Tito as liberator. OSS activity in Yugoslavia is also a topic of a 1976 book by Anthony Cave Brown,[2] the author of numerous other books, of which the biography and political experience of General William J. Donovan, published in 1982, is the best known. OSS operations in Yugoslav territory are also mentioned in Richard Harris Smith's[3] book on OSS, published in 1972 and reprinted several times, and Bradley F. Smith's[4] book from 1983. The latter deals with OSS operations in Yugoslav territory only cursorily, despite the fact that it remains one of the most comprehensive historical syntheses regarding the American intelligence agency during the Second World War. It is important to mention publications by Peter Pirker,[5] which examine the activities of Anglo-American intelligence services in Austria and the collaboration between the Austrians and Allied intelligence services, as well as the activities of OSS agents in Yugoslav territory. A book by Jaj Jakub[6] is also significant; the author touches on the origins of the Anglo-American "special relationship" in human intelligence collection and special operations.

This topic is also the subject of a book by Patrick K. O'Donnell,[7] published in 2004, for which he made use of oral testimonies and supplemented them with archival sources. Many new findings on the operation of OSS and its role in Yugoslavia are featured in a 1992 collection of articles edited by George C. Chalou, which is a product of work by several authors.[8] There are two more books that should not be overlooked: these were written by OSS veterans, Franklin Lindsay,[9] Robert McDowell,[10] Albert Seitz,[11] and Erasmus H. Kloman,[12] who supplemented their memoirs with analyses of archival sources. In his book, originally published in 1993 and translated into Slovenian in 1998, Franklin Lindsay describes his work as the head of the Anglo-American mission in the Fourth Operational Zone in Styria, Croatian Headquarters, and Supreme Headquarters of the National Liberation Army.

Only a few authors from the former Yugoslavia have published articles on OSS operations in Yugoslavia during the Second World War. A comprehensive in-depth study on OSS activities in Yugoslavia has not yet been written; however, several books, articles, and memoirs have been published that refer to the activities of individual missions with the Chetniks and the Partisans, and the role of Yugoslav emigrants in OSS. I will mention just a few of these, which I also reference and cite in my volume. The first are articles written by Dušan Biber, who touches upon OSS in his numerous publications on Allied views of the Second World War in Yugoslavia. Among these, I would like to highlight Biber's articles about Lieutenant Colonel Robert McDowell's mission at Mihailović's headquarters, Allied and Soviet missions, and intelligence services in the Partisan National Liberation Movement, the penetration of OSS missions into Austria, and assessments and reports of OSS liaison officers.

Another significant publication is a book by Miodrag Pešić[13] about an important OSS mission with the Chetniks, Operation Halyard, which saved the lives of many American airmen. Articles by Gorazd Bajc are also noteworthy. They deal with OSS operations in Yugoslav territory and Friuli-Venezia Giulia, particularly in the light of Yugoslav–Italian demarcation and the collaboration of some Slovenian liberal politicians with OSS intelligence. In addition to Biber and Bajc, I need to mention Vojislav Pavlović,[14] whose book concerns American–Yugoslav relations during the Second World War, and Bogo Gorjan, whose volume describes the main OSS missions and groups tasked with infiltrating Austria.

This book provides the most in-depth story of OSS operations on Yugoslav soil thus far. It is based on American, British archival sources and archival sources of former Yugoslav countries, especially on the previously unpublished documents of the Yugoslav Department of National Security, which gives the book even greater value. I express my appreciation for assistance in publishing this volume to McFarland & Company, Inc., Publishers, Gorazd Bajc, Božo Repe, Bojan Dimitrijević, Russell G. Rodgers, Donald F. Reindl, Simona Lapanja, Peter Pirker, Roderick Bailey, Obalne galerije Piran/Gallerie costiere Pirano, National Museum of Contemporary History from Ljubljana, and especially my family, Eva, Drejc, and Juš, who support me in all of my projects.

Blaž Torkar

1

OSS and the Beginning of the Second World War in Yugoslavia

From COI to OSS

Before the Second World War, the United States' use of covert, or shadow, warfare was limited. In the prewar years, the vital task of gathering foreign intelligence fell on the shoulders of four departments within the federal government: the State Department, the Office of Naval Intelligence (ONI), the War Department's Military Intelligence Division (MID), better known as G-2, and the Federal Bureau of Investigation (FBI). Although the FBI had no mandate to gather foreign intelligence until 1940, it indirectly gathered intelligence in conjunction with the investigation of crimes in the United States. In 1940, the bureau set up a Special Intelligence Service to conduct operations in Latin America.

Under pressure from the British to improve intelligence matters, President Franklin D. Roosevelt took a decisive action. On July 11, 1941, the president ordered the establishment of a new White House agency, the Office of the Coordinator of Information (COI), effectively creating America's first peacetime national intelligence agency. COI received a powerful mandate: the authority to collect and analyze all information that might bear upon national security, to correlate such information, and to make such information available to the president and to such government departments and officials that the president might determine.

The president could not have chosen a better qualified man to lead COI: the war hero, former assistant U.S. attorney general, Wall Street lawyer, and executive William J. Donovan. In Washington, Donovan's fledgling COI came under assault from the government agencies responsible for gathering intelligence, who viewed him as an intruder in their territory. The very agencies COI was attempting to coordinate—the FBI, the ONI, G-2, and the State Department—formed a loose anti–COI alliance that would continue throughout the war. The four departments took steps to curb the new agency's scope and influence. COI nevertheless expanded into research, analysis, and propaganda, collaborating closely with the British intelligence agencies. Special operations and secret intelligence lagged behind other divisions because spies and saboteurs took so long to train.

The date December 7, 1941, marked the United States' entry into the Second World War. COI, still in its infancy and mostly focused on the threat of Nazi Germany, did not play a role in one of America's worst intelligence failures of the war. Hawaii lay within the territory of ONI and G-2, and it was they that failed to detect the attack on Pearl Harbor. The advent of the war transformed COI's relationship with the newly formed Joint Chiefs of Staff, who largely sided with their own intelligence organizations and distrusted Donovan. In order to solve this perception problem and gain access to military support and greater resources, Donovan proposed bringing COI under the control of the Joint Chiefs of Staff.

On June 13, 1942, the president officially endorsed the idea. COI's name was changed to OSS, and the organization was placed under the authority of the Joint Chiefs of Staff. Part of the change also included the loss of COI's Foreign Information Service (FIS). FIS conducted America's "white propaganda" campaign, which consisted of truthful information publicly acknowledged to be of American origin. Nearly half of COI's Research and Analysis staff was placed in a separate, newly created organization, the Office of War Information (OWI).

While under the tutelage of the British, OSS developed many of its own independent concepts practically overnight, emphasizing an integrated "combined arms" concept of shadow-war techniques. Donovan's vision held that "persuasion, penetration and intimidation ... are the modern counterparts of sapping and mining in the siege warfare of former days." Propaganda represented the "arrow of initial penetration," followed by espionage. Sabotage and guerrilla operations would then soften up an area before conventional forces invaded. The integration of all shadow-war techniques was a groundbreaking approach to covert warfare. The British intelligence agencies were not integrated, but operated in separate divisions. A central element of the shadow war was special operations, a new concept that OSS would develop during the war. At the end of March

1941, Donovan urged the president to permit him to develop special operations forces, which would take the war to the Germans in an unexpected, irregular way.

Major departments and branches of OSS under Donovan included the Maritime Units (MU) for transporting agents, supplies to resistance groups, naval sabotage, and reconnaissance; Operational Groups (OG) for sabotage and guerrilla warfare, made up of highly trained foreign-language-speaking commando teams; Morale Operations (MO) for subversive, black propaganda, such as operating fake German radio stations from the United Kingdom, ostensibly manned by anti–Nazi groups; Research and Analysis (R&A) for intelligence analysis; Secret Intelligence (SI) for intelligence collection and espionage; Special Operations (SO) for sabotage, subversion, fifth-column movements, and guerrilla warfare; Counter Intelligence (X-2) for counterespionage; and Research and Development (R&D) for weapons and equipment. There were also other branches such as the Foreign Nationalities Branch (FNB), Communications Branch, Schools and Training (S&T), Special Funds, Censorship, and Documentation and Special.[1]

General Donovan in Yugoslavia

At the end of 1940, Donovan was sent to the United Kingdom, the eastern and western Mediterranean, and the Middle East as a special envoy of President Roosevelt. During his journey from January 23 to January 25, 1941, he also visited Yugoslavia. His task was to establish what influence the United Kingdom had in the Mediterranean, and to find out for himself about the new British subversive and counterintelligence agencies set up by the United Kingdom in 1940.[2] The aim of Prime Minister Winston Churchill was to unite Turkey, Yugoslavia, Greece, and Bulgaria into a Balkan union. Its purpose would be to serve as an obstacle to Nazi advances toward the Middle East, backed by American financial and material aid. Donovan expressed American support of fighting the Axis powers to the Yugoslav political and military leadership. His focus was particularly on the British influence in Yugoslavia and how the United States could help. As a representative of the American administration, he wanted the Balkan countries to jointly resist the pressure of the Third Reich; however, this was impossible without the active political and military assistance of the Allies.[3]

1. The Beginning of the Second World War in Yugoslavia

In one of his conversations with the prime minister of Yugoslavia, Dragiša Cvetković, Donovan said that the United States did not want to enter the war, but stressed that it would do everything in its power to prevent the British from losing it. Cvetković assured him that German units would not enter Yugoslav territory; however, he was quite reserved regarding the idea of a Balkan union, particularly because of Bulgaria, which was a rather unreliable partner. In addition, Prince Paul of Yugoslavia tried to make Donovan understand that a Balkan union was not a realistic option, and that Yugoslavia could attack Bulgaria, should it allow German units to cross its territory. The Yugoslav military leadership, however, was less convinced of Yugoslavia's ability to resist German pressure. In his conversations with the military leadership, Donovan received the impression that Yugoslavia would not be able to defend itself should German forces invade Yugoslav territory. The Commander of the Royal Yugoslav Air Force, General Dušan Simović, was the only one that believed Yugoslavia could resist the German attackers.[4]

Despite the concerns of the Yugoslav politicians, Donovan estimated that a coordinated American policy and military support could facilitate the creation of a Balkan union, serving as a defense against the German advance toward the southeast. Later, Donovan's presence in Yugoslavia caused accusations to be made by the American isolationist faction, accusing him of having cooperated in organizing the coup d'état in Yugoslavia in March 1941. According to historian Dušan Biber, the Soviet intelligence service was also allegedly involved in the coup d'état. Wilhelm Höttl, head of the Security Service (*Sicherheitsdienst*) in southeast Europe, claimed in his memoirs that before the war General Simović had secretly met with the lawyer Djordje Radin in the Planica Valley several times, and had maintained contacts with Donovan's confidants through him. General Simović denied that Radin had offered political and financial assistance to carry out the coup d'état. Donovan's alleged involvement in terms of intelligence in the coup d'état has never been sufficiently examined, and the alleged involvement of the Soviet intelligence service even less so.[5]

After his departure from Yugoslavia and the other Balkan countries, Donovan drafted a report for President Roosevelt, establishing that Great Britain should preserve and expand its influence and control in the Mediterranean countries, and prevent Germany from gaining access to the Aegean area. The British could maintain control in the Mediterranean with the help of military bases in North Africa. From there, they would provide assistance to the Mediterranean countries via Gibraltar and the Suez

Canal. According to his findings in the report, the military commanders of the Balkan countries firmly believed that Germany would also attack the Balkans, which did in fact happen in Yugoslavia and Greece. Germany's main objective was to prevent any attempt on the British side to maintain their influence in the Balkans. Donovan believed that the Balkans represented the last Allied deployment operational base where the Germans could be defeated. Donovan endeavored to back up his ideas by considering it important to persuade Yugoslavia, Greece, Turkey, and Bulgaria not to sign the Tripartite Pact, which in fact did not happen.[6] Despite Donovan's unsuccessful visit to Yugoslavia, he was praised by Churchill in his correspondence with President Roosevelt, saying that he had done a great job on his tour of the Balkans and the Middle East; moreover, he had delivered encouraging words for everyone he had been in contact with.[7]

The American Ambassador to Yugoslavia, Arthur Bliss Lane, believed that Donovan, through his presence in the Balkans, provided support to British policy and gave encouragement to the entire Yugoslav political leadership, particularly the masterminds of the coup d'état. He did not act immediately on the "Balkan strategy" because he expected a quick Soviet intervention and advance in the Balkans.[8]

The United States, the Coup d'État, and the April Occupation of Yugoslavia

In its initial phases, American policy toward the Kingdom of Yugoslavia was predominantly a continuation of the relationship that the United States had had with the Kingdom of Serbia. The American authorities did not consider it necessary to change their policy toward Yugoslavia because they had little interest in it. However, Yugoslavia played an important role for a short period of time during the presidency of Woodrow Wilson, specifically in relation to the secret London Memorandum. President Wilson opposed secret treaties, and he therefore promoted participation in the League of Nations and advocated the right to the self-determination of peoples. When he left international politics, postwar American politics became more passive; that is, the role of American diplomatic representatives was to listen and to report to Washington without interfering in other countries' internal affairs.[9]

In the United States, the Yugoslav government was represented by Konstantin Fotić, who had been the Yugoslav ambassador to the United States since 1935. Prior to the attack on Yugoslavia by the Axis powers, Fotić had submitted requests to the State Department for purchasing

1. The Beginning of the Second World War in Yugoslavia

weapons. At the end of 1940 and the beginning of 1941, almost all of Yugoslavia's neighbors signed the Tripartite Pact, and so Fotić was summoned to the State Department several times for talks because American politicians were concerned about the developments in the Balkans. On March 10, 1941, Churchill wrote to Roosevelt, saying that Yugoslavia still had the chance to withdraw from the influence of the Axis powers exerting pressure on it. He requested that the American ambassadors to Turkey, the Soviet Union, and Yugoslavia also put pressure on the Yugoslav government, which should take advantage of the opportunity and its current situation. On March 21, 1941, Arthur Bliss Lane let the Yugoslav government know that the United States was willing to offer Yugoslavia all possible assistance in accordance with the Lend-Lease Act, enabling Yugoslavia to receive American aid.[10] Lane sent a telegram to Prince Regent Paul of Yugoslavia, expressing his belief that the resistance of those nations that would be subject to attack would certainly contribute to both defense and the outcome of the war, which was in their vital interest. He believed that every nation offering resistance to either a diplomatic or a military attack by the Axis powers would enjoy great sympathy in the world. However, when the United States found out that the Yugoslav government with Prince Regent Paul intended to sign the Tripartite Pact, it informed the Yugoslav government via Fotić that it would be forced to freeze all of Yugoslavia's assets in the United States and change its policy toward Yugoslavia. Immediately after the coup d'état in Yugoslavia, which was a direct result of signing the Tripartite Pact, the United States informed the new Yugoslav government that the Lend-Lease Act was at Yugoslavia's disposal. Moreover, the Anglo-American Allies, particularly the British, were said to be making promises about changing the Yugoslav borders; however, these promises were not precise, and quite often they were merely rumors and prewar trafficking in territory.[11]

Perhaps no country has ever dispersed its forces as irrationally as the Yugoslavs did in April 1941, seeking to defend one of the longest land frontiers in Europe with old rifles and mule-borne mountain artillery against Panzer divisions and two thousand modern aircraft. The Yugoslav air force, which had masterminded the coup on March 27, was overwhelmed in the opening hours of the Axis attack on April 6. The German army's plan, which the Italian Second and Hungarian Third Armies were integrated with, nullified the Yugoslav strategy from the start. It turned on throwing armored columns against the mountain ranges that the Yugoslavs had counted on to protect their country's heartland; the columns would then turn to converge and so envelop the Yugoslav formations they had out-flanked. It proved brilliantly successful. As the official Yugoslav history of the war subsequently conceded, three initial attacks determined the fate of the Royal Yugoslav army, on April 6 in Macedonia, April 8 in Serbia, and April 10 in Croatia. On all three occasions, the Axis powers breached the frontier defenses, pushed deep into the interior, and dislodged the Yugoslav defenses from their positions. After the frontier defenses were broken through, the Yugoslav troops were soon outmaneuvered, broken up, and surrounded, without contact with each other, without supplies, and without leadership. What official history seeks to conceal is the active responsibility of much of the Yugoslav leadership for this debacle. Yugoslavia was in no sense a nationally unified state. It had inherited all of the tensions between the ethnic South Slavs within the Habsburg Monarchy before 1914 and sought to check them merely by imposing Serb dominance over other Yugoslav nations. The invasion of April 6 was seized upon by the Croat nationalists as an opportunity for secession: on April 10 the Croatian Ustasha, a group of extreme right-wing nationalists, proclaimed an independent state and accepted Axis tutelage.[12]

Shortly after the Axis invasion and subjugation of Yugoslavia the Allied propaganda services began to manufacture a legend, a heroic tale of a bearded and bespectacled Colonel Draža Mihailović. Chief of Staff of a Yugoslav Royal Army unit at the time his country's capitulation, he refused to surrender. Taking to the hills in the wake of the Axis victory, he formed a guerrilla army to fight the invaders. Calling themselves Chetniks,[13] Mihailović's troops pledged their loyalty and devotion to King Peter II. Shortly after the attack by the Axis forces, the Yugoslav government fled and sought British protection in emigration. The British established the first radio contact with the Yugoslav guerrillas in September 1941, and soon after King Peter II gave his official blessing to the Chetniks. Mihailović was promoted to the rank of general and appointed minister of war by the government in exile. The British began to herald the Chetniks as the first organized underground of occupied Europe, urging all patriotic Yugoslavs to join this irregular army. The American and Soviet press echoed London, and Mihailović became a symbol of the anti-Nazi resistance.[14]

Immediately after the attack on Yugoslavia, President Roosevelt sent the new Yugoslav King Peter II a letter expressing his tremendous shock regarding the unprovoked and ruthless attack on the nations of Yugoslavia. From the very beginning of the war in Yugoslavia, the first ideas of

1. The Beginning of the Second World War in Yugoslavia

changing Yugoslavia's borders and separating it into three independent states kept being introduced; Roosevelt himself often thought about it.[15]

In one of his letters to Churchill, Roosevelt expressed his doubts about the potential existence of the Yugoslav state. He wrote: "I think that you and I should bear some such possibility in mind in case the new government does not work out. Personally, I would rather have a Yugoslavia, but three separate states with separate governments in a Balkan confederation might solve many problems."[16]

The Yugoslav government in exile was also actively engaged in organizing aid to its invaded homeland. Soon after the April occupation, Fotić reported on the breakup of Yugoslavia, the recruitment of Yugoslav volunteers in the United States and Canada, the collection of aid to be sent to Yugoslavia in order to prevent crimes there, and the visit by the King Peter II to the United States. He also widely reported on the leftist propaganda against Draža Mihailović, and Partisan gatherings in Bihać and Jajce in Bosnia and Herzegovina. Fotić received information from the American diplomatic representatives in Belgrade (i.e., Ambassador Arthur Bliss Lane and Consul Karl Rankin), as well as the ambassadors in Budapest, Rome, Sofia, and Berlin, American Red Cross delegates, and individuals from Yugoslavia. These individuals provided much information about the Axis administration systems, the Ustasha crimes, and the deportations of Slovenians. During the war, the Yugoslav government in exile had a number of ministers and prime ministers. General Simović was replaced by Slobodan Jovanović in January 1942, by Miloš "Miša" Trifunović in June 1943, and by Božidar Purić in August 1943. After numerous replacements and the recognition of the Partisan National Liberation Movement, the United States and the United Kingdom wanted to choose a new candidate for prime minister. At Donovan's proposal, Ivan Šubašić became prime minister on June 1, 1944. Consequently, Fotić was dismissed from his function as ambassador in Washington and was replaced by Ivan Frangeš. The new American ambassador to Yugoslavia was Richard Patterson, who succeeded Anthony J. Drexel, Lincoln MacVeagh, and Rudolph Schoenfeld. In addition to the state of affairs in their homeland, the Yugoslav government in exile was constantly burdened by conflicts between the Serbs and the Croats.[17]

Armed Partisan resistance against the Axis forces began in the summer 1941, and this soon developed into a liberation struggle with a clear political program: to ensure national liberation and bring about political changes (communist revolution). When the Partisans in Yugoslavia decided on armed resistance against the Axis forces, they could only rely on themselves in the military sense. They were convinced that resistance was the only possibility for achieving national freedom, and that combat was the only means of driving out the Axis forces. The Partisan resistance movement in Yugoslavia soon turned into an organized military and political liberation movement. All of the Partisan resistance activities were based on the conviction that the military struggle against the Axis forces was the only way of attaining freedom and restoring the divided state. In their efforts they did not even enjoy political support because the Yugoslav government in exile, which represented the Axis-held and divided Yugoslav state, did not support the Partisan resistance movement. Instead it supported its own resistance units led by Mihailović. However, starting in the fall of 1941 his units also collaborated with the Axis forces and the Serbian quisling authorities, and otherwise, in the military sense, Mihailović was more or less passive as far as attacking the Axis forces was concerned.[18]

2

OSS in North Africa and the Mediterranean

OSS–SOE Agreements and British Primacy in the Balkans

From June 16 to June 22, 1942, negotiations commenced between OSS and Special Operations Executive (SOE) representatives, who reached an agreement on June 26, 1942. The two agencies divided their areas of interest between themselves: SOE received control over India, East Africa, the Balkans, and, with the help of the Americans, the Middle East; and OSS was to control special operations in China, Manchuria, Korea, Australia, the Atlantic, and Finland. Western Europe remained under SOE control, whereas OSS could operate in Europe only under the supervision of SOE. Special rules applied to North Africa and Spanish Morocco, which were deemed to be American areas of influence. The agreement also included a provision that permitted OSS members to train in paramilitary and advanced schools, which SOE had in the United Kingdom and Canada. Yugoslavia and the Balkans fell within the British area of interest, whereas OSS was allowed to provide help in Yugoslavia.[1] Up until this point in time, OSS had not had its agents in Yugoslavia, whereas SOE had already been successful in this regard.

According to agreement, OSS intelligence officers were under British supervision and had to use British radio communications. The British retained their central role until mid–1944, when the United States sent its first independent mission to Yugoslavia. This meant that OSS no longer used British radio communications, and OSS liaison officers were no longer part of British missions. The British were constantly worried that OSS would organize its own base in the Middle East, and so they concluded an agreement with OSS in January 1943, under which all activities in the Middle East were controlled by the SOE–OSS Committee, headed by an SOE representative, Lord Glenconner. He believed that such agreements were not significant for the Americans because they could be enforced when there were enough personnel, schools, communications, and aviation.[2]

The second important agreement between OSS and SOE was concluded between Donovan and Sir Charles Hambro in London on July 26, 1943. SOE welcomed the United States' presence in the Balkans at the time. The British decided that officers of OSS missions would be included in missions to both the Chetniks and the Partisans. These missions would be under British operational control, which meant that joint Anglo-American missions were under British leadership, with OSS officers taking part in each mission. Donovan and Hambro agreed that OSS would operate in the Middle East under the auspices of SOE Cairo, and that it would use the SOE communication code. According to the agreement, OSS would provide explosives, and demolition and sabotage groups. This arrangement was in effect until 1944, when the United States sent its first independent mission to Tito's Partisans.[3]

Further meetings followed, which defined relations between SOE and OSS. In a meeting between the OSS and SOE chiefs, Donovan and Brigadier Gubbins, it was decided that all American intelligence operations would be integrated into the SOE base that was being established in southern Italy at the time. Later, this decision came to fruition.[4] In a meeting between SOE and OSS on November 6, 1943, OSS introduced an initiative to send more liaison officers to Yugoslavia, which the British approved on the condition that the officers be under their command. General Henry Maitland Wilson, Supreme Allied Commander in the Mediterranean Theater, finally decided that the British had to permit certain OSS officers to enter Yugoslavia, and that the British would not have access to the contents of OSS reports from Yugoslavia.[5]

OSS Cairo and Bari:
Creation of the Yugoslav OSS Section

The Anglo-American liberation of North Africa thus provided the opportunity for starting psychological warfare operations, including psychological and morale subversion, black propaganda, and covert operations in North Africa and southern Europe.[6] Based on an agreement between SOE and OSS from July 26, 1943, Yugoslavia was part of the Middle East Theater of Operations (METO), which was under the control of the British. According to the agreement, OSS officers would become part of SOE missions, joint missions would be sent to Tito as well as to Mihailović, and OSS and SOE would use a common code.[7]

On October 11, 1943, Dwight Eisenhower and Henry Maitland Wilson agreed to relocate the SOE[8] base from Cairo to Bari. In this way, the base of SOE was closer to the Dalmatian coast, and its relocation was a step in establishing links between SOE and OSS. Founded in March 1944, Special Operations Mediterranean (SOM) was thus directly responsible to General Wilson. It included the operations of both OSS and SOE and was thus no longer subordinate to SOE in London. Due to the need for better coordination between OSS and SOE, a joint operations headquarters was set up in Algiers in May 1944, known as Special Projects Operations Center (SPOC).[9]

The establishment of American bases in North Africa was crucial because they included the OSS Yugoslav Section, where Yugoslav members of OSS missions were trained and then sent to Yugoslavia. The establishment of the base was only possible with the help of the British, who agreed to a mission in Africa under the condition that it be controlled by SOE Middle East.[10]

In spring 1942, Donovan wanted to establish a base in the Middle East, and therefore Cairo sent a representative who was tasked with establishing a link with the British and their intelligence agencies. They laid a foundation for establishing an OSS base in the region covering the Middle East and southeastern Europe. Donovan's representative was Commodore and later Assistant and Chief of OSS / Secret Intelligence Branch in Middle East Turner McBaine, who came to Cairo on April 9, 1942, as an assistant to the U.S. naval attaché. McBaine was personally responsible for the successful recruitment of a number of OSS agents. In addition, he established the first COI office in Cairo, which specialized in OSS / Secret Intelligence and Special Operations. On June 4, 1944, he left Cairo and assumed a new position in the Far East.

The main problems of the United States in the Middle East were related to the fact that they had no contractual rights that would allow OSS to establish wireless communications in the British sphere of influence. Initially, OSS had no authorization from the Joint Chiefs of Staff, and therefore McBaine had to return to Washington. In December 1942, the

Joint Chiefs of Staff issued a directive that gave Donovan authorization to establish an OSS base in Cairo and consult with the British military authorities. The directive provided specific operations in Yugoslavia, Albania, Bulgaria, Hungary, Crete, Romania, Greece, and the Dodecanese, and the establishment of special operations and communications centers in Turkey, Iran, Iraq, Saudi Arabia, Syria, and other neutral countries. The directive also set out the beginning of counter-subversive and counter-intelligence activities in all of these areas. After its establishment, OSS Cairo began operating within the United States Army Forces Middle East (USAFIME), which was subordinate to the British command in the Middle East.

The first OSS mission in Cairo was headed by Colonel Ellery C. Huntington, together with a team consisting of Colonel Julius Amoss, Lieutenant Colonel Lada Močarski, Captain Turner McBaine, Rodney Young, and Stephen Penrose. In Cairo, they were joined by Colonel Gustav Guenther.[11] OSS and SOE in the Mediterranean were subordinate to the Combined Chiefs of Staff (CCS), which was commanded by General Wilson. OSS Middle East commander became Colonel Gustav Guenther, OSS / Special Operations Branch was led by Major Louis Huot, and McBaine became OSS Middle East deputy commander.[12]

In the first days after the establishment of the Cairo base, OSS had difficulties recruiting officers that would be suitable for leading the Yugoslav Section and also for departure to Yugoslavia. Thus, it was decided that Lanning Macfarland would be the first head of the Yugoslav Section, although he quickly left that position and became OSS chief in Istanbul. However, soon after arriving in Cairo, Macfarland established relations with Lieutenant Colonel Lada Močarski and McBaine, so that in May 1943 all three prepared a plan of departure for the first missions to Yugoslavia with the help of some of the royal Yugoslav officers that showed greater willingness to cooperate with OSS. The purpose of the OSS Yugoslav section was to train agents mostly in secret operations and send them to Yugoslavia, where, with the help of the Partisans and Chetniks, they would create an effective intelligence network against Nazism.

OSS Cairo was often dissatisfied with the American policy toward Yugoslavia, and so on July 15, 1943, OSS / Secret Intelligence wrote to McBaine about the unwillingness of the American press and the Americans to deal with the situation in Yugoslavia. It also wrote that due to the United States' disinterest in Yugoslavia it did not closely follow the events in Yugoslavia and that it also received second-hand information. Only the

2. OSS in North Africa and the Mediterranean

Soviets and the British had first-hand sources because they had liaison officers in the Partisan and the Chetnik headquarters. OSS therefore proposed to have its own liaison officers in the two resistance movements. In addition, the United States had more suitable agents for departure to Yugoslavia than the British because they spoke Serbo-Croatian and the majority of them were of Yugoslav descent.[13]

McBaine also reported to Donovan about the problems encountered by the Yugoslav OSS Section, presenting him with the plan of infiltration in Yugoslavia and informing him that the British in Cairo were greatly advantaged and that the Yugoslav OSS Section did not have enough Yugoslav-born agents that would be suitable to be sent to Yugoslavia. McBaine also reported that he lacked qualified personnel that could train Yugoslav-born agents.[14] Shortly afterward, on September 23, 1943, McBaine appointed a new head of the OSS Yugoslav Section, Major Francis F. Arnoldy.

At the same time as Arnoldy, First Lieutenant Alexander Vucinich also came to Cairo. In OSS Yugoslav Section, he assumed the role of the analyst and reporting officer. After that, First Lieutenant Francis Likar, First Lieutenant Rex Deane, and First Lieutenant George Vujnovich arrived, all recruited in the United States. Despite the manning process, Arnoldy assessed the situation in the Yugoslav Section as poor because the superiors did not have much interest in Yugoslav problems. Thus Arnoldy, in spite of all the difficulties, continued training the Yugoslav-born recruits, improving their welfare and outfitting.[15]

OSS in Cairo also soon received news that among the Italian and German prisoners-of-war there were many soldiers of Yugoslav (Slovenian and Croat) origin that would be suitable for OSS operations. Therefore, in May 1943, with the permission of the Yugoslav government in exile, Lieutenant Colonel Lada Močarski was sent to Algiers. Among the Italian and German soldiers in prisoner-of-war camps, he gathered ten Yugoslavs that were eligible for secret intelligence operations. The Yugoslav-born agents were not trained as standard secret agents or liaison officers, but as wireless operators, coders, and interpreters. They never became equal to American OSS officers because they were not trusted. With the permission of the Yugoslav government in exile, this group of ten Yugoslav-born soldiers joined OSS.

Shortly after the successful Operation Husky and the advancement of the Anglo-Americans into the Apennine Peninsula, the Yugoslav OSS Section from Cairo was transferred to Bari. Part of the Yugoslav Section and OSS training school nevertheless remained in Cairo. In Cairo, OSS still retained some staff and the Yugoslav office, the management of which was taken over by Robert P. Joyce. On January 11, 1944, Joyce was relocated to Bari, where he became chief of OSS / Secret Intelligence, and the position in Cairo was taken over by an American OSS officer with Yugoslav origin, Captain Andrej Kobal, who was lent to OSS by the G-2 United States Army intelligence unit.[16] The Yugoslav OSS Section in Cairo was still giving broad guidance concerning operations in Yugoslavia and played an important role in the recruitment of personnel, while the section in Bari had to inform Cairo about its functioning. The Training School in Cairo remained there for almost a year and was finally closed on August 30, 1944.[17]

After the advance of the Anglo-Americans into the Apennine Peninsula, in addition to the OSS base in Cairo, the establishment of an OSS base in Bari was very important for OSS operations in Yugoslavia. OSS was thus closer to the Yugoslav coast, which facilitated the organization of sending missions and aid to Yugoslavia. In September 1943, Donovan approved the plan for sending aid to Tito's Partisans. Even before the approval, the officers of OSS / Special Operations discussed that topic at the meeting in Algiers. OSS officers were aware that they would have to work under the auspices of the British, which did not bother Donovan because he had his own plans for the future of the base, envisaging its increasing autonomy and independence.[18]

Upon Donovan's order, on October 2, 1943, Major Huot and First Lieutenant Robert E.S. Thompson left Cairo and went to Algiers, where they made all the necessary arrangements for setting up a base in Bari. That is when active cooperation between OSS and the Partisans began, in terms of the organization of military aid to Partisans and also in terms of assistance in the recruitment of Yugoslav-born agents, who, as former Italian prisoners of war, were accepted into the Partisan Overseas Brigades of the National Liberation Movement and then, with the permission of the Partisan leadership, entered OSS. In Algiers, Huot and Thompson met two Partisan envoys, Sergei Makiedo and Joze Poduje, who attempted to obtain aid from the Anglo-American Allies for Partisan units in Yugoslavia. OSS offered them aid, and hence this was the start of the successful organization of aid to the Yugoslav Partisans, who sent a strong team to Bari. As regards the cooperation between OSS and the Partisans, Captain Hans Tofte, who later joined OSS base and replaced Huot, wrote: "Under the command of two OSS officers, a permanent team of one hundred Partisan port workers and armed guards was located in Bari and was actually led by a Partisan delegation, authorized for this work by Tito."[19] Huot undertook also reconnaissance missions to the Yugoslav coast to determine the locations and capacities of receiving points under Partisan control. Later Huot had lots of problems with the British because Maclean lodged a vigorous protest with OSS headquarters over Huot's unauthorized trip to Tito's headquarters, which resulted in Huot being relieved from his duties in Bari.[20]

The OSS base in Bari was established on October 15, 1943 and was actually an advance base for the United States Army Forces Middle East (USAFIME). The Yugoslav Section in Bari was based at Villa Suppa and Villa Re David, which housed the main areas for training, and part of the premises for training wireless operators was also located at Villa Pasqua.[21] Bari base was the main base for deploying missions and for evacuating staff, as well as the address point for all of the reports coming in daily from Yugoslavia. All telegrams and reports of OSS missions to the Yugoslav Partisans and Chetniks were deciphered at this base and the information was then sent to senior commands. In addition, all of the directives, questions, and requests to OSS missions in Yugoslavia were sent from there.[22] In addition, the office of the OSS Yugoslav Section was created on the island of Vis, which was in Partisan hands. It collected intelligence from the Dalmatian islands and coordinated the work of OSS missions and groups. The island of Vis was also identified as the place for the distribution of all the Allied aid.[23]

Immediately after his arrival in Bari, Arnoldy established contacts with the Partisan representatives in Bari. At first, the Partisan representatives accepted Arnoldy with reservation and mistrust because they did not understand the purpose of his mission in Bari. However, over time, the tensions subsided, and Arnoldy obtained Makiedo's permission to recruit Yugoslav prisoners of war. This was the beginning of effective cooperation between the representatives of OSS and the Partisans. Arnoldy also noticed the mistrust of the Yugoslavs toward the British and toward some Americans. The Partisans did not trust them because of their dual politics, which supported both Tito and Mihailović, whereas they did not know much about American politics. The report on the development of OSS Bari also described the efforts of OSS officers that organized ship support in Bari for the Partisan movement, and part of the support was intended for the Yugoslav Partisans.

This project, better known under the name Operation Audrey,

was quite successful but hardly a secret operation. A direct supply line was established in October 1943, and the majority of OSS officers led the organization of sending aid to the Dalmatian coast independently, even though the British formally controlled the supply lines. Immediately after the supply line was established, OSS financial support was also organized because it had no material food and weapons supplies. Over time, OSS discovered that the financial support was inappropriate because they gave money to the Partisans, who in turn purchased food and other material goods from the British. It should also be emphasized that the British obtained the majority of food and other goods on the basis of the Lend-Lease Act, behind which was the United States supplying the British, which was further nonsense. After several meetings between the British and Partisan representatives at the end of 1943, a reorganization of the aid to the Partisans took place because the British Royal Navy assumed responsibility over the organization of aid. A special military mission (the Zed military mission) was established, which took over the organization and supervision of aid to the Partisans. In addition, the Americans were asked to include its representatives in this mission, which never happened. Thus, the British took over almost all of the supply lines for the Partisans. In addition to Bari, aid was also organized from Monopoli and Brindisi, whereas the majority of aid originated from the United States on the basis of this act.[24]

In January 1944, OSS sent Lieutenant Colonel Street to Vis. He was responsible for defending the Dalmatian islands in cooperation with the Partisans. After further discussions, which also included the head of the Partisan mission in southern Italy, Colonel Vladimir Velebit, they came to the conclusion that new OSS liaison officers would be sent to Yugoslavia. This was one of the OSS initiatives to increase the American role in Yugoslavia, which was later launched with the dispatch of an Independent American Military Mission to the Tito's Supreme Headquarters.[25]

Relations between the Yugoslav OSS Section in Bari and the Partisans were always friendly and increasingly confident. The missions intended for departure to Yugoslavia usually waited for two to three months, mostly due to the obstruction of the British. Toward the end of the war, the activities of OSS in Bari were reduced to a small unit with four people, which was included in the 15 Air Force and operated until May 20, 1945, when all of its personnel had to leave. Between October 15 and December 31, 1943, OSS managed to transport 6,500 tons of equipment, supplies, and weapons with thirty-seven ships to the Dalmatian islands. Compared to OSS, SOE at that time sent 125 tons of aid to Yugoslavia with aircraft, which was considerably less than OSS.[26] Soon afterward, the initial enthusiasm of OSS in organizing aid to the Partisans faded due to the takeover of the supply by the British. In addition, a number of OSS officers were transferred to other positions.[27]

In a short time, however, a change occurred because on July 23, 1944, OSS realized that the Yugoslav Section was not operating well, that the agents were poorly prepared, and that the personnel were suffering from low morale and distrust. In March 1944, Kobal proposed that Arnoldy be replaced. He labeled him as inappropriate, not to be trusted, being pro–Partisan and incompetent.[28] Shortly afterward, Arnoldy was recalled and Robert P. Joyce became the new leader of the Yugoslav Section. Joyce soon had to leave the position of section head. He was replaced by Lieutenant Holt Green and Arthur M. Cox. They took over the Yugoslav Section at a time when it was characterized by chaos, inefficiency and low morale.[29]

Allied military aid for the Partisans, 1944 (National Museum of Contemporary History).

Training Yugoslav and American Agents in Yugoslav OSS Sections in Cairo and Bari

At the very beginning of the operation of the Yugoslav OSS Section, a significant role in the selection and training of Yugoslav-born agents was played by Lieutenant Colonel Lada Močarski. In an agreement with the Yugoslav government in exile, he was already sent to Allied Force Headquarters in Algiers in May 1943 to determine the possibilities of recruiting a number of Yugoslavs that were held in British prisoner-of-war camps—specifically, in Camp no. 207 near the town of Alma. He interviewed approximately four hundred prisoners and selected ten agents for work in OSS. Due to disagreements with the British military authorities, Močarski failed to organize transport to Cairo. For this reason, the agents were temporarily sent to the Yugoslav Royal Guard Battalion, which was a military unit of the Yugoslav government in exile in North Africa and Palestine until its disintegration at the end of 1943.[30]

As late as August 7, 1943, Močarski managed to organize transport for the agents and sent them to Cairo for training in the region of Ras El-Kanayis, or Area A. They attended basic training in special and intelligence operations. After three weeks, the Yugoslav-born agents went to the British parachute school near Haifa in Palestine. Before their departure, they needed confirmation that they were physically fit enough to attend the parachute course. The course, which lasted nine to fourteen days, was physically demanding.[31] The Yugoslav-born agents stayed in Villa Re David and Villa Suppa in Bari, which were located near the training areas. Soon after his arrival in Bari, Arnoldy started to systematically gather new agents that were appropriate for work in OSS. He was authorized by the British authorities to gather the agents. He looked for them in a number of prisoner-of-war camps in North Africa and southern Italy. Thus, Carbonari prisoner-of-war Camp no. 1 housed approximately three thousand Yugoslavs, of which, according to OSS archival sources, 2,600 were pro–Partisan and four hundred pro–Chetnik. Within four weeks after his arrival, Arnoldy gathered thirty of them and then selected the eighteen best. They were sent to a three-month training course in radiotelegraphy and secret operations. When choosing or selecting Yugoslavs to enter OSS training system, Arnoldy was helped by the Chetnik and Partisan officials in Bari. Partisan official was Marjan Barišić, who carried out interviews with potential agents that were willing to go to Yugoslavia as members of OSS missions at Partisan headquarters. Yugoslavs that had completed the training participated in OSS missions as wireless operators, coders, and interpreters at Partisan headquarters. The only thing missing in the Yugoslav Section was American OSS officers that were supposed to lead the missions. The British SOE and MI6 faced the same problems because it was difficult to obtain appropriate officers to lead missions in Yugoslavia.

Yugoslav-born agents had already been trained in special operations and that their training focused on radiotelegraphy and secret operations, including techniques for writing intelligence reports with practical exercises and specialized reporting on economic, political, naval, and traffic developments. They were trained in encryption, identification of military vessels and vehicles, and the general principles of morale operations. Additional course subjects were techniques for carrying out interviews and interrogations, reading military maps and photographs and interpreting them, sabotage and demolition techniques, close combat, fighting with melee weapons, and shooting. The entire course lasted for three weeks and was adapted to the current situation, and the average monthly salary of an agent was forty American dollars.[32]

Agents were trained in groups. In this way, greater homogeneity and cohesion was achieved within the group, and it was also easier for an instructor to evaluate their work. Detailed interviews with the agents were already conducted in the prisoner-of-war camp, before the training. Later on, their biographies, fingerprints, and photographs were examined. According to the general guidelines, the agents also lived together, and therefore they were accommodated in rooms for four people. In the yard in front of the villa, they could conduct fire drills, play sports, and read newspapers.[33]

On February 11, 1944, Major Arnoldy sent a report on the situation in the Bari Yugoslav Section to OSS Headquarters in Washington. The section comprised twenty-eight people: four instructors, seven wireless operators, eleven agents, and six members of staff that took care of the house. The seven wireless operators were ready to depart, and new ones were not recruited due to the lack of space. The average period of training a wireless operator lasted eight weeks. Most wireless operators did not have more than a high-school education. They were between twenty and twenty-six years old and were talented in music. Six groups of three or four men were prepared and waited for departure. They were assessed as having high moral values and a desire to learn. Relations between the Yugoslav-born agents were good, and there were no signs of quarrels and tensions. Not all of them completed the training. For some, it was too demanding, and so they had to return to the Partisans. In Washington, Arnoldy also reported on Tito's wish that OSS not recruit agents for missions in Yugoslavia alone but through the Partisan authorities.[34]

American OSS officers destined for Yugoslavia did not attend the same course as the Yugoslav-born agents, but most often a program that was shortened and adapted for them. The first American OSS agents destined for Yugoslavia mainly attended the British RAF parachute school in Ramat David, Palestine, and later the British school STS 102. With the development of their own training, OSS soon introduced a nine-day training course on basic geography, political and military characteristics of Yugoslavia, secret operation techniques, reporting techniques, basic security in secret operations, sabotage techniques, encryption, decryption, and weapons handling, map reading, and other basic skills that they needed in their secret operations on missions.[35]

3

OSS Missions in the Chetnik Movement

OSS Officers and Missions with the Chetniks

On the night of August 18, 1943, OSS sent First Lieutenant Walter F. Mansfield to the Supreme headquarters of the Yugoslav army in the fatherland, where he remained until January 15, 1944. Mansfield's greeting party consisted of Colonel William Bailey, head of the British mission to Mihailović's headquarters, and Major Kenneth Greenlees, Bailey's chief of staff. Mansfield quickly gathered his gear and, with the other members of the team, set out for the British camp about an hour's journey away. The British mission consisted of a crude peasant hut and two parachute tents. Shortly thereafter, Mansfield was escorted to Mihailović's headquarters for his first meeting with him. Mansfield also met British Lieutenant Colonel William Hudson, who had been in Yugoslavia since September 1941 and was the first Allied officer to have established contact with the Yugoslav resistance movement. Hudson was the first Allied officer that reported on the collaboration between the Chetniks and Italians in Montenegro, and on the passivity of the Chetnik movement in the fight against the Axis powers.[1]

On September 24, 1943, OSS sent Lieutenant Colonel Albert Seitz to Mihailović's headquarters, who was added to the British mission headed by Brigadier Charles Armstrong. Seitz and Armstrong disliked one another personally and never developed a working relationship comparable to that enjoyed by Mansfield and Bailey. Mansfield, who witnessed the personal conflict between Seitz and Armstrong as well as the growing disillusionment with which Mihailović and the British viewed one another, observed that from the very outset relations between Mihailović and the British were tenuous. The attitude toward American officers, on the other hand, was one of warmth in which Mihailović made no bones about his dislike for the British.[2]

On October 18, 1943, OSS sent First Lieutenant George Musulin as a head of Repartee mission to Mihailović's headquarters. He was the only one that remained with Mihailović after the order to evacuate and return to base on May 29, 1944.[3] Musulin was supposed to join Seitz and Mansfield in the First Corps area, but for reasons that are not altogether

Foreground, left to right: Lieutenant Colonel Albert Seitz and First Lieutenant Walter Mansfield during inspection of the Yugoslav Army in Fatherland (the Chetniks) in Serbia, November 1943 (N. Dević collection, courtesy B. Dimitrijević).

clear was dropped into territory held by the Second Corps. Musulin remained constantly on the move, giving him the opportunity to witness firsthand the destruction and personal tragedy the people of Serbia had experienced during two and a half years of German occupation. In many respects, Musulin's report substantiated the conclusions of Seitz and Mansfield. Musulin estimated Mihailović's total strength at between sixty and ninety thousand, but pointed out that these figures reflected information supplied by various corps commanders and that strength reports have a tendency to be highly magnified in Yugoslavia. Regarding the question of German-Chetnik collaboration, Musulin reported that he never personally witnessed anything or found any evidence to support the charges that Mihailović and his forces were collaborating with the Germans. There were reports that some Chetnik commanders in Hercegovina, Montenegro were receiving weapons and supplies from the Germans.[4]

Shortly after the Teheran Conference in December 1943, where the Allies made a decision to support Tito's National Liberation Movement, Seitz, Mansfield, and Musulin were informed that they had to leave Mihailović. In January 1944, the Chetniks received detailed instructions for the evacuation of American personnel, and gradually members of the OSS mission to the Chetniks were evacuated. Mansfield arrived in Bari on February 14, whereas Seitz arrived in Bari on March 15, 1944. Unlike Mansfield and Seitz, Musulin, as mentioned earlier, remained with the Chetniks until May 1944 because he delayed his departure and at the same time saved Allied airmen. Musulin was ordered to stay with Mihailović even after the departure of the British and, despite strong British opposition to this OSS decision, Musulin took advantage of the delay and further procrastinated his departure. Upon his arrival at the base, Mansfield wrote a report that he sent to the State Department, where it was read and evaluated by numerous OSS analysts. Although he wrote favorably about the Chetniks, Mansfield nevertheless stressed that Mihailović was rather inactive in combat against the Germans. The essence of his policy was to wait for a "D-Day," when massive resistance would be organized along with Allied landings somewhere on the continent.[5] The problem with the Chetnik leader was that he failed to organize active resistance against the Axis powers. He was seen as a collaborator primarily due to the fact that he was basically interested in ensuring that the Chetniks were allowed to operate and move freely, and fight the Partisans.

An OSS expert on the Balkans, J.W. Lane, wrote that the weakness of Mansfield's report was that it only covered the territory of Serbia, northern Montenegro, and western Herzegovina. Although in that limited area activities were indeed mostly carried out by the Chetniks, the report failed to cover other parts of Yugoslavia, especially the north, which were of crucial importance for OSS. Seitz also held a positive view of the Chetniks, even though he noticed some shortcomings in Mihailović's movement. He recommended that the Chetniks should exercise better control of their operations and that they should receive more aid. A weakness of Seitz's report was that he was unable to estimate the number of the Chetnik units. He described the problems they had due to constant German reprisals, lack of weapons, equipment, poor communication, and inactivity after the capitulation of Italy. Seitz also stated that the Chetniks occupied some cities where they should begin combat action. The Chetniks also had poor relations with the British due to Mihailović's rejection of the British proposal that the Chetniks should carry out military operations in the eastern regions of Yugoslavia and stop attacking the Partisans. According to Seitz, the British requests were only feasible in the event that the amount of aid to Mihailović be increased.[6]

When Seitz and Mansfield returned from the Chetnik headquarters, they wrote in their report to Donovan in April 1944 that the Chetniks conducted effective military operations of great strategic importance for the Allies. According to information in their reports, accusations of the Chetniks' collaboration with the Germans and Italians were of no significance and therefore did not harm the Allied strategy. Accordingly, Mihailović deserved American aid mainly because he saved Allied airmen that had been shot down. After that, in July 1944, Washington learned that hundreds of Allied airmen were waiting for evacuation in Mihailović's territory, which in turn prompted Donovan to plan the deployment of new missions to the Chetniks. Both Seitz and Musulin positively assessed Mihailović's movement, noting a few weaknesses such as the fact that the Chetniks concentrated most of their power on the fight against the Partisans and were waiting for Anglo-American landings on the continent.[7]

The Halyard Mission

By May 1944, President Roosevelt had received all of the reports from Seitz, Musulin, and Mansfield. However, he also needed new and

3. OSS Missions in the Chetnik Movement

more up-to-date reports from the Chetnik headquarters. In the summer of 1944, OSS had to establish new relations with Mihailović because there were a large number of Allied airmen in his operational area that the United States wanted to evacuate. On July 26, 1944, upon the direct order of Roosevelt, a rescue mission for the evacuation of Allied airmen (Air Crew Rescue Unit, ACRU),[8] called Halyard, was quickly established and deployed.[9] American Colonel George Kraigher, a relative of Colonel Boris Kraigher, a Yugoslav communist leader, was responsible for the mission. He was the chief of Air Crew Rescue Unit for the Balkans and was especially active in carrying out both missions because they were accompanied by complications. The mission consisted of three officers that arrived at Mihailović's headquarters on August 2, 1944. The Halyard mission, which was a part of the Fifteenth Army Air Force, was initially led by Musulin, who had left the Chetniks only seven weeks earlier. In addition to Musulin, Sergeant Michael Rajacich and Arthur Jibilian formed the team. The mission was given clear instructions not to act as an official military mission or intelligence team, but only as a mission for evacuating airmen.

Evacuation of USAAF airmen in Serbia in fall 1944, carried out by the Halyard Mission (M. Samardžić collection, courtesy B. Dimitrijević).

After the evacuation of Musulin on August 27, 1944, Captain Nick Lalich came to Yugoslavia on August 9, 1944 as the new head of the Halyard mission.

After returning to Bari, Musulin prepared a report on the Halyard mission in which he praised those that had played a role in Halyard, including Mihailović and his forces. At the time of its operation, the Halyard mission evacuated 417 persons, of whom 343 were American airmen. The evacuation was organized from the airfield in central Serbia which was indirect confirmation that Mihailović controlled most of Serbia in mid–1944. However, not everything ran smoothly. The mission also caused a political incident because it sent members of Mihailović's political mission to Bari where they came in a conflict with Partisan authorities. Lalich and his Halyard mission remained at the Chetnik headquarters until December 27, 1944, when they left Yugoslavia.[10]

The Ranger Mission

During the Halyard mission, on August 26, 1944, the Ranger mission was also sent to the Chetniks, this being led by Lieutenant Colonel Robert McDowell.[11] McDowell's team included Captain John Miodragovich, wireless operator Sergeant Michael Devyak, and First Lieutenant Ellsworth Kramer. Ranger mission arrived at Mihailović's headquarters just a few days before the beginning of Operation Ratweek, a joint Allied-Partisan undertaking aimed at destroying German forces retreating from Greece and Yugoslavia into Austria. Furthermore, Mihailović had designated September 1 as the date for general mobilization, calling all men between the ages of sixteen and sixty to join his forces. After that date Ultra revealed a noticeable increase in Chetnik activity. Chetniks in eastern and central Bosnia had opened hostilities against the Germans, but according to Ultra the "Hercegovinian" Chetniks were loyal to the Germans.

McDowell was instructed that the mission was not political in nature, did not represent the State Department, and was aimed at collecting and handing over strategic military and political information that was useful for the joint fight against the enemy. Some of the tasks were also related to building relations with groups in Bulgaria, Romania, and Hungary. Those relations differed from those that could be set up through Partisan channels. McDowell was not authorized to promise aid to Mihailović, and there was also no plan to provide Mihailović with material or political support. During his tenure there, McDowell found no evidence of Mi-hailović's collaboration with the Axis forces. He even made contact with the representatives of the Wehrmacht in Serbia because he was advised in negotiations that the Anglo-American Allies should not hinder their withdrawal, and in turn the withdrawing German troops would then not be ordered to fight against the Anglo-American forces. The negotiations were subsequently suspended at the request of OSS. McDowell wrote that the Partisans had been falsifying and were continuing to falsify military and political information on a grand scale when it suited their purposes to do so.

McDowell's report was a defense of Mihailović and his resistance forces. Noting that the political dynamics of the Partisans and Chetniks were diametrically opposed, McDowell argued that different standards or means of evaluation had to be employed in analyzing the intelligence gathered on the two organizations. It was a valid argument, but to Brit-

Left to right: General Draža Mihailović, Lieutenant Colonel Robert McDow-ell, head of the Ranger Mission, and the Yugoslav Army in Fatherland Supreme Headquarters Chief of Staff, Colonel Luka Baletic, September–October 1944 (M. Samardžić collection, courtesy B. Dimitrijević).

ish and American analysts the most important criterion remained which group was, or appeared to be, killing the most Germans. After strong protests by Tito and British interventions, which were referred to in the correspondence between Roosevelt and Churchill, the Ranger mission left the Chetniks on November 1, 1944.[12]

4

OSS Missions in the Partisan Movement

OSS Officers and Missions with the Partisans

The first OSS agent to join the Partisans was Captain Melvin Benson,[1] who arrived at Tito's Supreme Headquarters on August 22 and remained there until December 22, 1943. The first American liaison officer dispatched to the Partisans was subordinated to the British mission, which consisted of two British officers, Major Basil Davidson and Captain William Deakin, and other supporting staff.[2] Benson wrote about the Italian capitulation on September 8, 1943. News of the Italian surrender reached the British missions at Tito's and Mihailović's headquarters, setting off a three-way scramble for Italian arms among the Partisans, Chetniks, and Germans. Both resistance leaders accused the British of giving the other side advance warning about the capitulation, but there is no direct evidence to substantiate these charges. Benson, who was with the British mission at Partisan headquarters at Jajce when news of the surrender arrived, recalled that Tito immediately requested that he and Deakin proceed to Split to assist in disarming the Italians there. Benson represented OSS during negotiations between Partisans and Italians but, like Deakin, more in the capacity of an observer than a participant. Benson was also stationed on the island of Vis, which was an important place for the distribution of all the Allied aid to the Partisans.

Just as the British strengthened their presence in September 1943 by sending Brigadier Fitzroy Maclean to Tito, OSS deployed Major Linn Farish to Tito on September 17, 1943. He was the senior American liaison officer with the Partisans and was subordinate to Maclean, who was the chief Anglo-American officer at Tito's Supreme Headquarters. Maclean was no ordinary Brigadier randomly chosen from the ranks to present

British interests in Yugoslavia. He was a man with extensive Foreign Office experience, a conservative member of Parliament, and a personal acquaintance of Churchill. Clearly, his arrival in Yugoslavia marked the opening of a new chapter, political as well as military, in Britain's relations with the Partisans. By comparison, Armstrong, selected to go to Mihailović's headquarters, was a professional soldier with a distinguished record of service in India, who, by virtue of being known by Field Marshal Montgomery, was asked to go to Yugoslavia.[3]

Maclean had quickly established a very amicable relationship with Tito. Maclean's famous report of November 6, 1943, which called for the abandonment of Mihailović and the transfer of all support to Tito, found its way to Churchill and Roosevelt before the Teheran Conference. At Teheran, Roosevelt also shared with Stalin a copy of Farish's findings, which the president described as most interesting report from an American officer that had spent six months in Yugoslavia in close contact with Tito. In reality, Farish had not been in close contact with Tito. He was removed from the center of events. Maclean had sent him to the town of Glamoč, where he remained for several days with a radiotelegraph device that did not work and a wireless operator that could not fix it. Farish was strongly involved in organizing drop areas in Yugoslavia and with the rescue of the Allied airmen. He believed that the Partisans had great military and political importance, and he described their struggle against Axis forces. Farish's conclusions and recommendations paralleled many of those in Maclean's report, particularly regarding Chetnik collaboration, support for the Partisans, and the suggestion that through such support the Allies might secure some political advantage in the postwar period. The Farish report therefore had little, if any, impact on the course of Allied policy. Its true significance lay in the fact that it supported a strategy to which the Allies, particularly the United States, were already committed.[4]

Farish was in Yugoslavia twice, and the most influential report addressing the Partisan–Chetnik civil war came from his second report. Farish reentered Yugoslavia with Maclean on January 20, 1944, as the head of the Columbian-Gargantuan mission. Farish believed that the United States could and should play an effective role in bringing the Yugoslav civil war to an end, and he argued that it was morally wrong for his country to continue providing supplies, arms, and ammunition without regard to any other consideration except the military outcome. He remained with the Partisans until June 15, 1944, when he was again evacuated from Yugoslavia.[5] Shortly before he was relieved as the highest American represen-

4. OSS Missions in the Partisan Movement

Evacuation of wounded Partisans from White Carniola (*Bela Krajina*), February 1945 (National Museum of Contemporary History).

tative to Tito, Farish had already begun to question his work. In his final report of July 1944, he wrote:

> I personally do not feel that I can go on with the work in Yugoslavia unless I can sincerely feel that every possible honest effort is being made to put an end to the civil strife. It is not nice to see arms dropped by one group of our airmen to be turned against men who have rescued and protected their brothers-in-arms. It is not a pleasant sight to see our wounded lying side by side with the men who had rescued and cared for them—and to realize that the bullet holes in the rescuers could have resulted from American ammunition, fired from American rifles, dropped from American aircraft flown by American pilots. At one time I worried because America was not getting the proper recognition for her participation in supply operations. Now I wonder—do we want it? The issues in Yugoslavia are ones which will have to be faced in many parts of the world. The Yugoslavians with their wild, turbulent, strong-willed nature have abandoned reason and resorted to force. Is this the shape of things to come? Are we all of us sacrificing to end this war only to have dozens of little wars spring up which may well merge into one gigantic conflict involving all mankind?[6]

However, later on during the war, in one of his trips to Greece, Farish died in a plane crash.

On December 4, 1943, OSS Captain George Selvig, in the company of a number of British officers, infiltrated into Bosnia, where he joined the British Fungus mission at Tito's Supreme Headquarters. Selvig was under the command of Maclean, although Farish was his immediate OSS superior. Selvig moved into western Bosnia to the town of Potoci and travelled to Bosanski Petrovac on January 17, 1944, to greet Maclean, Farish, Eli Popovich, and Churchill's son Major Randolph Churchill, who arrived three days later. Maclean ordered Selvig to the Partisan Eighth Corps headquartered at Tičevo, where he relieved British liaison officer Major John Henniker as head of the Relator mission on January 25, 1944. Selvig had many difficulties in working with the British, and he reported that there was always a tendency for them to take credit for everything that was done for the Partisans without regard for the person doing the work.[7]

In early April, Selvig left the Eighth Corps in Bosnia and in the company of Major Churchill travelled to Croatia, where he coordinated supply drops and distribution to Partisan forces operating in that area. Acting largely on his own initiative, Selvig oversaw construction of a much-needed airfield at Gajevi, near Topusko. In fact, while Selvig was in Croatia, approximately 150 Allied airmen, nine hundred Partisans and six hundred refugees were evacuated from this airfield. Selvig did note in his report the extent to which the peasants gave support to the Partisans in return for the protection of the army. In his opinion, this was "not of great importance, because the army always runs from the enemy on an offensive and the poor peasant either stays behind and gets shot, or goes on the move and loses all of his worldly goods."[8]

The Reedwood mission, led by OSS officer Rex Deane, parachuted to the Partisan Second Corps with its headquarters at Kolašin in Montenegro. Deane sent many reports about the situation in the Partisan Second Corps. He was surprised that the Partisans were storing away substantial quantities of the supplies they were receiving, apparently for use against their internal enemies. Deane also wrote that there was no fighting spirit at the Partisan Second Corps and that there was a lack of organization there and, although tons of ammunition and demolition equipment had been dropped, no use had been made it. Deane wrote that the Americans were tolerated to supply the goods with constant inquiries for more aid and that the Partisans were far more interested in attacking the Chetniks and their supporters than in fighting the Germans. Deane also noted that speeches given at Partisan political rallies made frequent references to Stalin and the Red Army, whereas "there would be a reference to England and America, but very seldom."[9]

4. OSS Missions in the Partisan Movement

First Lieutenant Holt Green parachuted to the Partisan Second Corps area in early February 1944 as the head of the OSS Rakeoff mission and was impressed by what he saw there. In a report filed with Bari in late February, he encouraged full support for the Partisans, arguing that Allied supplies were being used to fight the Germans and were not being employed against the Chetniks. Later in early April, Green and a member of his mission, Stephen Galembush, began to notice the very poor condition of the weapons carried by most of the Partisan patrols and became curious about what was happening to the supplies they knew were being sent into the area by the Allies. They learned through a young Partisan that the Partisans were hiding supplies in barns throughout the countryside.[10] Green also wrote about Partisan efforts to restrict the freedom of action of Anglo-American officers operating in their territory. Green wrote, "the only items of enemy intelligence we are in a position to get are those which funnel through Partisan headquarters, and of course this would apply to a large extent if you are in the field."[11]

On February 27, 1944, the California mission arrived at Tito's Supreme Headquarters in Drvar. The mission, which was led by Colonel

Transfer of wounded Partisans of the Fourteenth Division (National Museum of Contemporary History).

Richard Weil, worked more independently than the other OSS missions, especially in terms of information and political needs, whereas in fact all of the channels for the operational links and supply were still controlled by the British through Maclean. Weil remained in Yugoslav territory for only three weeks and then left Yugoslavia. Despite his short stay among the Partisans, he became well acquainted with Tito and his movement. In his reports, Weil was critical and rather negative about the Partisans because he believed they were not able to fight the enemy and prevent him from withdrawing. Nevertheless, he viewed Tito primarily as a liberator, and only secondarily as a communist. He argued that the war in Yugoslavia was exclusively a guerrilla war. At the same time, he was not in favor of the contact between the British, Soviets, and Partisans because he believed that Partisan successes would continue throughout Yugoslavia and that it was therefore necessary to support them. The American ambassador to the Yugoslav government in exile, Lincoln MacVeagh, believed that during his stay with Tito, Weil did not comprehend the actual picture of the Partisans, and therefore his interpretations revealed a lack of Mihailović's authority. Weil believed that Mihailović was saving his army for a possible Allied landing. He thought that, although it might be true that he did not cooperate with the Axis powers, he certainly did not intend to cooperate with the Allies. Weil's report was delivered to the highest echelons of the American administration.[12]

In September 1944, the Willow mission reached Serbian Partisan headquarters and the leader was Captain Charles B. Grimm. In his reports, Grimm wrote about the good contribution of the Partisans in the fight against the Germans, but he also complained that after mid–October 1944, when his men were allowed contact only with Partisan sources, their presence in Yugoslavia as a military mission was utterly worthless. Grimm also reported that the hostility that the Partisans had exhibited toward the British and American missions diminished considerably after the Partisans had their first glimpse of the glorified Soviet Union. Grimm noted that it took only a few days for the Partisan officials to realize the blunder they had committed in their propaganda because an army depending on American trucks, jeeps, medical aid, and food would definitely be unable to supply another nation with like items.[13]

Major Scott Dickinson, who headed the Spike mission in Serbia and Macedonia, reported about the effectiveness of Partisan warfare and Partisan relations against OSS missions. Dickinson reported that the Partisans obviously exceeded the limits of polite obstructionism. In early December 1944, Dickinson and some of his men drove out to view a large power station near Skopje. During the course of their inspection, a young officer from the Department of National Security arrived, confiscated the mission's camera and film at gunpoint, and forced the British driver to take the men back to headquarters. Although Dickinson and his men later received an apology for this treatment, the Partisans made it clear that they saw no need for the continued presence of an OSS mission in their area. Dickinson reported that in late October 1944 he and his men tried to persuade the Partisans to destroy railroads and bridges that were being used by the retreating Germans. Although the Partisans argued that they were not adequately prepared to confront the Germans directly, Dickinson suspected that they simply did not want to destroy the facilities in question. When he argued that the Germans would destroy them in any case, the Partisans paid no attention to this advice and made only feeble and temporary attempts to stop the Germans. Dickinson also reported that it was difficult to decide which enemy would do Yugoslavia more harm. For Mihailović, Tito's Partisans were more of a menace to his country than the Germans, and Mihailović was willing to fight the Partisans even if it meant temporary collaboration with the Germans.[14]

The joint OSS/SOE Geisha mission led by First Lieutenant Robin Nowell operated among the Partisans in Croatia between May and October 1944. Members of the mission expressed anti–Partisan views and soon had to leave the country. Soon after their arrival to the Croatian Partisans, they cancelled Nowell's permission to remain in the country. One of the members of the mission, Joseph Veselinovich, was questioned by the Partisan commissar about why the Americans still had a military mission with the Chetniks. When Veselinovich replied that there was no mission with Mihailović, the commissar said sarcastically that he knew a mission was continuing to operate with the Chetniks.[15]

Between September 1944 and March 1945, the OSS Walnut mission was led by Captain Robert Weiler, operating among the Partisans in Croatia. Weiler wrote a report in which he wrote about a strange incident that might account, in part, for Partisan General Petar Drapšin's concern for security. According to Weiler, the British had succeeded in establishing undercover agents in Hungary and were maintaining contact with them through Partisan channels. Apparently, one of these agents had been captured and "sweated" by the Germans because a package, sent to the British mission through regular channels, contained a bomb that exploded and killed Colonel Malinković, Drapšin's chief intelligence officer, as he opened the container.[16]

The Ash mission led by Don Rider operated among Serbian Partisans in Vojvodina. Like Dickinson, Rider also reported about Partisan passivity regarding active fighting with the Germans. On more than one occasion, he accompanied Partisan columns that passed within one hundred yards of German tanks and bunkers and neither side fired on the other.[17]

In Croatia, in the Partisan Tenth Corps operated Air Crew Rescue Mission Hacienda, which was led by John Hamilton.[18] In his early report, he admired the Partisans and their fight against the enemy, but later on he wrote that the Partisan movement was not an expression of the people's will. Hamilton characterized Partisan claims of holding liberated territory as "pure bunkum." In his opinion, Partisan territory was free simply because the enemy did not care to use it at the time. When the enemy wanted to, it marched in and the Partisans took to the hills.[19]

There were also some other OSS and OSS/SOE missions in Partisan headquarters, but there is not much information about their work in the archival sources. These missions were: the Altmark mission led by First Lieutenant Nels J. Benson, which operated in Bosnia, the Bethesda led by Captain Miller, which operated in Bosnia, the Abbeville mission led by Captain Rainer, which operated in Macedonia; the Deposit mission led by Everett Greaser, the Idaho mission, the Ohio mission, the Mine mission which operated in Montenegro and Serbia, the Dunklin mission led by First Lieutenant Pfeiffer, the Darien led by Captain Plowman, the Toledo mission led by Robert Phillips, the Oak mission (agent Milos Kosec), the Pine mission (agent Radko Bajt), the Belaware mission and the Mulberry mission led by John Goodwin, which all operated in Croatia.[20]

American Mission at Tito's Headquarters and the Arrival of the First U.S. Diplomats

In February 1944 Churchill decided that the American and British missions in Yugoslavia would be separate, which in turn stimulated the Americans to start more preparations for the first independent military mission. The British tried to dissuade the Americans from their intention by using Maclean because they wanted him to remain the only official information channel between the Allied Force Headquarters and Tito.[21] In May 1944, Donovan sent the State Department a proposal for the ex-

4. OSS Missions in the Partisan Movement

tension of OSS activities in Yugoslavia. Its basic purpose was to increase the power of the independent American mission, which would operate at the Supreme Headquarters of the National Liberation Movement. The State Department answered that they supported his proposal because the future mission would need to operate independently and in parallel with the British against the enemy. Moreover, the State Department emphasized the role of increased OSS activities, which should be supported by the Joint Chiefs of Staff.[22]

Thus, on June 9, 1944, the Joint Chiefs of Staff approved the arrival of the first Independent American Military mission in Yugoslavia (IAMM), which would be sent to Tito's Supreme Headquarters. It was formally activated at a meeting between Donovan, Huntington, and Tito on Capri in August 1944. At the meeting with Tito, Donovan explained the tasks of the new mission. The mission was supposed to include military and intelligence tasks, special operational tasks, organization of supply, and morale operations for the Partisans, with the condition that the United States refuse to support any political group in Yugoslavia. Donovan argued that the United States was not primarily interested in the Balkans because its purpose was to develop the intelligence network in central and eastern Europe. However, it did not oppose the Soviet and British politics of support for Tito.[23] Initially, Colonel Holdahl was assigned as head of the mission. However, he soon fell ill, and so the new commander became Colonel Ellery Huntington, who was previously the head of the OSS / Special Operations Branch in Washington. In August 1944, Tito then visited British General Wilson in Caserta, who also received the American delegation led by Donovan. They agreed that the Americans would send an independent mission to Tito, under the leadership of Huntington. The objectives and policies of the mission were consistent with the policy of the United States toward Yugoslavia and the Memorandum from Cavendish Cannon dated May 19, 1944. According to the Memorandum, the United States did not intend to intercede in the internal affairs of Yugoslavia. Furthermore, the interest of the United States was the establishment of a government after the war that would be elected and would reflect the freely expressed desires of the peoples of Yugoslavia. The memorandum also stated that the United States had no obligations toward King Peter II or any other government in Yugoslavia.[24] Donavan also sent the Memorandum to Huntington to be used as a guideline for his political activities.

Although the tasks of the Independent American Military Mission were more military in nature, they were also related to the social, political, and economic developments in Yugoslavia. The mission also reported about healthcare and diseases in the country. It also summarized the activities of individual OSS missions to the Partisans, pointing out that OSS staff, which organized ship and aircraft support, was particularly effective. The mission was responsible for all American personnel in Yugoslavia, as well as controlling the sending of American aid to the Partisans. The Partisans provided the mission with access to intelligence information, along with the possibility to travel throughout the country and to visit other OSS missions that were located at the Partisan headquarters. All American personnel working along the supply line were transferred from British to American jurisdiction. The Independent American Military Mission was especially warned not to interfere in the internal political affairs of Yugoslavia. Initially, the mission had its headquarters on the island of Vis. Later on, it moved to Valjevo, then to Aranđelovac, and finally to Belgrade in October 1944.[25]

The Independent American Military Mission was responsible for all subordinated OSS missions in all parts of Yugoslavia. Their main objectives were sending military intelligence about the German armed forces,

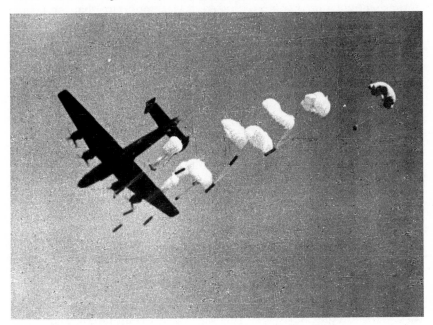

Allied aircraft dropping military aid for the Partisans (National Museum of Contemporary History).

49

the organization of aid to the resistance movements, and the dissemination of political and economic information to OSS bases in North Africa and southern Italy. Especially in the fall and toward the end of 1944, it became increasingly clear that military intelligence from Yugoslavia had declined in importance, whereas reporting on the political situation on the ground, especially in Slovenian and Croatian territory, had increased in importance. For this reason, as early as August 10, 1944, Donovan sent a letter to Huntington in which he explained that the United States had not yet publicly expressed its policy toward Yugoslavia. Therefore, he defined some main points that had to be followed.

The basic policy was that the United States would not interfere in internal Yugoslav affairs because it did not have any special interests in the area. What was also important was that after the liberation a democratic government was to be established, cooperating with the governments of other countries and elected by the people. Moreover, Donovan wrote that the main U.S. wish was to create cordial cooperation between the Serbs and the Croats. They also expected that the Yugoslav peoples would continue to strive for the liberation of Yugoslavia and that the resistance groups would be further strengthened. It was important that the United States, together with the British and the Soviets, wage a joint struggle against Germany, and therefore in Yugoslavia a common policy of all the Allies had to be developed. Donovan stated that the United States would not support the interests of the British or the Soviets in Yugoslavia, but common interests because they were consistent with the American doctrine of non-intervention. Donovan concluded that the United States was realistic and did not expect the unity of all the Yugoslav peoples to result. However, they expected the unity of all the Yugoslavs across the world because they could help Yugoslavia in its reconstruction along with the United States. He placed special emphasis on the fact that the Yugoslavs in the United States were not an objective indicator for measuring the public opinion of Yugoslavs.[26]

Since its arrival in Yugoslavia, Huntington maintained friendly relations with the Soviet mission of Colonel Melnikov and also had good contacts with Maclean. With the Soviet advance into the Balkans and the liberation of Belgrade in October 1944, OSS gradually reduced the number of its personnel in Yugoslavia, while directing its activities toward northern and northwest Yugoslavia and therefore maintaining its missions in Croatia, Slovenia, and western Bosnia. Before his departure, Huntington established an OSS city mission in Belgrade (the Belgrade

City Team), which was part of his mission. He made all the necessary arrangements for the arrival of the American diplomatic personnel in Yugoslavia. At the time of Huntington's command, OSS evacuated large numbers of Allied airmen from Partisan territory. The official air force statistics from October 1, 1944, reveal that 1,088 Allied airmen were evacuated from Yugoslavia, and 732 received assistance from the Partisans. Subsequent evacuations raised this number appreciably, although the Partisans claimed to have been responsible for the evacuation of around two thousand airmen.[27] After his return to base, he wrote that the mission made great efforts to ensure independent reporting, although that was very difficult because the relations with the Partisans were merely formal and not friendly, and because the intelligence reports were still based on Partisan intelligence extracts.[28]

In the spring of 1944, after the liberation of Belgrade, Šubašić and Tito met again and agreed to establish a common government, composed of the so-called progressive democratic elements that had not collaborated with the Axis powers. The agreement itself was opposed both by King Peter II and American Lieutenant Colonel Charles Thayer, who replaced Huntington on November 13, 1944. Thayer, a West Point graduate with more than eight years of diplomatic experience in Germany and the Soviet Union and a personal friend of Maclean, seemed well-suited to head the mission during the transition from military to political affairs. He believed that the agreement between Šubašić and Tito was not specified in detail because the government was dominated by Tito's people. Up until the elections to the Constitutional Assembly on November 11, 1945, and also beyond, the United States was increasingly critical toward Tito and the new Yugoslav authorities and therefore viewed Yugoslavia as the first ally of the Soviet Union. This was the guiding principle of U.S. policy toward Yugoslavia until the Tito–Stalin Split, when more active support for Yugoslavia started.[29]

Thayer, wrote about the activities of the Department of National Security in Yugoslavia on January 30, 1945. He said that arrests and executions continued; the press placed great emphasis on the trials of Yugoslav collaborators and the number of victims varied greatly. Thayer estimated that the truth was probably somewhere between the rumors and the official reports, and that the Department of National Security controlled all spheres of life. He believed that the Partisan movement should not be condemned because their moral values were held in high regard. Furthermore, they were strongly convinced and devoted to their ideals. In his estimate of the Department of National Security and its agents, Thayer observed that it was difficult to distinguish between a Department of National Security agent and the rest of the population because the agents wore civilian clothes and most certainly cooperated with the Soviet People's Commissariat for Internal Affairs (NKVD). Their agents were especially active in Belgrade after its liberation. Many Yugoslav agents had been educated in the Soviet Union, and for this reason Thayer assumed that the Department of National Security had developed into a service identical to the Soviet People's Commissariat for Internal Affairs.

On April 19, 1945, Thayer was replaced by Major Franklin A. Lindsay, who led the Independent American Military Mission until its end. Furthermore, the United States established its embassy in Belgrade. Toward the end of the war, the number of intelligence reports from Yugoslavia increased considerably. These reports mostly contained information about Yugoslav territorial demands in Istria, Trieste, Carinthia, and Styria. In addition to the Belgrade City Team or the American diplomatic mission, the following missions were active in 1945 on territorially disputed areas of Yugoslavia: Arrow, Grady, Spike and Dunklin.[30] On May 12, 1945, the commanding officer of the American diplomatic mission in Belgrade, Lindsay, together with Air Vice Marshal Lee, met with Chief of the General Staff of the Yugoslav Army[31] Arso Jovanović. Jovanović told them that, upon Tito's command, all British and American missions had to leave Yugoslavia because they were being replaced by military attachés. Lindsay tried to explain to Jovanović the important role the missions had played in the recognition of the Partisan movement and organization of aid to Partisans. However, Jovanović underestimated the role of the Anglo-American Allies and believed that the Partisan movement would have won regardless of the Anglo-American aid and recognition.[32] Soon after that, Allied Force Headquarters instructed Lindsay to reduce the number of personnel even while the mission had to remain in Yugoslavia. At that time, the Belgrade City mission consisted of eighteen members and was later reduced to ten people, of which seven members were under the command of Lindsay and three acted as attaché assistants.[33] After his meeting with Jovanović, Lindsay sent the American ambassador to Yugoslavia, Richard C. Petterson, a message saying that at Tito's command Jovanović had ordered the withdrawal of Anglo-American missions from Yugoslavia because it had been decided that military attachés would take over their work. OSS sadly ordered its Belgrade mission to withdraw from the country. The American diplomatic mission was formally abandoned on July 2, 1945.[34]

OSS Missions with Slovenian Partisans

The Alum and Amazon Missions

Already in the summer of 1943, OSS in Cairo and its Yugoslav Section started to train a group of Slovenians called Amazon, which was supposed to be sent to Yugoslavia (Slovenian territory). The first group of Slovenians in Cairo was gathered and trained with the help of Lieutenant Colonel Lada Močarski and Major Arnoldy, who was the head of the Yugoslav Section in Cairo. Due to a number of complications, this group was ready to deploy no sooner than the end of October 1943. Its departure was delayed due to the German offensive, poor weather, and the opposition of the British, who hindered the deployment of OSS missions to Yugoslavia. In addition to the Amazon mission, OSS also deployed the Alum mission, which belonged to the OSS / Secret Intelligence.[35] It was not only the Amazon mission that was unsuccessful; the Alaska mission, the composition of which is not known, as well as the Arizona mission, which was apparently active in Venezia Giulia, also failed. The latter was composed of Slovenian agents Ivo Pahor and Radko Zuodar. Zuodar's death ended the Arizona mission and Pahor joined the Alum mission.

While the Alum mission was being prepared, its leader, Captain George Wuchinich, wrote to Močarski about the progress in training the group. He reported that not all members of his mission were ready for departure because some of them were still attending training. Due to the lack of adequate maps of Slovenian territory and the lack of more accurate data on the area where the missions were to be sent, Wuchinich sent Lieutenant Stampados to Cairo to gather as much information as possible on the situation of the resistance in Slovenian territory and in the region itself.[36] As the head of the mission, Wuchinich understood that his personnel must be well prepared for any demanding task, which was not easy because sources of information on the political situation and the military and economic situation in Slovenian territory were difficult to obtain in northern Africa. This was one of the key reasons for the deployment of OSS missions to this part of Yugoslavia.

Planning the deployment of the first OSS missions to Slovenian territory lasted several months. On October 9, 1943, it had been decided that the Amazon mission would be composed of Franc Menčak, Anton Galun, and Venčeslav Šaly. The Alum mission, on the other hand, would be composed of an OSS first lieutenant and sergeant and a Slovenian,

Captain George Wuchinich, head of the Alum mission, August 1944 (National Museum of Contemporary History).

Jože Stante. Both missions were commanded by Captain Wuchinich, and therefore the missions are often called the Wuchinich team. The initial plan was to deploy the missions on October 12, 1943 on the night before the full moon, but the first flight was aborted. Finally, the missions were ready to be deployed on November 26 and November 27, 1943; the Amazon mission was deployed on the first day and the Alum mission on the second.[37]

The task of the Amazon mission was to report on the enemy's activities, the communications situation, German traffic between Celje and Maribor, monitoring OSS infiltration groups from Yugoslavia to Austria, and sending reports via the Alum mission or directly to the base.[38] On the night of November 26, 1943, due to incorrect navigation and signalization, the Amazon mission landed at the Slovenian Home Guard[39] post in Velike Lašče. However the group of three Slovenians, who lost all of their equipment, soon managed to escape to the Partisans. After the arrival of the mission at the Slovenian Partisan headquarters, the wireless operator sent a message in which he reported on the situation and the state of the mission. The investigation later showed that the guards lighting fires for signaling the unit were not responsible for the incorrect landing by the group. A day after the Amazon mission, the Alum mission successfully landed at the Slovenian Partisan headquarters. It has been recorded that the Partisan headquarters received the Americans and that Wuchinich was well on the way to gaining the trust of the Partisans. The analysis confirmed that the Amazon mission landed at the Home Guard post due to the pilot's mistake. The members of the mission were thus sent to the Home Guard prison. They later managed to escape during the chaos caused by the alarm, when it was believed that an Anglo-American invasion was occurring. The mission apparently missed its target because the pilot did not see the fires and the signal signs, because there were not any. The Partisans found the members of the Amazon mission to be suspicions from the very beginning. However, they soon accepted them. Their information proved to be extremely useful when the Partisans occupied the Home Guard post in Velike Lašče. All three members of the Amazon mission were included in the Alum mission and nominated to receive British military decorations for their courage and resourcefulness. It must also be stressed that the stories of Anton Galun and Franc Menčak differed from the story of Venčeslav Šaly, with whom they quarreled.[40]

The American and the Slovenian archival documents state that, soon after the arrival of both missions in Slovenian territory, one of the three members of the Amazon mission, Venčeslav Šaly, showed signs of bad behavior, was becoming mistrustful, and wanted to transfer to the Partisan side, which was unusual for Slovenian agents of OSS missions. Wuchinich demanded that the base replace Venčeslav Šaly because he allegedly entered into a quarrel with colleagues from the Arizona mission. Menčak and Galun did not want to work with him ever since their imprisonment in Velike Lašče. They characterized him as selfish and also said that he gave the Partisans their code, letting his colleagues down when they needed him.[41]

Bari responded to Wuchinich's criticism of Šaly regarding his inappropriate conduct and the desire to join the Partisans as follows: "Does that mean that the Partisans do not want Wensel to stay with you? If the Partisans explicitly reject this, we would prefer it that Wensel stays with you, for you will soon be needing another wireless operator who will be arriving from New York and of whom we will soon be reporting. This work will be directly beneficial to the Partisans, so try to keep Wensel and let us know the result."[42] They did not manage to keep Šaly, who transferred to the Partisans and was the only Slovenian agent included in an OSS mission that ever did such a thing. On the other hand, the Slovenian agents of the British missions transferred to the Partisans in great masses: They were guided by the desire to be able to liberate their homeland as part of the Slovenian Partisan army. However, one should not neglect the successful role of those Slovenians that worked for OSS; as members of OSS missions, they followed the same objective: the liberation of their homeland.

The next night, November 27, 1943, the OSS sent the Alum mission (code X-18), composed of six members. Other members landed between January and June 1944. This team was composed of Captain Wuchinich, Sergeant Peter Sfikas, and the Slovenian Jože Stante, who were joined by the members of the aforementioned Amazon mission and a few Slovenians at the beginning of 1944. The Alum mission already started sending reports in December 1943 and continued sending them until April 1944. Altogether over one hundred reports were sent, and they covered Slovenian territory, southern Austria, parts of Croatia, and northeastern Italy. The reports were full of personal experience and unverified hearsay. Some of them, however, proved to be useful because they included a lot of reports on the evacuation of Allied aviators, political developments, the economic situation in Slovenian territory, combat formations, the fortification of the Adriatic coast, bombing targets, and Partisan ethics. The main intelligence task of the Alum mission was to control and to provide daily reports on the railway traffic on the lines from Maribor to Trieste via Ljubljana, and from Maribor to Belgrade via Zagreb. They also had their own observation point for surveillance of the railway traffic in the Sava Valley near Litija, which stopped operating after the death of Viljem Štamol. He died because he went to a neighboring village to obtain food despite the prohibition and fell into a German ambush.[43]

Wuchinich was very popular among the Slovenian Partisans and, in comparison to other agents of the Anglo-American missions, also enjoyed greater freedom of movement. The German newspapers also wrote about him; most often they declared him dead. Before Wuchinich's departure, the Alum mission was composed of a wireless operator and the head of the signals in the Alum mission, Sergeant Peter Sfikas, and Franc Menčak and Jože Stante, who were both part of the encryption section at the Alum mission. Stante together with Viljem Štamol, Ivo Pahor, and Vladimir Kumar composed the observation group for the railway observation point near Litija, and Vladimir Kumar together with Stante and Galun composed the observation group for the area of Celje and Maribor. The Arkansas meteorological mission (Alum Amet) is mentioned in the context of the Alum mission on a number of occasions; its leader was Lieutenant Robert Schraeder. Other members included in the mission were the wireless operator Marjan Česnik, Sergeant Ralph Baker, and Staff Sergeant Joseph Newmayer. The meteorological group operated independently until its dissolution, at which point its members—with the exception of Česnik, who joined Alum—returned to Bari. Some members of the mission even changed their duties; in other words, Jože Stante and Vladimir Kumar also operated in the observation mission, where they observed railway traffic near Litija. Wuchinich wrote a number of reports on the economic, political, and military situation in Slovenia. He never hid his enthusiasm for the Partisans, and so the OSS considered him biased and influenced by the Partisans.[44]

For almost six months the mission received no relief supplies, and so they had to ask the British for assistance. Wuchinich blamed the poor coordination between OSS and the British base because the supplies ordered were sent to other places and, in addition, were delivered by British aircraft. The mission also did not receive any of the military equipment it requested. The meteorological station that transmitted weather reports every six hours was transported to a safe location in a mountainous area after the German air strike in 1944, from where it transmitted without interruption.

During his stay, Wuchinich became familiar with the organization of the Slovenian Partisans, and their training and military actions. He also visited the Partisan Officer Candidate School and established contacts with the British mission. He assessed Partisan commanders and political commissars, and was especially impressed by General Franc Rozman (nom de guerre Stane) and political commissar Boris Kraigher

Slovenian members of the Alum mission (National Museum of Contemporary History).

(nom de guerre Janez). He was also impressed by the fighting morale, endurance, self-discipline, and idealism of the Partisan units.

In his report on the military situation in Slovenian territory, he described that here the Germans encountered a homogeneous population where there existed no antagonistic, racial, or religious contradictions among the population. When evaluating the Partisan tactics, he wrote that they preferred to fight at night, and that they used the tactics of the American Indians and were masters of camouflage. They knew the territory they were fighting in, meaning that the forest was their ally. They often concealed the positions of machine guns and their artillery positions, and urgently needed anti-tank weapons, explosives, and medical aid. It was almost impossible to deliver supplies to the Partisans from the air; therefore a secure bridgehead near the coast was more than needed. He also reported on the negotiations between the Partisans and the Germans, which were unsuccessful.[45]

In one of his reports, Wuchinich described the economic and medical conditions and the overall situation in Slovenian territory, particularly in the territory of the former Ljubljana region. In the introduction he described the medical situation, which he assessed as good. He assessed the teeth of all Partisans to be in poor condition, and stated that the most widespread disease among the men was thyroid disease, whereas combatants suffered from rheumatism and arthritis. The Partisans suffered from the cold and lack of vitamins. He also stated that many women stopped having periods and acquired more manly facial features. There was little or no sexual promiscuity. He also wrote about the Partisan hospitals.[46]

Wuchinich mentioned the lack of salt and sugar in nutrition. Tea and coffee were not available; lunch and dinner were mainly potatoes and meat, and breakfast was most often brown roux soup. The bread was hard and dry. In his opinion, personal hygiene was at a surprisingly high level. OSS marked his report B-2, which usually signified a reliable or a most likely true report.[47]

In one of his reports he also assessed the political situation in Slovenian territory and wrote that it strongly resembled the American Revolution. A united Slovenia within a federal Yugoslavia was one of the military objectives of the Partisans. The Slovenian Catholic priests also assumed different positions; some of them joined the quisling Bishop Rožman, while other joined the Partisans. He was also interested in the position of the communist ideology among the people, and established that the Communist Party was in fact the core of the Partisan movement. In his opinion, the Slovenian communists did not want to force their ideas. They followed the line of nationalism and did not welcome any kind of intervention by the Soviet Union in their internal affairs The credit for managing, assisting in developing, and diffusing the movement among this nation of conservative and religious farmers, primitive in their political thinking, went to the communists. Wuchinich believed that the people understood the call for freedom, not paying attention to who was a communist and who was not. In his belief, their only concern was who was fighting for freedom and who was not. Based on this, the communists enjoyed trust and popularity unlike any other political party. In his report, Wuchinich warned that postwar Yugoslavia would include the Slovenian Littoral and Carinthia, and that the issue of Trieste was also often mentioned.[48]

In the part of his report in which he mentioned collaboration, Wuchinich wrote that the Partisans usually let captured traitors go with an oral warning only, allowing them to join their families. The anti-communist units that the Partisans called the "White Guard" and later the "Home Guard" initially collaborated with the Italians and, after Italy's capitulation, with the Germans. He wrote that the Home Guard was led by General Leon Rupnik and that sadly these people did not know that the Allies were on the Partisans' side. Wuchinich estimated that there must be approximately seventy thousand hostile units in Slovenian territory, five to six thousand of which were White Guard or Home Guard units collaborating with the Germans. The Home Guard units were manned mainly by farmers from the regions of Dry Carniola and Lower Carniola. In April 1944, they were organized in thirty-two companies each numbering 160 men. He also described their leaders, saying that they received political and spiritual support from important "clerical politicians" and Bishop Rožman. The uprising in Slovenia started on April 27 and was led by the communists, but the White Guard remained active in Dry Carniola and in Inner Carniola. He also wrote about the German minority—the Gottschee Germans—who were transferred to the area near Brežice and the Krško Basin, and on political slavery resulting from the fact that Slovenians had never been free because they were under foreign rule for the past 1,200 years. In Wuchinich's belief, the Slovenians were not used to elections because there was no democracy prior to his arrival and everything was subordinated to the military.

He was convinced that the Partisans would allow the widest possible participation of the people in the decision-making process regarding the type of government they would like to have. He was honored that he could witness the first elections in the territory held by Axis forces. He saw many Partisans attending Sunday Catholic mass, because they had a positive attitude toward religion, whereas the "great clericals" collaborated with the Axis forces. Wuchinich believed that they had a high opinion of the communist leadership and their contribution to the establishment of the Liberation Front, meaning that the communists there did not possess the same aura of fear as they did in the west.

He concluded his report with visionary words because Wuchinich predicted that Slovenians would follow neither the Soviet Union nor the United States, but would find an intermediate path that would ensure private entrepreneurship, comprehensive development, and at the same time not allow for too much unemployment. Wuchinich believed that the new postwar Slovenia would be democratic and that the communists would not turn out to be extremists, but prudent and realistic.[49]

Wuchinich participated in political conventions and attended various cultural events. He consequently sent a report on his participation at the Slovenian Cultural Congress in Semič, where he addressed the delegates in the name of the United States. He also met Metod Mikuž, who invited him to a Partisan Catholic Congress.

At the time when the Alum mission was led by Wuchinich, the relations between the mission and the Partisan leadership were fairly good, which was also reflected in the freedom of movement of his members. After Wuchinich's departure on July 25, 1944, when the mission was taken over by First Lieutenant Daniel Boško Desich, the relations started to become increasingly more strained. This, however, occurred not because Desich was unpopular, but because of the overall straining of relations between the Anglo-American Allies and Partisans.

Some tension was already felt during Wuchinich's time because he wrote in his manual on covert operations that freedom of movement was limited and that the Partisan authorities might well be harsh and sensitive. He added that the Partisans were hospitable, but that they let you know that you were a guest and nothing more. They had their own intelligence department, an intelligence service that overreacted to all hostile activities. The main problem that he stressed in his report was communication and information, which always came too late. The Partisan leadership insisted that the missions remain at the headquarters, that their movement remain limited, and that the intelligence information be provided by their intelligence departments. Communication was one of the greatest challenges because almost no one could speak English. He also wrote in his manual that there were also some Slovenians in OSS missions that seemed suspicious to the Partisans because they expected them to join them.

The British never managed to build such friendship with the Partisans as they did with the Soviets and the Americans. The Partisans greatly esteemed the Americans. From their point of view, they were immediately after the Soviets. On the other hand, they did not trust the British due to their foreign policy.[50]

The Alum mission had friendly relations with the Soviet mission. One day they sent a message to the base in which they described the critical posture of the Soviet mission toward the Partisan movement. In his conversation with the Soviet colonel, the head of the Alum mission heard a lot of criticism on behalf of the Partisan army, saying that they lacked discipline and that they talked about politics a great deal but did nothing much about it.[51]

A Slovenian member of the Alum mission, Marijan Česnik, stated that the relations with the Soviets were correct, respectful, and friendly, even though the Soviets were heavy drinkers and also proposed establishing an Allied officers' club at a time when a German offensive was right around the corner. The Soviets ate Partisan headquarters' food, whereas the other Allies ate the food of common soldiers.[52] The Partisan trust in the Soviet missions was increasing even though the Soviet officers strongly and openly criticized the Partisan movement and their manner of fighting.

In his book *Beacons in the Night*, Major Franklin Lindsay assessed Wuchinich as a resolute communist and a Slovenian American that shared Major Jones' colonial prejudice regarding the British officers. His behavior was crude, and he also became a victim of the anti-communist purges by Senator McCarthy.[53] The analysts of OSS assessed Wuchinich as an energetic, hard-working, and sincere officer that clearly acknowledged his devotion to the Partisan cause in Yugoslavia. The officer of OSS / Secret Intelligence, Daniel DeBardeleben, believed that Wuchinich could not objectively observe the complicated Yugoslav scene in such a role. He wrote that Wuchinich's reports were biased and should be limited in number and written in a more concise manner. Wuchinich was completely devoted to the Partisans and proudly stood up for Tito and his fight.[54]

Wuchinich sent only a few reports with actual intelligence content to OSS; however, they included much propaganda material, which bothered his superiors because he was too pro–Partisan oriented. Major Lindsay also believed that Wuchinich's reports were emotional and poor in information. In addition, Wuchinich had sympathized with the Partisans emotionally. He believed that Wuchinich almost never reported on the actual intelligence objectives, the German combat formation, their tactics and the protection of railway tracks, the power and the weaknesses of the Partisan forces, and their effectiveness in the demolition of German communication lines.[55]

On June 16, 1944, Desich parachuted 1944 to Ravna Gora, Croatia together with the Slovenian Viljem Štamol and later came to Slovenian Partisan headquarters.[56]

More strict control of the Anglo-American missions in Yugoslavia and the Alum intelligence mission was carried out on September 18, 1944.

Based on an order received by the Slovenian Partisan headquarters and Tito's Supreme Headquarters, Desich received a message that he did not have approval for operation of the mission, and he was therefore ordered to halt any activities and to call off all groups sent to the field. He was advised to ask for permission through Brigadier Maclean. Only after November 15, 1944, was any further operation of the mission allowed.[57]

The mission structure under Desich's leadership was almost the same as under Wuchinich's. A newly arrived member was Stanley Drozdowski, whereas the others remained the same: the wireless operator and coder Marijan Česnik, the interpreter and coder Franc Menčak, the wireless operator Vladimir Kumar, the coder Ivo Pahor, and the coder Jože Stante. Two other were mentioned: the wireless operator Romeo Gaudet and George Hobson, who worked in the British RAF team for receiving material at the Partisan airport.[58]

Under the leadership of Drozdowski, Kumar, Pahor, and Stante formed an observation group near Litija that surveyed railway traffic. Because they did not have permission from Tito's Supreme Headquarters to operate after the situation became strained between the Anglo-Americans and the Partisans, Deisch sent them home due to the lack of any other suitable work. Their work had no more meaning; the Partisans would not accept any advice on how to improve intelligence reporting. For this reason, all three of them left Slovenian territory on December 11, 1944, and were evacuated to Bari.

Desich continued Wuchinich's work and cooperated well with the intelligence section of the Slovenian Partisan headquarters. He submitted all of the questions that he received from Bari directly to the intelligence section. Desich was especially interested in military intelligence information on German railway transports and the locations of important German industrial facilities. He did not always receive answers to his inquiries, and Partisan intelligence agents often eliminated questions because they either found them inappropriate or simply did not have any answer to them.[59]

The base in Bari was mainly interested in information on the movements of German troops, battalions, and larger units. It required precise information on the location and direction of the movement of a specific unit and as well as the time a specific unit arrived at a certain location. This was important information for the Anglo-American Allies because they used it to bomb German units and posts. At the beginning of 1945, the OSS base in Bari was interested in the Partisan activities in Austria. For this reason they addressed questions to Desich on a number of occasions; he then forwarded these questions to the intelligence section of the Partisan headquarters. He wanted to know whether the Partisan units had crossed the Drava River in Austria or whether they crossed the defense line near Klagenfurt, as well as the locations of certain hostile units. The answer he received from the intelligence section was as follows: "The units of the National Liberation Army and the Partisan Detachments of Slovenia have also been operating on the left side of the Drava River in Carinthia from the very beginning because this is Slovenian ethnic territory. However, the connections were relatively poor due to guards at all of the crossings on the Drava River and especially due to the heavy snow in the winter. The Drava River crossing is considered fairly dangerous."[60]

On January 21, 1945, the Alum mission moved from the Seventh Corps to the Ninth Corps, where it arrived on February 11, 1945. It reported useful and important information on the movement of hostile units in northeast Italy. On its way, the unit lost all of its equipment with the exception of the radiotelegraph device. In addition, its members, Menčak in particular, suffered frostbite. The mission returned to the Slovenian Partisan headquarters on March 31, 1945. Desich later flew to Bari together with the wireless operator and the coder on April 2, 1945.[61] Desich believed that there was no major resistance by Slovenians against the communists because the communists were leading the fight against the invading forces and had thus gained a reputation based on their actions. Regarding the postwar arrangement of Yugoslavia and the role of the communists in it, he was optimistic. He believed that the communists would not act in an extreme manner and that democracy would rule in postwar Yugoslavia. He wrote that the communists were showing the people an image of a federal Yugoslavia in which prewar Slovenian territory together with the Littoral and Istria would be included, but the issue of Trieste was becoming increasingly complicated.[62]

In his reports, he was also critical of the events around him because he believed that the Partisans were exploiting the United States and the British purely for assistance purposes, whereas they respected the Soviets as their real allies. He concluded his report with the statement that, after the departure of the Germans from Slovenia, British and American troops would also try to enter this territory, and that it would be only then that the Partisans would show their true attitude toward the Allies. After the departure from the Slovenian Partisan headquarters, he returned to the area of Venezia Giulia because his name can be found in a message of June

1945. OSS received information from Desich that the Yugoslavs were deporting between five and ten thousand Italian citizens from the territory west of the Isonzo River and that they would thus allow the success of the plebiscite for the return of the disputed areas to Yugoslavia. Information on deportations referred to the arrests and deportations that occurred after May 1, 1945, in Venezia Giulia. This information, however, was not of interest for OSS analysts, who thus requested a reexamination and, in addition, required that the rumors of Yugoslavs running concentration camps for deported Italians be verified.[63] In comparison to Wuchinich, Desich was much more critical of the Partisans, especially at the end of the war, when Desich had already left them. Based on his reports, one can clearly see when he left the Partisans because the content of the messages that were critical of the Partisan movement changed after his departure from Yugoslavia.

The Arkansas Mission

The Arkansas meteorological mission, which is often mentioned in documents under the name Amet, formally operated within the Alum mission, even though it was an independent mission until the departure of most of its members. The mission parachuted into Slovenia on March 13, 1944, and soon arrived at the Slovenian Partisan headquarters. The mission was composed of Staff Sergeant Ralph Baker, Staff Sergeant Joseph Newmayer, and Private Marijan Česnik (Martin Chester). On May 14, 1944, they were joined by the head of the mission, First Lieutenant Robert J. Schraeder, and the mission arranged its own meteorological station in the Gorjanci Mountains.[64]

The arrival of the Arkansas mission was approved by Partisan Colonel Vladimir Velebit, the head of the Partisan mission in southern Italy, and British Force 133 in Cairo because OSS was not allowed to make independent decisions on the mission deployment plan for Yugoslavia. The task of the Arkansas meteorological mission was to install its observation posts near German airports. This was very important for the Anglo-Americans because they received the most precise picture of the weather above Axis-controlled European countries through decoding German messages and could thus set the goals for their bombers up to twenty-four hours in advance. Every German airport had its own observation post in order to be able to report the data every four hours. Hence, the intention of OSS observers was to get as close to the German airports as possible. In this way, the Anglo-Americans soon decoded the German weather code by comparing it to the reports of their own weather observers.[65]

OSS intended to send a number of meteorological missions to Slovenia but failed to do so due to the nature of Partisan combat and constant movements. Major Lindsay, who operated in the Partisan Fourth Operational Zone, was asked to investigate where in Styria it would be possible to install an observation post, but he could not guarantee that the post would be able to operate in the same location for as long as a month. Because the OSS was unable to send a number of meteorological missions to Slovenian territory, other non-meteorological missions were assigned the task of reporting on the weather situation.[66]

In Drage near Metlika, the members of the mission set up a meteorological and wireless station and sent weather reports four times a day to the air base in Bari. Due to constant transmissions, the location of the mission was detected by the Germans, who attacked the mission with fifteen rounds of assault on April 20, 1944, during which one of Česnik's assistants was killed. For greater security, the mission moved to Trdina Peak in the Gorjanci Mountains and later to Črmošnjice.[67]

On June 16, 1944, Schraeder wrote that he and Baker were ill and that they had suggested that the base to evacuate them from Slovenian territory due to medical problems. Schraeder already left Slovenia on August 2 and Baker on September 2, 1944. Newmayer, on the other hand, had already left on July 25 together with Wuchinich. The only one left was the Slovenian Marijan Česnik, who joined the Alum mission as a wireless operator.[68]

The Cuckold Mission

The Anglo-American Cuckold mission (code X-84) at the Partisan headquarters of the Fourth Operational Zone in Styria was led by OSS Major Franklin A. Lindsay. In addition to Lindsay, the mission was also composed of Lieutenant Gordon Bush and wireless operator Sergeant James Fisher. The documents also mention Edward O'Malley Welles and British Army Sergeant Vučko Vučković, who apparently joined the mission at a later time. Together with the Cuckold mission, First Lieutenant Robert Schraeder, the head of the Arkansas (Alum Amet) mission, arrived in Slovenian territory. Lindsay's group, which belonged to the OSS / Special Operations Branch, parachuted into Slovenian territory on May 14, 1944, and arrived at the Slovenian Partisan headquarters with the help of the Partisans, where members of the mission met with Goodwin and Wuchinich. On May 27, 1944, the group traveled to the north toward the headquarters of the Fourth Operational Zone, where it finally managed to arrive after numerous complications on June 15, 1944.[69]

During Lindsay's stay among the Styrian Partisans, living conditions were extremely difficult because they were constantly threatened by German patrols. In addition, much rain fell and the food was scant. Due to the difficult terrain, the constant German presence, and constant movement, it was very difficult to organize assistance for the Partisans, which was one of the key tasks of Lindsay's mission. In addition, the mission had to report on the enemy's traffic and the movement of his forces, and organize the evacuation of shot-down Allied pilots and prisoners of war. It is therefore not surprising that Lindsay is also mentioned as working with the British secret service (Military Intelligence 9, MI9), the task of which was to evacuate personnel from the Axis-controlled countries and to debrief them.[70]

One can find many reports on the movement and the location of hostile units, military transport, and evacuation among the American and British documents of the Cuckold mission. In contrast to the reports of some other OSS and British officers, who soon after their arrival to the Partisan or Chetnik lines came under the influence of the propaganda of either movement, Lindsay's intelligence reports were highly esteemed. On his last assignment, Lindsay traveled to Croatia and at the end of the war became the head of an Independent American Military Mission.[71]

Lindsay's mission was an Anglo-American mission, which in fact represented one part or a submission of the mission of Maclean, He sent his messages to two bases at the same time (SOE and OSS base), which also sent him his questions with similar military topics, which he submitted to a Partisan intelligence agent. The British SOE gave Lindsay an order: "Major Lindsay is appointed as commanding officer of the Allied military mission at Partisan forces in Styria. As such he is authorized to represent the Allied military authorities in this area. He or his delegate is the only representative of Brigadier Maclean and through him the Allied Supreme Commanders in all matters referring to the connection with the Partisan military authorities in Styria, including the military plans and supplies."[72]

Lindsay wrote a final report on his operation in the Fourth Operational Zone between May 14 and December 7, 1944, which was later supplemented by the remarks of the historian Tone Ferenc and published in the journal *Borec* in 1983. Other Anglo-American liaison officers at Partisan headquarters had to write similar reports. Their reports were similar;

4. OSS Missions in the Partisan Movement

they all portrayed the Partisan struggle as positive, but assessed the Partisan leadership—which constantly controlled intelligence operations and limited the movement of Anglo-American missions—in a negative way.

Lindsay sent reports to the SOE base in southern Italy (Force 399). The same reports, however, were also received by OSS base with an active OSS / Moral Operations. The OSS / Moral Operations had extremely unrealistic demands because Tito's Supreme Headquarters wanted to send an officer that would be in charge of the propaganda and psychological operations against the Germans. These requirements were unrealistic for both the Partisan leadership and the other OSS branches because the content of the propaganda messages contradicted the American strategy in the Balkans and in Yugoslavia. The OSS / Moral Operations gave Lindsay a Memorandum on the proliferation of propaganda and the methods of propaganda operations. In addition, the OSS / Moral Operations wanted to provide information for him on occasion so that he would spread false news or rumors among the Slovenian Partisans, Slovenian collaborationists, and Austrian farmers, depending on the type of rumors.

One of the pieces of advice he was given on how to act toward the Partisans and the civil population was not to praise Tito too much, except in the territories under Partisan control, because the peasant population was generally not keen on orthodox communism. It was not desired to spread rumors about any disputes between the Soviets and the Americans, and no criticism of the Catholic Church was allowed. It was acceptable to criticize the Catholic Church only in the event of its open collaboration. The Home Guard was marked as a collaborationist force even though it was pro-western oriented. The OSS / Moral Operations submitted instructions to Lindsay regarding any political issues that were not in accordance with the orders received. Disputable were the instructions that he should convince the Slovenian Partisans that Venezia Giulia and Istria, including the area of Klagenfurt, would be granted to them, should they lead an active uprising.[73]

The instructions were as follows:

> Your main objectives in Slovenia should be: demoralization of the enemy army. You should carry out pressure on all traitors and their supporters (with the exception of priests) and demoralize them. You should encourage all separatist tendencies among the Austrians and warn them of the Moscow Declaration in reference to Austria. You should encourage unity of resistance in Slovenia and prevent misunderstandings and disputes. Encourage the Slovenians to actively resist the enemy and convince them to get support from the Allies for the endeav-

ors invested in the successful combat against the enemy. The more Slovenians that are to fight in the resistance, the greater will be the Allied assistance for the postwar reconstruction of the land and the realization of their territorial requirements toward Austria and Italy. You should convince the Slovenians of the military, economic and political power of the United States of America and their victory in the war.[74]

The Anglo-American officers apparently acted on their own conviction and belief on a number of occasions, giving no promises regarding the borders. The instructions above were, as is well known, in total contradiction to the American policies that stipulated that all conclusions on postwar territorial changes would be postponed until peace negotiations following the war. The British regarded the border issue in a similar way. In addition, OSS / Moral Operations gave instructions that OSS officers were to suggest that the United States would occupy Slovenian territory before the Soviets did, which contradicted the non-interference policy of the American Army in the Balkans.[75]

The general conclusions of Lindsay's mission in the final report[76] on his stay in the Fourth Operational Zone between May 14 and December 7, 1944, were as follows:

1. The Partisan forces of the Fourth Operational Zone greatly contributed to the destruction of German communications between Italy, the Balkans, and Germany.
2. This contribution was not as much as it could be given the number of shipments and the teams available to the Partisans and taking into account the feeble German resistance. This is especially true of the period after September 1944, when the Partisans almost completely lost their initiative.
3. Through obstruction and indifference, the Partisans in the Fourth Zone prevented the representatives of the Anglo-American Allies from obtaining anything more than a small percentage of the available intelligence information on the enemy's movements across this important area.
4. In general, the Partisans obstructed all efforts by the Anglo-American Allies to receive intelligence information from Austria in order to infiltrate agents into Austria and to start an Austrian Partisan movement against the German "occupation."
5. The incompetence and negligence of the Allied base, as far as supply was concerned, was to be blamed for the failure of numerous actions and for the frequent ineffectiveness of the Partisans

because urgent supplies were not delivered to the right place and at the right time.

The general conclusions of Lindsay's report must be explained because he was forgetting the successful operations of destroying the German communications Bearskin and Ratweek[77] in his second conclusion because they were organized together with the Partisans and it is hence difficult to claim that the Partisans almost lost their initiative after September 1944. In addition, the last conclusion can offer an incorrect interpretation of the claim that the Anglo-Americans saw Austria as an occupied land and that its inhabitants were ready for organized resistance to Nazism. The reports of other Anglo-American missions for infiltration into Austria claim the exact opposite because according to them there was no resistance among the Austrian people or such resistance was negligibly small. The report was divided into separate thematic chapters describing different phases of the Cuckold mission. Lindsay initially analyzed the Partisan power, which included the battle formation of the Fourth Operational Zone and the Partisan military operations, which in his opinion were both successful and efficient in combat against the enemy and his communications. In his report, he described the Partisan organization, locations and movements of German units, the use of military equipment, Germanization, emigration, and aviation operations in detail. Especially interesting were his assessments of intelligence activities. Like the majority of the Anglo-American officers, he also wrote that the Partisans allowed no independent action in collecting intelligence information for the Anglo-American Allies. They received all intelligence information from extracts from Partisan intelligence reports. He assessed the Partisan intelligence agents as poorly trained and few in number, and thus unable to carry out their work effectively. The Anglo-Americans were not permitted to interrogate prisoners, fugitives, or any other person of that kind arriving from territory held by the Germans, except upon and after the end of the war.

The tasks of the Cuckold mission were exclusively military and not political, which meant that in his reports Lindsay never sent any political assessments of the Partisans or any other information of a political nature. He saw the Liberation Front as a coalition of several parties; however, in his opinion there was no interest in the existence of any other party except the Communist Party. He described the simple Partisan fighters as pro–American and pro–British, whereas the Slovenian communists and officers glorified the Soviet Union and its role in the war. They were mistrustful toward the British because they understood their every move as aiming to return the Yugoslav king to the throne and thus limit the Partisan aspirations to annex certain territories disputable to the British. Following the examination of Tito's Supreme Headquarters, the Cuckold mission likewise did not have written permission for its operation, and so its members ended up in an unofficial detention of some kind. The new Partisan politics became obstructionist politics, which was reflected in limitation of the freedom of movement and restrictions on access to intelligence information for all Anglo-American missions. The Partisans rejected all initiatives for conversation. Therefore he wrote to his base in October 1944 that he had literally been put under house arrest during the previous month.[78]

One of Lindsay's tasks was the evacuation of prisoners of war and shot-down Anglo-American airmen, which was also the task of the British MI9 service or the A Force service. The A Force service sent Major Matthews to the Fourth Operational Zone, who from his arrival onward could do nothing to liberate and evacuate prisoners and avia-

Major Franklin Lindsay, head of the Cuckold Mission, speaking at a Partisan celebration in Styria, 1944 (National Museum of Contemporary History).

tors. This only caused relations between the Partisan leadership and the Anglo-Americans to deteriorate. Many Partisan officers occupied certain positions based on the time they spent fighting on the Partisan lines and due to political reasons, meaning that professionalism did not always play the key role. He also noticed the different types of food received by the Partisan officers and ordinary soldiers.

In the analysis of the infiltration of OSS groups and missions into Austria, Lindsay was convinced that all Partisan operations related to Austria were covered in extreme secrecy and included a number of machinations. He also claimed that to this end the Partisans hindered and sabotaged all Anglo-American efforts in every way possible. Major Lindsay was firmly convinced that the Partisans maintained contacts with Villach, Klagenfurt, Graz, and Vienna, although they claimed to have lost all connections and were thus unable to provide safe addresses in Austria. Lindsay's claim raises the question of how involved the Slovenian Partisans were in organizing resistance in Austria and the connections they had with possible Austrian organizers of anti–Nazi resistance. In the archival documents there is no record of any kind of connections between the Slovenian Partisans and Austrian rebels. The Partisans were not very obliging to the missions and groups headed to Austria. and therefore in August 1944 they demanded that all members of the Anglo-American mission for Austria leave. This was supposedly a consequence of the fact that the Germans had captured ISLD agent Dick Black and that the Gestapo had discovered some Anglo-American and Partisan identities. They were not allowed to meet the Allied airmen and prisoners of war that the Partisans brought from Austria.[79]

In his report, Lindsay listed a number of reasons for poor relations between the Anglo-Americans and the Partisan leadership. Specifically, they did not want the Anglo-Americans to know how strong the Slovenian anti-communist camp really was because they were aware that their postwar situation was not very stable; the proximity of the Red Army gradually encouraged the Partisan leadership, even though it only managed to reach the Prekmurje region; they feared that the British would bring the Yugoslav King back to Yugoslavia; the Partisan leadership was afraid that the Anglo-American endeavors in Austria would contradict their territorial claims; the assistance of the Anglo-Americans was not as great as promised and expected by the Partisans.

Lindsay also endeavored to build airports with the approval of the British Royal Air Force that would facilitate the shipment of assistance and the evacuation of wounded Partisans in the Fourth Operational Zone. Royal Airforce wanted to send an officer prior to the beginning of the construction. This officer would have to approve and prepare everything necessary for building the landing site; however, the Partisan leadership was unwilling to accept him. The Partisans later started building the airport at the same location where the Anglo-Americans were planning to build it. However, the airport was never used because the severe winter and the German offensive by the end of 1944 prevented it.

Lindsay was also critical toward OSS staff in Bari, who planned their missions poorly on a number of occasions and were also very poorly coordinated among themselves. Lindsay heard about the arrival of twelve agents of the Fisher group for infiltration into Austria only when the group arrived at the headquarters of the Fourth Operational Zone, due to which he was very disappointed by the OSS base in Bari because nobody had asked his opinion or told him about the arrival of Fisher's group. Lindsay believed that all Allied matters would be much better handled by only one combined mission composed of two officers, two wireless operators, and one coder.[80]

He believed that his superiors were sending too many personnel representing too many organizations and secret services, such as OSS, ISLD, and SOE, to Styria. SOE members often demanded identical information from the Partisans, and so he proposed that it would be better if one mission only carried out work for everyone else.

In his final report, Lindsay concluded that in September 1944 the Anglo-American mission in the Fourth Operational Zone counted altogether twenty-seven officers and soldiers. That caused problems because the Anglo-Americans were represented by different organizations and could thus not always stand behind a united policy in relation to the Partisans; they made a poor impression on the Partisans when they saw the number of people with little or no work; different missions requested the same information from the Partisan headquarters; and it was very difficult to provide food, shelter, and guards for all of the Anglo-American officers and soldiers. In contrast, all of the Soviet interests were represented by one officer only.[81]

He also put down in his report that the American and British endeavors to infiltrate Austria were less successful, and also criticized the agents, who were poorly prepared for infiltration. They came without documents, false stories, secure addresses, and civilian clothing and were thus at the mercy of the Partisans. Lindsay also stated that he did not perceive any proof of any kind of resistance in Austria against the German regime. He stated that there were some Austrian organizations, but none of them ever took weapons in hand and carried out any kind of sabotage action.

During his entire stay among the Styrian Partisans, Lindsay was supervised by the Department of National Security because he was a critical observer, which is evident from the reconstruction performed by the Department of National Security's successor, the State Security Department (UDBA), after the war. Some of Lindsay's statements about the Partisans not portraying him in a positive way are also analyzed. Part of the statement is as follows: "due to the sabotaged shipments declared that he (Lindsay) will attack the base, but told me in confidence that he does not believe to be successful and that he is convinced that there will be no promised descent/descend promised by comrade. Luka/, as the Allies do not have airplanes at their disposal." Another statement states that: "On 7 October, Lindsay declared that the Partisan commissar will not see him; due to the arrival of the Soviets to the territory of Yugoslavia, the relations are apparently deteriorating—he declared that he apparently used to be good enough for advertising purposes at rallies."[82]

He assessed the relations with the Soviet mission as good, especially with the liaison officer Bogomolov, who believed that the problems the members of the Cuckold mission experienced with the Partisans were not incited and fueled by the members of the Soviet mission. Lindsay was convinced that the Partisans were praising the Red Army and the Soviet Union far too much, even though their mission arrived later. The members of the Soviet mission were exclusively soldiers and did not have any established political or Communist Party connections with the Partisan Politburo. Lindsay supported the Partisan enthusiasm over the Soviet mission with the following words: "The Partisans were thrilled to finally have their Russian brothers and comrade communists at their side. However, the mutual relations soon cooled down, which was carefully concealed from us by the Partisans. The Russians evidently expected to have a strong influence on the Partisan commanders. But the Partisans decided to fight their own fight."[83]

On November 18, 1944, Lindsay received an order to return to Bari from the Partisan Fourth Operational Zone. He became a head of the Durand mission and left his intelligence work to Captain Charles Fisher and together with Edward Wells and Jim Fisher, he traveled from Gornji Grad toward Lower Carniola and continued his way to the Croatian Partisan headquarters on December 18, 1944, where he was to arrive on Christmas

Eve. He left for the base for a couple of days and then returned to Yugoslavia. Wehrmacht General Edmund Glaise-Horstenau, the German military plenipotentiary at the Croatian Ustasha puppet government with whom OSS from Switzerland established contact, wanted to discuss surrender and also requested a secret meeting with the American officer. Lindsay received this message from his command. The negotiations were to take place in Zagreb under the greatest possible secrecy, and so he established contact with the Glaise-Horstenau group through a wireless connection as an OSS agent. When Tito authorized his route, he was replaced by the British officer, Captain Owen. Allen Dulles, the head of OSS in Bern, established contacts with Glaise-Horstenau through agent K-6. Prior to that, the Partisan delegation sent an agent to Zagreb, who returned with a message that the German general had already been arrested by the Gestapo. However, this information is questionable even today because Glaise-Horstenau never mentioned it in his memoirs.[84]

On June 9, 1945, he went to Caserta for three days, where he coordinated arrangements regarding Trieste and Rijeka with the officials of the Allied Force Headquarters and Ambassador Kirk, returning to Belgrade on June 23, 1945. All of these areas were occupied by the Yugoslav Fourth Army and the British Eighth Army; the resolution of these political affairs was essential. They also discussed the decentralization and reduction of OSS Belgrade City Team. It was arranged that First Lieutenant Pfeiffer would continue to the north with the Dunklin mission and the Fourth Army to establish contacts with the Slovenian Partisans, while First Lieutenant Welles would stay in Trieste.

At the end of the war, Lindsay was present in Trieste at the conference in the company of General Frederick Morgan and the representatives of Tito's Yugoslav government. Lindsay's view on postwar borders was interesting because he defended the thesis that the Anglo-Americans should receive Trieste. Unlike Lindsay, the British Lieutenant Colonel Wilkinson was more inclined toward Yugoslav demands regarding the Slovenian Littoral and Trieste even though he established that the Slovenian Partisans were strongly influenced by the Soviet Union.

It is risky to generalize that Lindsay's and Wilkinson's opinions really do reflect the different standpoint of British and American politics regarding the Yugoslav postwar territorial requirements. Based on Lindsay's and Wilkinson's case, it can be established that despite the instructions of their superiors the Anglo-American officers were quite liberal in expressing their opinions, which they put down in their reports.

4. OSS Missions in the Partisan Movement

The Flotsam Mission

The Flotsam mission was an Anglo-American mission headed by the Canadian liaison officer that worked for SOE Major William Jones from June 1943 onward. At the end of March 1944, Major Jones was replaced by OSS liaison officer Captain James Goodwin, who headed the mission until October 4, 1944. He flew to Bari for a short time in August 1944 to give a report, and then returned. Immediately upon his arrival in Cairo, at the end of 1943, Goodwin was assigned to join the mission headed for Yugoslavia. He wrote the final reports on his activities in the Flotsam and Mulberry missions in Slovenian territory and Croatia. The archives on the reconstruction of OSS missions, written by State Security Administration after the war, present Goodwin as an officer deeply hostile to the Partisans. He was negatively critiqued by the Department of National Security, whereas OSS archival documents presented him as a diligent and hard-working officer that was not much involved in political action, but rather in the organization of Partisan assistance and the evacuation of Allied airmen.[85] At the end of December 1943, OSS Lieutenant Colonel Toulmin ordered Goodwin to join the Anglo-American mission, under the command of Brigadier Maclean. The mission was sent to Yugoslavia on January 19, 1944. Goodwin, along with Maclean, Farish, Major Churchill, and Lieutenant Eli Popovich, ended up in Bosnia.

At the end of February 1944, Maclean informed Goodwin that the Anglo-American mission at the Slovenian Partisan headquarters, headed by Major Jones at the time, was not being conducted in a satisfactory manner, and he asked him if he would like to be transferred there to improve the situation. Goodwin accepted the offer and headed from Drvar to Slovenia on February 1, 1944, with a small group. The journey proved to be extremely difficult because the soldiers had to walk a long way over many hills covered by 60 to 90 cm of snow. After a grueling journey, they arrived at the Slovenian Partisan headquarters in Semič on March 22, 1944. This mission also operated at the Partisan Seventh Corps headquarters.[86]

Soon after joining the Flotsam mission, the mustached twenty-four-year-old engineer, who also became a hero of the American comic *Goodwin's Guerrillas*, found it impossible to cooperate with Major Jones in a way that would improve the situation of the Anglo-American mission. He spoke of this with British Lieutenant Colonel Peter Moore, who relieved Major Jones of his duty and appointed Goodwin as head of the mission. In the trial month that included the organization of Anglo-American air assistance to the Partisans, Goodwin convinced the Slovenian Partisan commanders and Maclean with his results.

At the beginning, the Flotsam mission, in addition to Goodwin, included the British doctor Major Rogers, Major Scott from RAF, responsible for landing fields, Captain Saggers from the American Air Force (USAAF), Captain Leonard, a British Royal Engineer, Lieutenant Jack Wick, two American Sergeants, eight British Sergeants, and two Canadian Yugoslavs.

Goodwin spent most of his time organizing evacuations of shot-down Allied airmen and prisoners of war, ordering air assistance for Slovenian Partisans, accepting and recording assistance, submitting intelligence information, and maintaining communications with the Slovenian Partisan headquarters. He provided questions and suggestions from the Anglo-American headquarters in North Africa for the chief Partisan commanders. He also advised them on tactics and on how to organize attacks on the enemy without having to resort to unreliable Partisan methods. He submitted locations of important road and rail communications that presented suitable targets for Anglo-American bombing, in particular the route between Ljubljana, Pivka, and Rijeka, which supported the main German transport. Moreover, he submitted requests for gas, oil, emergency medical aid, and new generators for radiotelegraph devices.[87]

As a liaison officer, Goodwin encouraged the Partisans to control the important railway line from Trieste to Ljubljana to an extent that prevented the enemy from transporting supplies and units to the Italian front. Goodwin was personally involved in the attack on the rail bridge over the Sava River in September 1944, in which he was slightly wounded. His participation in the attack was reported from the Slovenian Partisan headquarters to Tito's Supreme Headquarters.

The head of the Anglo-American mission personally participated in our operation on the bridge over the Sava River at Litija, which included several Allied airplanes that, prior to the attack, dropped bombs on enemy positions. "Contrary to our advice and warnings, the head of the mission refused to remain in the division headquarters and moved on. He sustained a very slight leg injury, inflicted by a fragment of an Italian hand grenade. He continues to head his mission, but will soon be evacuated to Bari to have the iron fragment removed from his leg (above the knee). He has declared that he attended the campaign at his own risk. Parts of this operation were captured by Mr. Phillips, a photojournalist for *Life* magazine."[88] Goodwin's role was especially important for organizing evacuations of shot-down Allied airmen and prisoners of war. Goodwin viewed the

Captain James Goodwin, head of the Flotsam Mission, speaking at the funeral for American airmen, May 7, 1944 (National Museum of Contemporary History).

Partisan army as well organized with developed guerrilla warfare doctrine and execution. However, he was also critical. All intelligence on the enemy and the Partisans was submitted to the mission through daily Partisan intelligence reports. To an extent, however, these were superficially composed, inefficient, and biased. All requests forwarded by the mission first had to be sent to the Partisan intelligence unit under the watchful eye of the political commissar. Goodwin wrote that the Partisan leadership was very unwilling to accept any recommendations on improving its system; even when it agreed with the proposals, these were never realized to a satisfactory extent. It usually took a week to ten days for intelligence on operations, troop movements, and rail transport to reach the mission.

On September 30, 1944, by order of Tito's Supreme Headquarters on the limitation of the Anglo-American missions, Captain Goodwin was informed that the Anglo-American mission had no written authorization for its operation. Moreover, Goodwin was asked to submit detailed information on his mission's members. The team, as cited by the Slovenian archival documents, consisted of Assistant Head of Mission British Lieutenant Jack Wick, American Sergeant Romeo Gaudet, British Sergeant S. Booth, American Sergeant George Hobson, British Sergeant Mihajlo Klobučar (Mike Clark), British Sergeant Frank Pavletich, British Sergeant Reginald Reffold, British Sergeant Less Westerby, British Corporal Tom Gordon, Major L. Scott RAF, Sergeant G. Brombey RAF, Sub-Sergeant C. Lowell RAF, Sergeant E. Poole RAF, and Corporal Wright RAF. Major Scott's team also lacked a license for the operation and use of drop zones and airports. On September 30, 1944, Major Scott was called to return to Italy. He was succeeded by Captain Wiley.[89]

Goodwin described the Partisan military commander and the political commissar as nervous and suspicious people that behaved very coldly in relation to all matters official. Over time, Goodwin managed to convince both that he was able to manage their affairs for them and that his sole reason for staying in Slovenian territory was to help. After three months they were willing to cooperate, although it turned out that some arrangements and principles were only slowly implemented in practice. Goodwin was convinced that the current Partisan political organization was controlled by the communists. Communists were pulling all the strings and holding the highest positions in the National Liberation Movement. He doubted that farmers and the middle class could understand the concept of democracy because it was impossible to organize a party that would be opposed to Tito. Moreover, he had concerns about the future democratic regime in Yugoslavia.[90]

Goodwin described relations with the Soviet mission as good and appropriate. At meetings and parties, Soviet officers appeared quite fun and intelligent, and came across as good military officers. In formal meetings, however, where discussions focused on problems and politics related to the United States, the United Kingdom, and the Soviet Union, these officers proved extremely difficult. They were unwilling to cooperate with the Americans and British, and they disagreed with all proposals unless suggested by them. Goodwin slowly realized that, if they did agree to a compromise, they made no effort to comply with it, or only complied with it if it suited them. The Partisans offered them everything they wanted, and the Soviet mission took great advantage of this.

Like all American and British liaison officers, Goodwin realized that the Partisans accepted the Soviets more warmly. The Soviets appeared to have greater access to information on Partisan operations and German intelligence. In a way, however, not even the British trusted the Americans because they felt threatened by the growing American involvement in the Balkans. Goodwin felt that the British in Yugoslavia were only led by economic interests. Not only did they behave as though they were natives, but the Partisans also lost many ships at the expense of misdirected bombings by the British Royal Air Force.[91]

Goodwin was evacuated on October 5, 1944, because, as the war progressed, his presence in the area was no longer needed, and also because he required surgery due to a minor leg injury which he sustained in the attack on the bridge over the Sava River at Litija. When he returned to Bari he was instructed to prepare his final report while waiting for orders related to his return to the United States. The orders, however, came earlier than expected and Goodwin wrote his report in a rush, not being as detailed as he had intended.

After Goodwin's departure and before the arrival of British Major William S. Pears in January 1945, the Anglo-American mission was headed by the deputy commander, First Lieutenant Jack Wick.[92] Later, Goodwin returned to Yugoslavia (to Croatia), where he remained until March 9, 1945.

The Arrow Mission

Captain John Blatnik was an American OSS officer of Slovenian origin.[93] The main reason for his recruitment was his knowledge of the territory, his understanding of the political and geographical situation in Yugoslavia, and his knowledge of Serbo-Croatian and Slovenian. He was of great interest for the Department of National Security and the later State Security Administration because he was constantly supervised even after the war. On January 8, 1945, Blatnik took over the OSS mission at the Slovenian Partisan headquarters. During his stay in Slovenian territory he established contacts with the Partisan cultural activists, with his neighbors, and people with whom some members of his mission shared their dwellings. In their postwar elaboration on OSS missions, State Security Administration officers wrote that Blatnik presented himself as a supporter of the National Liberation Movement in public, but was in fact its enemy. In his personnel folder it is mentioned that he was only thirty-two years old at the time and was from Minnesota and a captain in the American Army. Some of his most distinct characteristics that were mentioned are: "He speaks loudly and slowly. He speaks Slovenian with an accent typical for the Lower Carniola and Inner Carniola region. He is correct and politely pushy with his propositions."[94]

Blatnik's final report[95] includes a chronological report of his stay, an accurate analysis of the political and military situation in Slovenian territory and Croatia, relations with the Partisan leadership and other Allied missions, and proposals for improving fieldwork. A large part of Blatnik's work was included in diplomatic cables and other military reports on the military situation in Yugoslavia, which he regularly sent to his superior base. In his final report, he states that he flew from the Italian city of Brindisi to Glina, Croatia, on August 12, 1944, where he led a team to rescue Allied airmen. The rescue team was composed of Staff Sergeant Joseph Bradshaw, Jr., and Corporal Arthur S. Kern. They were one of the groups under the command of Colonel George Kraigher, whose mission was to search for and evacuate Allied airmen shot down over Yugoslavia and those that parachuted into Yugoslav territory. At that time, the Anglo-American mission at the Croatian Partisan headquarters was led by OSS Captain George Selvig. During his stay in Croatia, among other things Blatnik also reported on the poor relations between the Anglo-American missions and the Partisans. Many Anglo-American missions became stuck at the Partisan headquarters because they did not have permission with Tito's signature for their stay in Yugoslavia. Blatnik's mission ended in September 1944, and therefore the personnel were evacuated to Bari.[96]

Blatnik returned to Croatia with OSS's Durand mission again on November 20, 1944, when he was sent to Korenica south of Bihać from Bari in Italy. He was again accompanied by Staff Sergeant Joseph Bradshaw, Jr., and Sergeant Arthur S. Kern; they were commanded by Colonel Lanning MacFarland.[97] He first came to Slovenian territory on November 25, 1944, when he, Colonel Ellery Huntington, and Staff Sergeant Musulin departed from Croatia to visit the Slovenian Partisan headquarters, where he became familiar with Partisan General Dušan Kveder, the head of the British mission Lieutenant Colonel Peter Moore, and the political commissar Boris Kidrič.

He came to Slovenian territory for a second time on January 4, 1945, together with Sergeant Arthur Kern and Major William Pears. They stayed in Paka near Črnomelj, where the British, the American, and part of the Soviet mission were accommodated. Prior to Blatnik's arrival, OSS mission was led by First Lieutenant Daniel Desich. The mission was located at the Slovenian Partisan headquarters until December 1944, and it then moved to the Seventh Corps, where they mainly operated in the neighborhood of Paka and Žužemberk, and finally left for Croatia. From Croatia they once again traveled to Slovenia, where together with the Slovenian Partisan headquarters in May 1945 they went to Ajdovščina and then continued their way to Gorizia and Trieste, which they returned to in June 1945.[98]

In his report, Blatnik carefully analyzed the relations with the Partisans in both Croatia and Slovenian territory. He wrote that the Partisans were very fond of the Russians, that he had not seen many signs of communist indoctrination, and that their love for the Soviet Union derived from their traditional fondness for "Mother Russia" and its strength, which was slowly destroying the Germans. Due to the ignorance of the ordinary people, he had many problems explaining the role of the United States as their ally. The Partisans had many problems accepting the American role during the war until the Anglo-Americans opened the second front. Blatnik wrote that the regular soldiers knew only little of the American and the British share in the war. According to Blatnik's assessment, the Slovenians' relations toward the British were cold, whereas they accepted the Americans with more open arms.

Like other Anglo-American liaison officers among the Slovenian Partisans, Blatnik also stated in his report that relations between the Anglo-American missions and the Partisans were deteriorating, which was best reflected in the limitation on their movement because the members of the missions were not allowed to move anywhere without the Partisans accompanying them or without their permission. Stricter surveillance of the Anglo-American missions started in the summer of 1944 and in the winter of 1944 and 1945, which was also felt by Blatnik. The reduction of the Anglo-American military and material assistance, OSS mission to the Chetniks in Serbia, and the increasing Yugoslav reliance on the Soviet Union strained the relations between the Anglo-Americans and the Partisans. Blatnik also established that the relations and the atmosphere in the corps' headquarters and the Slovenian Partisan headquarters were completely different than in the lower units. At higher headquarters the influence of the political commissar, the great fondness toward the Soviet Union, and the lack of affection toward the United States, and especially toward the United Kingdom, was strongly felt. He had many problems with acquiring authorization for conducting movement across the field, where they could also visit lower headquarters and units.

With the help of Partisan Major Boris (Boris Čižmek) and two first lieutenants, the Anglo-American agents established contacts with the Slovenian Partisan headquarters. They received all intelligence reports essential for their operation from the Partisans. All requirements and important questions had to be typed and sent to appropriate Partisan officers. In contrast to the British and the Americans, the Soviets had a higher position and many more benefits, which were also reflected in their mobility: they had their own car, better food, a driver, and better access to intelligence information.

He describes the relations between the British and the Americans between January 8 and May 19, 1945, characterizing them as follows: "I had a feeling that several officers from their mission are not very fond of the United States. In June and February, I have often come to them, while they only seldom returned the visits, and so I stopped visiting them. They were extremely secretive even regarding completely ordinary things."[99]

He mentions the Soviets as cold, conceited, and reserved. They most often met at official events. The contacts with the Soviet representatives

Captain John Blatnik, head of the Arrow Mission, saluting at a funeral for American airmen, April 5, 1945 (National Museum of Contemporary History).

were hindered by the Partisans, who demanded that they accompany OSS missions at their every attempt at making connections. Finally, following several visits, the ice was broken and they established friendly relations. Blatnik states that the relations between OSS personnel and the Partisans improved in April 1945, which was a consequence of the good American relations with the Soviets, especially after the meeting of American and Soviet units in Germany. In Blatnik's opinion, the Soviets respected the United States more because they were impressed by the great power and the greatness they demonstrated in the war. The changes in the relationship were soon also reflected in the field because the American personnel were suddenly allowed to move more freely and visit the natives and their relatives. The Partisans paid much more attention to possible espionage activity by the British intelligence agencies and their missions than OSS.[100]

For his superiors Blatnik also prepared proposals for improving work in the field. The proposals included demands for promotion of their ranks because OSS officers had lower ranks than the Soviet and the British ones. The Partisans often understood this as belittling and underestimating their movement. He also proposed establishing better connections among the groups in the field and the base in Italy, and required that the personnel in the missions be notified of current events. He also presented proposals for a more transparent policy on what the Anglo-American missions were or were not allowed to do at lower Partisan headquarters. Blatnik's conclusion in his report clearly demonstrates the poor cooperation between the commands of the Anglo-American missions because some commanders of OSS and British missions received contradicting directives and demands regarding the same intelligence information, which was also requested at the Partisan headquarters. In this way, the British and OSS missions simultaneously expressed demands for the same information, which often led to annoyance on the part of the Partisan intelligence officers.[101]

After the takeover of the Arrow mission by the Slovenian Partisan headquarters, Blatnik became actively involved in everyday reporting on the military situation in Slovenian territory. The daily diplomatic notes sent by Blatnik included intelligence information on locations, movements, and identification of hostile units. He often included a list of required material assistance. Therefore, soon after taking over the leadership of OSS military mission, Blatnik asked for additional material assistance; specifically, a radiotelegraph device, a gasoline-powered generator, a battery for the radiotelegraph device, a voltmeter, and other accessories.[102]

On January 23, Blatnik requested that OSS base send him information on the number of Partisan units and their plan regarding their advance into Austria. The Partisan intelligence officers, however, refused to respond to his requirements because they did not feel competent enough, and so they directed him to the political commissar at the Slovenian Partisan headquarters. One can see from the answers that the Slovenian Partisan headquarters sent all important information on the enemy and his activities and purposes, but sent nothing on the Partisan political plans or their numbers.[103]

In February 1945, Arthur M. Cox wrote to the chief of the Secret Intelligence Mediterranean Theater of Operations that they should consider reducing the number of OSS personnel in Yugoslavia. He proposed that all activities of OSS that were not important or were the same as those of the British be abandoned. Soon after, on March 5, 1945, Blatnik asked his superiors in the Yugoslav OSS Section for permission to leave for the United States for a short period of time because he had certain obligations as a member of the Minnesota Senate. However, his request was rejected. He believed that during his absence he could be replaced by an appropriate liaison officer. In addition, he also wrote that the relations at the Slovenian Partisan headquarters had become calmer and that the atmosphere was much friendlier. In March 1945, the freedom of movement of the mission was still limited; they had very little contact with Partisan officers, Partisan soldiers, and the civilian population. As stated above, the relations between the Partisans already improved the next month. Like most Anglo-American officers, Blatnik was also responsible for taking care of the shot-down Allied airmen. Hence he inquired at the Slovenian Partisan headquarters on March 28, 1945, about the shot-down pilot Larry Usher, about whom the Partisans had no information. In February, March, and April he was also interested in the results of the bombing of Maribor, the German plans in Istria, the deployment of German antiaircraft guns, the locations of the SS divisions, members of Decima Mas (X^a MAS),[104] railway traffic, oil transports to Germany on the railways, and the locations of the German units and headquarters at the Sežana hospital. His requests were predominantly of a military intelligence nature, and so he received the requested information.[105]

As the end of the war approached, the territory of Venezia Giulia became increasingly important for the Germans and the collaborationist units. In February 1945, the number of German soldiers in Venezia Giulia decreased because some of the units had already left toward the north to Austria. However, during the next month many new units arrived in the Gorizia and Trieste region. Hence, in April 1945 Blatnik informed his superiors that the Germans were to counter any attempt by Anglo-American forces to land in the Slovenian Littoral. He was also interested in the changes that had occurred in the liberated territories from February 1945 onward because the Anglo-American Allies wanted to know which areas were safe and appropriate for landing in the event of an aircraft accident.[106]

On April 18, 1945, he established in his intelligence report that the Red Army was the main favorite of the Slovenian Partisans. He also participated in formal diners and rallies, where he had the opportunity to observe the Partisan enthusiasm for the Soviet Union. At these events, only the material assistance of the United States and the United Kingdom was mentioned. There was no talk about the British or the American contributions in the war against the Axis powers. According to Blatnik, the political commissar Boris Kidrič was the key person leading the pro–Soviet propaganda. He warned that the Partisans were firmly decided on occupying and annexing Trieste, Carinthia, and the Slovenian Littoral and joining them in a new state.[107]

The Partisan leadership did not want the Anglo-American Allies to know about their actual power and the locations of individual units wanting to occupy Yugoslav ethnic border areas by the end of the war. All of the questions of the American and the British liaison officers that referred to the territorial aspirations of the Partisan army and the movement of individual Partisan units were unanswered. Blatnik also perceived the loss of independence of Slovenian Partisan units that were included in the Yugoslav Fourth Army, which he wrote about on May 1, 1945. He reported on that day that the Yugoslav Army occupied key enemy positions along the railway from Rijeka to Postojna and had managed to reach to Trieste. He was under the impression that the Fourth Army determined all of the military operations in Slovenian territory and that the Slovenian Partisan headquarters merely followed its plans. On May 4, 1945, he reported arriving in Ajdovščina and that he would be leaving for Gorizia on May 5, where the Slovenian Partisan headquarters was also headed. On May 8, 1945, he went to Trieste, which he also returned to on May 13 and May 18, 1945. Afterward he left Trieste and went to Caserta. Based on Blatnik's statements, the Slovenian Partisan headquarters moved in extreme secrecy and disclosed no information on its future movements. After a long period of time, he was once again granted complete freedom of movement and freedom to communicate with the people, who were glad to see Italian supremacy come to an end. In the same month Blatnik was reportedly instructed to report on the question "Tito or Slovenia?" but his answer to this instruction cannot be found in the archival documentation.[108] The issue of credibility of Blatnik's intelligence reports is that in the period when he operated as the head of the Arrow mission he, like all other Anglo-American officers, received all intelligence information from extracts submitted by Partisan intelligence officers. All intelligence reports were thus selected by the Partisans and not by Blatnik because he was not allowed to move freely and to collect information himself.

At the end of the war, OSS withdrew all intelligence groups from Yugoslavia, with the exception of the one that remained in disputed Trieste, which Yugoslavia wanted to annex. Trieste was thus becoming the scene of the new conflict. However, like Lindsay, Blatnik also appeared on the list for Trieste in June 1945; he returned to Trieste from Caserta as a member of a new and larger team. OSS from Trieste had numerous problems, especially due to the opposition of the British secret agencies, which by all means possible wanted to have the leading position in terms of intelligence gathering in Trieste. The historian Biber also believes that the diplomatic cables of OSS of May 1945 offered a dramatic image of the disputes between the British and the American intelligence agents. In contrast to the Americans, the British had a number of services and undercover agents in Trieste.[109]

In addition to helping with the demobilization of some Slovenians from OSS, Blatnik also participated in the search for missing people that were believed to have been captured by the Yugoslav authorities. Hence the parents of the Italian officer Vinicio Lago asked Blatnik to investigate the whereabouts of their son because they were afraid that the Yugoslav authorities had arrested him on May 1, 1945, on his way between Udine and Trieste and sent him to a concentration camp. Lago was head of the mission that was apparently connected to the Italian intelligence service (SIM),[110] which was sent from southern Italy in September 1944 to Udine, where it was to establish contact between the Italian resistance in Udine and the Slovenian Littoral and the government and the military circles in the south. Lago was apparently the only one that provided connections between the Trieste anti-fascist and anti–Italian circles and the military circles in southern Italy, and at the same time maintained contacts with Italian non-communist Osoppo Partisans and the National Liberation Committee for the Venezia Giulia (CLNG). On May 1, 1945, on his way between Udine and Trieste, he was apparently killed by Garibaldi Partisan units; however, the circumstances of his death remain unclear.[111]

After the war, Blatnik already operated outside the Partisan headquarters, and therefore the nature of his intelligence reports changed. He also reported on the measures of the new Partisan authorities that were apparently imprisoning and liquidating numerous potential adversaries of the Yugoslav regime. On August 25, 1945, he submitted information to Lieutenant Colonel Chapin that he had received on the basis of testimonies from forty-five people that fled to Trieste or were visiting it. These unverified oral sources stated that, after liberation, between sixteen and twenty thousand people were killed and that the Partisans killed between thirty-two and thirty-six thousand Slovenians, which are definitely exaggerated statements. Most likely most of the imprisoned persons were released, and the number of those killed (i.e., between thirty-two and thirty-six thousand) is questionable because Blatnik received this information from oral sources, which cannot be backed up by archival documents. Blatnik submitted these narratives without commenting on their credibility through military and intelligence lines. The American Embassy in Rome later enclosed this report with their report of the State Department dated October 9, 1945. No response by the State Department to the report of the American embassy has yet been found in the archival documents.[112]

The documents of OSS and the Department of National Security contain records on and interrogations of Michael Hollinger (sometimes spelled Hilinger),[113] an American citizen, who ended up in Slovenian territory on his way from Serbia after being captured by the Germans and then escaping from captivity. He arrived at the Slovenian Partisan headquarters in December 1944 together with Allied evacuees. The Department of National Security arrested him as a Gestapo agent. In addition, they found the latest OSS documents on him. Blatnik endeavored to help Hollinger and thus inquired about him and his citizenship with his superiors on January 17, 1945. They confirmed Hollinger's claims that he was a citizen of the United States, and Blatnik helped him evacuate from Slovenian territory. The State Security Administration documents incriminated Blatnik because he supposedly arranged a flight from Slovenian territory to the Bari base for Hollinger and handed him certain documents on this occasion. Blatnik defended Hollinger, who admitted that he was forced to work for the Gestapo.[114] Hollinger was psychologically completely demoralized and exhausted by the arrest. He believed that everyone was conspiring against him and he was planning to commit suicide. Finally, he was re-leased by the Partisans and Blatnik arranged a flight for him to Bari. In Bari, they sent him to a hospital, where a neuropsychiatrist evaluated him as suicidal and a constitutive psychopath.[115]

According to the assessments of the State Security Administration, Blatnik's circle was also frequented by the painter Božidar Jakac and his spouse Tatjana, Čoro Škodler and his spouse, and Marjan Kozina. Ac-cording to the State Security Administration, the connection with Blatnik was supposedly also maintained by the spouse of Božidar Jakac, who was providing him with intelligence information. His other connection was Milan Kocjan, who was part of the theatre of the Partisan Seventh Corps. In his intelligence activities in Novo Mesto, Blatnik supposedly used con-nections with the spouse of Milan Kocjan and Ana Sitar from Toplice, who was well known for her connections with the British mission. Other persons that Blatnik supposedly had contact with and frequently visited after the war are also mentioned. The documents of the State Security Administration most frequently mentioned as Blatnik's collaborators the Yugoslav-born OSS agents.[116]

Blatnik was a critical observer of events around him throughout the entire time because he dared to criticize both the Partisan leadership as well as his superiors. He was aware that the Partisan were trying to ensure its power through revolution and that the leaders of the movement were communists. At the same time, he was aware that the Partisan struggle was essential for defeating of the Axis powers in Yugoslavia.

OSS Missions in the Slovenian Littoral and Connections with the Slovenian Partisans[117]

The landing of Anglo-Americans in Istria could have opened the door for the Allies to central Europe through the Postojna Gate, and therefore they—especially the British—often contemplated this idea in the Venezia Giulia region, particularly in Istria. Their leading circles wanted the mis-sions to obtain as much relevant information as possible about the actual situation on the ground. OSS was also present with its missions in Istria, in the Udine area, the southern part of the Slovenian Littoral, and especially in the Trieste area, where the first missions had been sent starting in Jan-uary 1944. Between January and June 1944, individual Italian-American missions landed in Istria and were tasked with preparing the area for a potential landing of Anglo-Americans and maintaining contact with the base. They arrived in Trieste, but the majority of them were captured and destroyed, and so only a few of them established contact with the local national liberation committee (*Comitato di liberazione nazionale*, CLN).[118]

Meanwhile, OSS initiated its activity in the Udine area during the summer of 1944, which coincided with the arrival of first SOE missions to this area (to the Italian Partisans, Garibaldi Partisans, and Osoppo groups). Some OSS missions also established contact with Slovenian Partisans from the Ninth Corps, who were suspicious about them and forbade them to move across Slovenian territory and the territory under the control of the National Liberation Army without permission from Tito's Supreme headquarters. The reason for the suspicion among the Partisans was the fear of a potential Anglo-American landing or increased presence of Americans and the British in the territory claimed by the Partisans.

Suspicious OSS agents joining the Slovenian Partisans were also mentioned in May 1944 in a message by the Ninth Corps to the Slovenian Partisan headquarters, concluding that none of the groups that had arrived were willing to provide any statements and that it was impossible to compel them to provide more information about their work and their superiors. The report also mentioned the settlement of disputed collab-

British liaison officer at a shooting party together with Slovenian Partisans from the Ninth Corps in Lokve, 1944 (National Museum of Contemporary History).

oration of a Partisan officer with the British. Moreover, the intelligence staff of the Ninth Corps noted that the statement of British Major Bakston and some agents indicated that the British and Americans landed between Rijeka and Udine or dropped some groups of agents designated particularly for Trieste. The Ninth Corps informed the intelligence bodies of the military and civilian authorities that they should reveal and find those agents.[119]

The first mission that was part OSS / Secret Intelligence was led by Valeriano Melchiori, who faced several operational problems. The mission landed near the Gorizia Hills on February 14, 1944, and ignored the demands of the Partisans when it landed; it also allegedly lacked discipline, which was probably noticed by the Partisans and the local population. After three days, the mission met the Garibaldi Partisans headed by Mario Fantini (Sasso) and moved in the field with their escort. On April 9, 1944, the mission was captured in the Gorizia Hills by the Chetniks and it lost all of its equipment, money, and a radiotelegraph device. The mission was held for twenty-eight days in Gorizia, and they suggested that the leader of the Chetniks accompany them to the Chetnik headquarters in Trieste. The Chetniks decided to help them secretly and took them to Opatija, where an unknown local group wanted to meet with the mission. They spent three days in Opatija and the Chetniks promised them that they would be released provided that they would work for them, but the mission rejected this proposal because it was informed that the Chetniks were cooperating with the Germans. The Chetniks then received confirmation that this was an OSS mission and they let the mission go. There is no information on how the Chetniks verified the identity of the OSS mission.

The mission claimed its equipment and returned to Trieste, where it found out that its equipment was in Ljubljana. They were told that the radiotelegraph device would be given back by the Germans, so the group instead decided to return to Trieste, and in the meantime the Germans had also determined their identity. The group evaded the Chetniks on the way to Gorizia and established contact with the Partisans of the Ninth Corps. The British mission at the Ninth Corps requested a new radiotelegraph device for the group and warned the group that it had no permission from Tito's Supreme headquarters to remain with the Ninth Corps. Some OSS archival documents mention that Melchiori's mission supposedly engaged in provocations among the Partisans and threatened to escape to the Germans rather than waiting in a certain village for further instructions. When pleading with the Ninth Corps headquarters, the group sought excuses for the threats expressed. Afterward, the British Captain helped the group establish contact with Goodwin and Wuchinich at the Slovenian Partisan headquarters. With their help, the mission received assurance that it had been sent by OSS and was then evacuated with Partisan help to Bari.[120]

This particular mission was also recorded in some testimonies collected by the Italian author Aldo Moretti, which, however, differ from the story found in OSS archives. He notes that the mission arrived in January 1944 and was captured by the Home Guard. Their leader established contact with OSS Cairo in Ljubljana, which confirmed their American identity. He sent them to Trieste and ordered their release because the Home Guard was not at war with the United States. Their stories also did not convince the leadership of the Garibaldi Partisans. Their leaders Fantini and Padoan accompanied them to the Ninth Corps, and then they disappeared. After the war, Fantini met them in Pieriso, where they stayed with the Fifth Allied Army. Moretti concludes that there was no information about their previous whereabouts and activity.[121]

The Plum mission was prepared by OSS / Secret Intelligence and led by Lieutenant Ego de Baseggio. He was accompanied by wireless operator Giuseppe Bucalo. In January 1944 they landed in the vicinity of Poreč in Istria, and were joined by Giovanni de Manzini and Livio Corsi. Through De Manzini, the mission established contact with Italian communists from Monfalcone, with whom they had cooperated until they were discovered. The mission retreated toward Slovenian territory, and de Baseggio and Bucalo were arrested by the Slovenian Partisans. They told them that they were establishing contact between the Americans and the Partisans. In August 1944, after confirming their identity, they were allowed to return to the base.[122]

A report on the Plum mission is also preserved in the Archives of the Republic of Slovenia, where the materials of the Slovenian Partisan headquarters include the following information supplementing the story of the mission. The mission is believed to have consisted of Lieutenant Ego de Baseggio, Aldo Naglia, wireless operator Giuseppe Bucalo, Giovanni Buccalli, and agent Livio Corsi, who had been hired in Trieste. The Lieutenant provided a statement saying that the mission had arrived in Istria on January 3, 1944, in the vicinity of Poreč. In Brindisi they had been tasked to make contact with the Partisans, who were to help them with their information activity. De Baseggio stated that they arrived in Trieste on February 6, 1944, and sought contact with Italian communists. On

February 15, 1944, they established contact with Giovanni de Manzini, a member of the Italian Communist Party, who promised them he would support the activity of the wireless operator. He provided contact with Boris Strojko from Monfalcone, who worked for Slovenian Partisans and reminded them that they would not be allowed to work in Partisan territory without a pass, and so they waited for permission. Strojko was shot soon afterward. In De Baseggio's opinion, his death was attributed to the Slovenian Partisans.

On March 16, Manzini was arrested by the Gestapo, and therefore OSS sent Egidij Walsenfeld instead, who was apprehended by the SS on April 29. After a while they became suspicious to the Italian National Police, and the mission members Corsi and the wireless operator were able to leave the town. In the end, De Baseggio received the radiotelegraph device and started working, and the Monfalcone communist also promised him assistance from the British wireless operator. De Baseggio met for the last time in Ronchi with Egon from the Slovenian Partisan Ninth Corps, who gave him a pass for free movement. He went to the village Šebrelje, where he hid his radiotelegraph device and was waiting for the wireless operator, but received a female agent named Corsi, about whom no detailed information is available. The three of them found themselves together in the first days of May 1944. The Slovenian Partisans provided him contact with a certain Slavko, who reported on everything that he had been doing. They were promised to receive instructions on their work in Partisan territory within a week, but the waited a whole month and sent several letters to the corps commander. Initially, the Partisans did not allow them any contact with the representatives of the Anglo-American mission at the corps; however, having established contact, they were allowed to return to the base.[123]

On the night of August 2, 1944, OSS sent the Eagle mission to Mount Pala close to the town of Clauzetto above Carnia, which landed together with the Mercury mission. Both missions were prepared by OSS / Secret Intelligence. The Eagle mission consisted of the leader Lloyd G. Smith (Smitty), Lieutenant Joseph F. Lukitsch (Joe), wireless operator Joseph S. Zbieg (Stan), and interpreter Victor Malispino (Vic). Later on they were joined by interpreter Godfrey Hall, who came from the Garibaldi Partisans. The mission was tasked with establishing contact with the Garibaldi Partisans and Osoppo Partisans in the Tramonti di Sopra area in order to train and help them in subversive activity against the enemy, to collect intelligence, and to prepare drop zones for deliveries of Allied help. The mission soon realized that there was no unity among the Garibaldi and Osoppo Partisans. Moreover, the mission was constantly threatened by enemy reprisals in the winter of 1944–1945. Smith therefore decided to advance east, where he met with the Slovenian Partisans in the town of Taipana on December 25, 1944. With their help they proceeded to Yugoslavia and were evacuated to Bari.[124]

OSS archival sources also include a document probably written at the end of 1944 or beginning of 1945 about a Slovenian named Dušan Humar from Maribor, who had been allegedly sent to a mission in the region of Venezia Giulia. He probably carried a letter signed by Slovenian Minister in Yugoslav government in exile Miha Krek and cooperated with the Partisan Liberation Front. Supposedly he was active in the area between Gorizia, Trieste, and Ljubljana as a courier between these towns in support of Slovenian counter-revolutionary circles. His task was to establish contact between Anglo-American Allies in Italy and the Slovenian non-communist underground movement. The movement was prepared to start fighting against the Germans, carry out acts of sabotage on the rail line from Ljubljana to Trieste, and provide information from the areas of Ljubljana, Gorizia, Trieste, and Lower Styria. This was probably one of the attempts of counter-revolutionary circles in Rome to offer cooperation to Anglo-American intelligence services.[125] The attempt to send Humar to the Venezia Giulia region probably failed because there are no reports or information available on his activity in this region.

As for the interwar activity of OSS intelligence in Istria, there was the previously mentioned OSS Dunklin mission led by First Lieutenant Pfeiffer. Based on OSS archival documents, it can be concluded that this mission operated in the field between 1944 and 1945, and was located in Dalmatia (close to Split), and in Istria and Slovenian territory at the end of the war. In April 1945, the superiors inquired with the mission head if Pfeiffer was able to join the Yugoslav Army as the first to possibly arrive in Trieste and whether any of the mission members spoke Italian. The mission went to Trieste and made contact with the Slovenian Partisans. Soon afterward Pfeiffer's mission was told to stay in Istria, where it obviously accomplished its tasks successfully, reflected through abundant praise by the superior base.[126]

5

The U.S. and the Anti-Nazi Resistance in Austria

INFILTRATION TO AUSTRIA

In the last year and a half of the Second World War, the primary goal of the Allied intelligence services was to infiltrate Germany, including Austria, with the aim of establishing an intelligence network and Austria's resistance, which would spread across the Austrian borders to Germany and Hungary. The same goals were pursued by OSS, which tried to establish connections with members of the Austrian Communist Party and other resistance groups to encourage them to engage in anti–Nazi activity. As early as March 1944, OSS contemplated the idea of establishing a special Austrian Section in the Middle East to be integrated in OSS Bari, which directed OSS activity in Yugoslavia. One of the possible starting areas for potential infiltration was the Partisan area of the Fourth Operational Zone along the Yugoslav border with Austria. An important role in the penetration of the Anglo-American missions toward the north was played by the Partisan Eastern Carinthian and Western Carinthian Detachments, initially led by the Carinthian Detachment Group Headquarters.[1]

At the end of 1943 the Anglo-American intelligence agencies were enthusiastic about the possibility of infiltration toward the north; however, already during 1944 their enthusiasm dampened. In November 1944, the joint Anglo-American military mission, 1, was divided in two; namely, an American and a British mission. All of the previous members of the Anglo-American military mission of the Fourth Operational Zone were recalled from Slovenia, leading to only eight British and American soldiers and civilians within the Fourth Operational Zone at the beginning of 1945.[2]

The British SOE was to develop plans for Austrian infiltration from the Fourth Operational Zone. Lieutenant Colonel Peter Wilkinson, head of SOE Central European Section and chief of the Clowder mission along with his assistant Major Alfgar Hesketh-Prichard (cover name Alfgar Cahusac) visited Tito's Supreme Headquarters in December 1943 to obtain approval for the Fourth Operational Zone as a transition point to the Third Reich. Tito approved the plan, and Wilkinson and Prichard arrived in Slovenian territory on December 24, 1943.

The mission was tasked with establishing conditions for sending British agents to Austria. Initially they made a stop at the Slovenian Partisan headquarters and proceeded to Carinthia on the northern side of the Karawank Mountains. Upon an unsuccessful attempt to cross the Karawanks during winter, Wilkinson returned to Italy to organize support for deploying agents to prewar Austria from the Italian side; that is, from Carnia. On May 15, 1944, Lieutenant Colonel Charles Villiers (known as Buxton), Wilkinson's deputy, joined the Partisans of the Ninth Corps, and together with Hesketh-Prichard set off across the Karawanks for the Carinthian Detachment. Hesketh-Prichard was then killed by the Partisans.[3]

From OSS bases in Italy, a growing number of teams and missions designated for infiltration to north were dispatched in the second half of 1944 to Slovenian territory, and to Austrian Carinthia and Styria. The Fourth Operational Zone headquarters received a number of Anglo-American missions, and the quantity of Allied weapons and equipment dedicated for the Partisan movement gradually increased. On March 3, 1944, the head of the OSS Labor Section for Italy, which was tasked with initiating resistance against Axis Forces of the labor party team, Edward A. Mosk, arrived in Bari and met with Colonel Vladimir Velebit two days later and Vladimir Dedijer on March 28. They devised a plan for OSS to set up a camp in the territory controlled by the Partisans and, with help of Partisans, to establish contact with underground resistance groups and labor organizations in Austria, Hungary, and Germany. The team designated for Austria was to include two trained agents and a wireless operator. OSS therefore trained eleven agents and six wireless operators to be initially deployed to the area of Villach, Klagenfurt, and Graz. On August 12, 1944, the head of the Austrian OSS Section, Lieutenant Colonel Howard M. Chapin, together with Mosk, informed Tito in detail about those agents and their biographies, at the same time making a joint recommendation to request permission from Tito to join the Partisans, disclosing as little information as possible because those men were not expected to stay long in the territory controlled by the Partisans.[4]

Based on initial reports from Austria in the fall of 1944, both the United States and the British began to change their assessments about the resistance situation in Austria. They concluded that there were no indications of resistance among the Austrian population. They eventually had some information about some minor anti–Nazi groups, but those were rather inactive. At the same time, it can be noted that the American personnel were increasingly dissatisfied with the unwillingness of Slovenian Partisans during the infiltration to the north, and they therefore decided at OSS to send their teams directly into Austrian territory. The teams mainly consisted of Austrian citizens, German Army deserters, and left-wingers that found their tragic end in Nazi capture.[5]

The Department of National Security noted the following message about the intentions of OSS missions for Austrian infiltration: "The American mission located with the Slovenian Partisan headquarters also sent a team to the Fourth Operational Zone in Styria with the task of organizing and directing underground organizations in Austria, to spread its propaganda and agents among those revolutionaries. However, their work was based not only on the infiltration of agents in Austrian underground organizations, but it also involved an active interest in our officials and the National Liberation Movement itself."[6] Allied intelligence services therefore hoped to see the evolution of resistance toward the end of the war with the help of Italian, Slovenian, and Croatian Partisans, and that Austria would become an active entity in the destruction of Nazism and the creation of the postwar situation—which, despite great efforts, never happened.

The Orchid Team

On August 27, 1944, a team of twelve OSS agents led by Captain Charles Fisher landed at the Nadlesk airfield. Eight members of this large OSS team were active within the teams Tunic, Fern, and later on Orchid. All of them were headed by the forty-year-old German socialist Robert Weichmann. Weichmann's eight agents, also known as Mosk's team, belonged to the OSS Labor Desk from Bari under the leadership of Edward A. Mosk, and the other four agents under Fisher belonged to the Austrian Desk of the Secret Intelligence Branch headed by Lieutenant Colonel

5. The U.S. and the Anti-Nazi Resistance in Austria

Howard M. Chapin and were subordinate to OSS for Central Europe (OSS/SICE). Although the members of Mosk's team rejected Fisher's authority, the Partisans also held Fisher responsible for the Labor Desk agents. The twelve agents operated in the area of the Fourth Operational Zone, where Lindsay acted as the senior responsible Anglo-American officer. Mosk's team hence included the Tunic[7] team with three Jewish agents: the wireless operator Ernst Knoth, Charles Deutner, Guy Justin, Walter Hass, and Robert Weichmann. The Fern team consisted of the soldier Arthur Bartl (Art), First Lieutenant Joseph (Julius) Rosenfeld, and Charles Martin. In addition to the Tunic and Fern teams, the Rose team was mentioned as part of the OSS Labor Desk but with no detailed information about its agents. Later on, the Tunic and Fern teams were called the Orchid team, and consisted of eight Austrians under the Weichmann's leadership.[8]

The twelve agents under Fisher also required Tito's permission to enter Yugoslavia, and therefore on August 12, 1944, Colonel Huntington was requested by OSS Bari to reach an agreement with Tito on sending those agents to Yugoslavia to allow their infiltration of Austria. Huntington was evidently successful because Tito's Supreme Headquarters issued a note on August 22, 1944, stating that the OSS team under the leadership of Captain Fisher was granted approval to set up an intelligence base on the Austrian border at the section of the Partisan Fourteenth Division for dispatching agents to Austria. Weichmann also prepared a final report about the Orchid team covering the entire story of Weichmann's team and its members that had left the Fourth Operational Zone and the members that were reported missing.[9]

After several weeks of waiting at the base due to bad weather and for the appropriate phase of the moon, the entire team with four radiotelegraph devices joined the Partisans on August 27, 1944. There was another option available for some time—namely, to send the team to Italy and from there to Austria—however, the initial plan prevailed. From Nadlesk the team moved to the Slovenian Partisan headquarters, together with the Partisan patrol and a team of British soldiers, including Joseph Phillips, a photographer for *Life* magazine. The team then proceeded north and soon reported that it had arrived at Gornji Grad and was momentarily incapable of advancing north due to the lack of any Austrian resistance group.[10]

OSS regarded Weichmann as a mature and intelligent person, loyal to democratic principles while maintaining an extraordinary level of objectivity in his reports. The group was tasked with infiltrating Austria with the help of the Slovenian Partisans, obtaining useful intelligence on the situation in Austria, and establishing contact with labor groups. In the report by the Orchid group, Weichmann noted that after landing in Slovenian territory the mission waited at the Fourth Operational Zone Headquarters to cross the Drava River. Major Lindsay and British Major Mathius had doubts about the possibility of bringing such a large mission across the Drava in the Pohorje Hills sector, which allowed three members of the Orchid group to join the Partisan Eastern Carinthian Detachment. The remaining five members of the Tunic and Fern groups realized that it was impossible to advance north and therefore decided on September 30, 1944, to return to Bari, where they flew on October 11, 1944. In contrast to Weichmann, Lindsay stated that the remaining four, and not five, agents were sent back by Fisher without the consent of Mosk, who wanted to keep all of his agents among the Slovenian Partisans. Mosk complained about Fisher on several occasions, claiming that he had prevented Mosk's infiltration toward the north, although Fisher had never been subordinate to Mosk.[11]

According to Partisan sources that were also mentioned by the historian Ferenc,[12] the Fourth Operational Zone was presumably left only by four persons—namely, Deutner, Haas, and Justin, who departed on October 11, 1944, and the soldier Bartl, who had been evacuated three days earlier. The fate of the potential fifth member, Ernst Knoth, can be speculated from various sources. In line with the most likely version, Knoth did not leave for Bari but spent the winter of 1944 with Rosenfeld in a Carinthian Partisan Hospital. All traces of him were lost and he was pronounced missing at the end of the war. Several sources have been preserved about OSS soldier Arthur Bartl, who had been preliminarily sent to Bari on October 8, 1944. He was also mentioned in the accounts by Lindsay and Fisher, who reported to Mosk and Chapin about sending Bartl home for "blabbing" everything to the Partisans and because his talking verged on subversion. Bartl also made up a story about being a member of the American Communist Party and the fact that OSS had no intention of helping the Partisans. Among other things, he proposed that Partisan commissar Benčič remove Lindsay and let him take over the mission and wireless connections with Italy. The Partisan leadership obviously questioned Bartl's stories because Fisher also received complaints from the Partisan commissar and officers about improper talk and behavior by the Bartl. He reportedly became very drunk and attempted to rape a female Partisan.[13]

The Partisan commissar received instructions in October 1944 from the Slovenian Partisan headquarters about facilitating the penetration of the OSS mission to the north, and therefore on October 17 the remaining three members of the Orchid group, Lieutenant Julius Rosenfeld, wireless operator Ernst Knoth, and Robert Weichmann, set off to the north. On October 22, 1944, they reached the Partisan Carinthian Detachment and sent their first report from Austria on the very next day referring to the military and economic situation in Austria.[14] The group stayed a full six weeks with Carinthian Detachment waiting for their departure across the Drava River to the north despite the promises of the Partisan Headquarters about providing all necessary assistance. The main reason for postponing their departure was the Partisan requests for new deliveries of weapons, which were approved by the Bari base but never shipped. The Partisans explained the postponement of their departure with other excuses, such as they wanted to help them across the river but had no weapons. Later on, the entire group had to withdraw from the Drava Valley due to continuing German attacks, so that the three agents could not penetrate into Austria. On December 3, 1944, Weichmann decided to leave the Fourth Operational Zone and return to Bari, where he flew in on January 8, 1945. An interesting part of the Orchid message addressed to Mosk on November 29, 1944, concludes that something wrong was going on in Partisan circles because the Communist Party was holding several meetings with the "opposition."[15] More detailed information about who the communists kept contact with or what the "opposition" meant could not be found in OSS archival materials.

After Weichmann's departure, Rosenfeld and Knoth stayed with the Partisans and continued their work. An increasing number of German units interfered with the area of their activity, and therefore on December 18, 1944, they informed Mosk that after ten days of fighting with the Germans they were exhausted and starved, and had lost contact with Fisher. Moreover, the group lost all of its equipment and had to sleep in severe cold. In January 1945, the base at Bari lost contact with the Orchid group upon receiving the team's last message on December 25, 1944, in which Orchid reported about its inability to continue with the work and the intent of the remaining members of the mission to attempt a breakthrough toward the south to major Partisan teams. The base learned through British channels on January 2, 1945, that Rosie and Ernst ended up in a Partisan hospital due to chilblains.

Biber, Lindsay, and Gorjan[16] mentioned that both OSS agents were injured in the December German offensive and that they most likely died during the German attack and fire in the Partisan hospital. Similar information can also be found in the archival material of the Slovenian Partisan headquarters, according to which, following the German offensive in December 1944, the two of them were at the Partisan hospital, whereas the May 1945 reports claim that they were declared missing. In December 1944, Fisher sent a telegram to Bari briefly mentioning that Rosie and Ernst were in the Luče area, where the situation was becoming "hot." They were reported to be on the move and unable to establish contact or receive a shipment. Nevertheless, they intended to continue with their plan of crossing the Drava River.[17]

The historian Linasi questioned the likelihood of the death of OSS agents during the hospital fire and notes that they spent only two days there before being released. They allegedly departed for the Partisan Carinthian Detachment, yet it was not known if they eventually reached it. As indicated by Bob Plan, OSS agent in this zone, they lost their lives under unknown circumstances soon after their return from the hospital, and their bodies were allegedly buried in a mass Partisan grave in Solčava. According to other unverified information, they were seen in Eisenkappel after the war. Linasi also refers to two undated statements by both OSS agents describing the Partisans in a rather negative tone. Their statements are full of impressions, self-infatuation, and excessive self-praise, whereby they do not hold back in their accusations against the Partisan movement. Their assessment of the resistance and Slovenian territorial aspirations is particularly interesting:

> What are you fighting for? All of the people that we met are dissatisfied with you. Such an army makes no sense. The war will be decided neither by the Partisans nor the Yugoslavs, nor by any other country; it will be dictated by Washington instead. Because we Americans will not tolerate having a war every twenty-five years. We Americans do not care at all about where Carinthia or the Littoral or any other part of your country belong; all we want is peace. In Carinthia, for example, people speak Slovenian and German. Those people will always support the winner. If the winner speaks Slovenian, they will be Slovenians, and if he speaks any other language, they will support him. Masses of people are opportunistic, and the golden key opens heaven's door. We support the idea of removing national borders all over Europe and of establishing only economic...[18]

Judging from the statements, it can be claimed that they could be victims of Partisan revenge, although information can be also found in OSS sources that the two members of the Orchid team might have been captured and killed in the spring German offensive while attempting to infiltrate Austria.[19] The question of the fate of these two OSS agents remains open despite investigations about their disappearance carried out by several commissions.

Weichmann notes in his report about the Orchid team that weather conditions led to unsuccessful penetration to the north and that the concentration of German forces in Austria was too high. Weichmann was also ignorant of the fact that there was supposedly a certain Austrian resistance group in his immediate vicinity, but he did have unverified information about Austrian resistance groups, which were rather passive. The main tasks of the Partisan Carinthian Detachment were to control German movements, to send the information collected to the Fourth Operational Zone headquarters, to disrupt the Germans during penetration into the interior of Slovenian territory, and to carry out continuous assaults on small German units protecting the roads and rail lines.

Weichmann had many contacts with the civilian population and established that all of the farmers were good patriots and liked the Partisans. In his opinion, there was no difference between the farmers north of the old Austrian border and those living in the Solčava region. He noted that seventy percent of the Carinthian Detachment's fighters were Slovenians from mountainous areas; they were pious, but not overly rigid, Catholics and were intensely loyal to their country. The majority of fighters were unencumbered by ideology and politics, and were genuinely enthusiastic about Tito and reserved about Stalin. There were no non–Slovenian Austrians in the detachment. Weichmann indicated that common soldiers and people only rarely discussed political issues, and that the soldiers were forbidden to discuss politics with Americans and other foreigners. He noticed that the Partisan commissars praised the Soviet Union more than the United States or the United Kingdom. Common soldiers had simple goals: to drive the German soldiers from their country and to provide freedom and a good deal of independence to Slovenians in postwar Yugoslavia. The Orchid team also provided relief material for the Partisans and sent several reports to Bari, which were particularly useful for the Allied air forces. All of the intelligence of the mission was obtained through the commissar, who often rejected the Allies' requests. The Partisan leadership supplied the mission with information of a military nature, but withheld information about the Partisan leadership and its future plans. Weichmann noticed that the Partisan leadership and the majority of fighters supported the annexation of southern Carinthia, including Villach and Klagenfurt.

The Partisans explained to OSS personnel that they deserved those lands that were mainly populated by Slovenians on the basis of historical rights and sacrifice of Slovenians in their fight against Nazism.[20]The analysis of the Orchid team activity shows that it never accomplished its goal of penetrating Austria and obtaining appropriate intelligence and contacts. The team nevertheless regularly sent intelligence to Bari, which contained specifically valuable information on damage caused by bomb attacks and information on locations of Nazi factories and railway traffic. Every attempt by the team to penetrate north was obviously prevented by the Partisan leadership.

The Maple Mission

A team of twelve agents under OSS Captain Charles Fisher, also known as the Maple mission (designated as J-9), comprised eight agents from OSS Labor Desk (Mosk's team). Mosk's team formally rejected Fisher's authority, but the Partisans also regarded him as the commander of Labor Desk agents. In addition to Mosk's team, three agents of the Austrian secret intelligence section operating within OSS Central Europe (OSS/SICE) reported directly to Fisher. Fisher's team of the Austrian Section, also referred to as the Maple mission in OSS sources, consisted of Bob Plan (Robert Perry), Lieutenant Quinn, and Sergeant Thabit. After several days, the mission finally awaited Tito's permission and landed safely at the Partisan airfield at Nadlesk on August 27, 1944. In his report, Quinn mentioned that Fisher and four other men were allowed to move north together with the Partisan commissar on September 29, 1944.[21]

The mission was tasked with penetrating Austria with the help of the Partisans to organize an uprising there and send intelligence to Bari. The task was set optimistically, and moreover the OSS Austria Section did not inform Lindsay as the competent Allied officer in the Fourth Operational Zone about the arrival of Fisher's team in his zone. Even Lindsay himself questioned the successful penetration of such a large team into Austria. Moreover, the team had no clear plan for how to carry out the penetration into Austrian territory, nor did it possess appropriate civilian clothing and documents.[22] Prior to departure, mission members conducted preparations in OSS Austria Section composed mainly of Austrians, among them also many prisoners of war and fugitives that left Austria after its annexation to the Third Reich in 1938.

Fisher's reports were full of accusations regarding delayed Partisan assistance, which was critical for the mission's penetration across the

Drava River. Several reports deal with restrictions on the movement of the entire mission and constant excuses by the Partisan leadership claiming that postponing the mission's departure to Austria was linked to German forces and the security concerns of the Allies. Fisher was convinced that the reasons for such behavior by the Partisans were political and not military, and he mentioned the following in his report:

> Every conversation ended almost at the same point. Every time, the words used were different, the reasons mentioned were different, the duration of every conversation differed, everything was different apart from the common outcome, which was always the same: "We have to wait a few more days, the situation has changed, and it would not be sensible at the moment to embark on such a dangerous mission." I will have better news for you shortly, and so on and so forth, from one end to the other.
>
> The tone of conversations was polite, friendly and gave the impression that everybody was trying to help us as much as possible. Our relations are not tense and everything is perfect, except that we are getting nowhere.
>
> After a few conversations like those above, I assured the political commissar that we have not asked them to provide for our security. I explained to him that we are fully aware of all potential risks and that I am ready, capable and willing to give my written assurance that he will under no circumstance be held responsible for anything that might happen to us.
>
> I explained to him that it was necessary for us to go on with our work and to accept obstacles or risks on our way should there be any. Namely, we could not wait for a golden path to open in front of us studded with orange flowers and covered with a red carpet. We must go on irrespective of the danger, and therefore I asked him to give us permission to move north, with their courier showing us the way. Not only once, but more than ten times he rejected this request politely and evasively, but resolutely.
>
> In my opinion, the Partisans are pursuing the politics of complete obstructionism.... Let me emphasize once and for all that Partisans do not allow under any condition for an Allied officer or his team to go on reconnaissance missions outside his headquarters with the intention of gathering additional intelligence. Intelligence in Slovenia is currently limited to daily or weekly Partisan intelligence extracts, covering only the desired content.[23]

In Fisher's opinion, the Partisans even contemplated the occupation of southern parts of Austria, which would also allow the integration of Slovenians living there into the new Yugoslavia. Yugoslavia namely demanded those areas as a reward for its contribution in the fight against Nazism and due to the fact that those areas were predominantly populated with ethnic Slovenians that should become part of Yugoslavia for geographic, traditional, and historical reasons. He supported the opinion that the Yugoslav demand could not be denied, but remarked at the same time that he had not been in a position to learn about the Austrian view. He also sensed some potential obstacles in Soviet demands because the Partisans wanted the Red Army to reach Austria before the Anglo-American forces. According to him, the Partisans did not want the Anglo-Americans forces to penetrate Austria and made every effort to prevent them from doing this.

As for the reasons for the Partisan ban on the penetration of the Maple team toward the north, Fisher had the following opinion:

> They do not let us or cannot let us proceed north and finally penetrate Austria for one of the two reasons or the combination of both. The first reason is of a political nature and refers to the issue of the Slovenian-Austrian border. As they are not fully aware of our intentions with regard to this border, it may be possible that they do not want us to rummage about up there because they cannot control us and know what we are doing. Perhaps the Russians have their hands in this. Another reason as already mentioned is of course their concern about our security.[24]

Despite all the obstacles, Fisher made it to the Pohorje Hills. The team soon came under German attack, which was followed by adverse weather conditions. Following the beginning of German offensive in December 1944, Fisher reported to Bari that severe fighting was going on between the Partisans and the Germans. They also came under two severe attacks from Home Guard battalions and an Ustasha division from the Lower Carniola direction. Reports also mention fierce fights for Mozirje, and the German use of howitzers, mortars, light tanks, and armored vehicles.[25]

Eight out of twelve members arriving with Fisher in Styria decided to return to Lower Carniola due to the emergency situation and, as previously mentioned, from there to Bari. Fisher stayed with the Styrian Partisans along with the three-member team of OSS Austria Section, First Lieutenant Quinn, Bob Plan, and Sergeant Thabit. On December 21, 1944, Quinn left Fisher and Plan, and set off south for the Slovenian Partisan headquarters and then arrived on January 5, 1945, in Bari. Meanwhile, Plan and Fisher were caught in an ambush in the Tuhinj Valley on December 26, 1944, together with other Partisans, and Fisher allegedly died in the fighting with Germans. In his report, Plan mentioned that the team was attacked by German units at Velika Lašnja and then split up. That was the last time Plan saw Fisher, who was together in the team with British Major Mathius and Lieutenant Parks. Fisher presumably lost his life together with sixteen Partisans in fighting with the Germans somewhere close to Nova Štifta in the upper Tuhinj Valley. The archival materials of the Slovenian Partisan headquarters on the fallen, captured, and missing members of Anglo-American missions show that Fisher had been missing since the German offensive in Styria in December 1944. Plan was later told that Mathius and Parks had been wounded, and all traces of Fisher had been lost. Close to and after the end of the war, OSS investigated the reasons for Fisher's death; however, no immediate witness, grave, or confirmation of Fisher's actual death was found. Some hoped or gossiped that he was still alive.[26]

On September 25, 1945, General Donovan sent a letter to Fisher's mother explaining to her that her son had been declared missing and that they would inform her if there was any new information.[27] OSS also made inquiries about Fisher in the Arrow and Alum missions. In March 1945, Alum wrote that absolutely no information was known about Fisher's death.[28] Fisher most likely died in fighting with the Germans at Nova Štifta, where a monument was erected in his memory.

In State Security Administration reconstruction of Anglo-American missions, the Orchid team and the entire mission of Captain Fisher are recorded as the "Hollywood-SBS" problem or under the designation "Hollywood." According to the Department of National Security information, the Fourth Operational Zone involved teams of OSS for central Europe known as Austrian infiltration teams. Mission members allegedly had constant contact with resistance groups in Austria, although no concrete evidence on these connections is available. As claimed by the Department of National Security, the team was headed by Captain Fisher and comprised the following agents: John Quinn, W. Thabit, R. Peru, A. Bartl, Charles Quetner, W. Haas, G. Justin, Charles Martin, J. Rosenfelt, R. Wishman, and M. Roht. The Department of National Security's opinion was that the real reason for the arrival of these intelligence staff at Styria had never been established. Members of the team also showed interest in the National Liberation Army and Partisan officials.[29]

Comparing archival documentation, it can be concluded that the Department of National Security had no verified information about the existence of effective resistance by the communist organization in Austria, which should also be reflected in contacts with the Partisans from Lower Styria. The Department of National Security obviously grew alarmed at the likelihood of a parallel organization of an Austrian resistance movement, which could have been organized by OSS missions and would not be under the Partisan control, which explains its opposition to autonomous activity by OSS missions in Austrian territory.

The Grady-Mansion Mission

After the death of Captain Fisher, the remaining members of the Austrian OSS / Secret Intelligence—Lieutenant Quinn, Bob Plan, and Sergeant Thabit—stayed in Styria and continued their intelligence activity in the Fourth Operational Zone. In spite of this it would be difficult to talk about active intelligence activity by Lieutenant Quinn and Sergeant Thabit in Styria because at the time of Fisher's death they apparently set off to the Slovenian Partisan headquarters and then to Bari.[30] The team apparently operated under the name Grady or Grady–Mansion (designation "Oyster"), although eventually only the wireless operator Plan carried out fieldwork.[31] Plan continued his work under the name Grady and submitted information of a military nature on enemy plans and defense preparations. He made a great effort to locate the grave of Captain Fisher and all witnesses to the heavy fight with German units. He explored the military situation in Slovenian territory and Austrian Carinthia, which he broke through into in December 1944. Already between December 5 and December 15, 1944, he attempted three times to reach the Pohorje Hills with Quinn, but all the efforts failed due to strong German units in the area. Plan managed to reach the Pohorje Hills with the Partisans on February 20, 1945. He noted that three out of twelve members of Fisher's team had been evacuated due to illness, five members for other reasons, two were in the Partisan hospitals, and their leader Fisher had been declared missing in fighting with the Germans. The analysis of the OSS Maple-Grady report mentions that Plan's reports were important and useful for OSS. His understanding and interpretation of Partisan tactics was that the Partisans always carried out attacks from an ambush, and during attacks they always split up into smaller groups and engaged in pursuing and destroying the enemy.[32]

Plan also presented detailed information about the number of Partisan units in Styria and their movements. He determined that the Partisan losses in engagements were small because they always managed to withdraw in a timely manner from the center of conflict. He also analyzed Partisan military commanders and commissars by focusing on their leadership abilities and military skills. Military commanders dealt with military operations, and commissars made sure that every Partisan performed his duty. The discipline was not strict, the food was not bad, and the combat morale was better with volunteers than with mobilized soldiers. The

Partisan soldiers were not communists, except for some individuals that were swayed by intensive communist and pro–Soviet propaganda.

In his opinion, the people were more likely to accept Anglo-American control than that of the Soviets. Partisan propaganda was focused on the issues of Trieste and Carinthia. In May 1945, Plan was present during some minor incidents between the British and Yugoslav units in Carinthia. He was convinced that the people had the feeling that the Anglo-Americans were unwilling to give the Yugoslav people the territory they were entitled to. The people in Carinthia were generally against the Partisans, except for local Slovenians that backed Slovenia as part of a new democratic federal Yugoslavia but outside communist influence. Plan noted that the Slovenians were ready to fight for the entire territory of Carinthia and Styria where an ethnic Slovenian minority lived. He had no information about the connections between Slovenian and Austrian communists.[33]

He also judged that a large portion of the Slovenian population was in favor of the Partisans because they regarded them as an army of liberation. Together with the Partisans, he also crossed the Yugoslav-Austrian border and established contact with the Klagenfurt OSS Section. He assisted during negotiations for the surrender of the German army group E and acted as a mediator and then as an interpreter between the British on the one side and the Croatian Ustasha forces on the other. After the Partisans promised that nobody would be shot without a trial, a total surrender was achieved. Plan also acted as an interpreter for British Brigadier Scott, and then left for Trieste and arrived in Caserta in June 1945.[34]

The Dania Mission

The Dania mission was organized by the Austrian branch of OSS / Secret Intelligence and comprised well-trained agents from whom OSS expected much. The team's missions resembled those carried out by other teams: infiltrating Austria and researching the possibility of gathering intelligence. It was led by Captain George Gerbner and the wireless operator was Sergeant Alfred Rosenthal (Ronald). They were accompanied by a deserter from the German army, George Mitchell (Paul Krock), who had relatives and acquaintances among his left-wing friends around Graz. His mission was to find a refuge for the team leader and the wireless operator among his friends. The team also carried a large sum of money.

They were supposed to parachute over the town of Deutschlandsberg, west of Graz, but on February 7, 1945, the air crew dropped the team in Yugoslavia (somewhere near Vuhred in Slovenian territory) owing to poor navigation and incorrect instructions. Gerbner and Rosenthal failed to recover all of the necessary equipment, as well as find Mitchell, who lost them after the plane jump. Mitchell had a key role in the trio because he had contacts with relatives and friends around the city of Graz. On February 9, 1945, Rosenthal and Gerbner, listening to conversations from their hideouts by the road and talking to farmers, discovered that they had landed in Slovenian territory and not Austria. Being unable to locate either Mitchell or their equipment, they realized they could contact the Partisans with the help of the local population and then make their way to Bari. Both succeeded, sending intelligence reports after coming into contact with the Partisans.[35]

The team members remained in the field for over four months. In mission reports to OSS they recounted their experiences with the Slovenian Partisans in the area north and south of the Sava River, where they were stationed between February 7 and May 15, 1945. On February 17, they made their way to the Fourth Operational Zone with the assistance of the Partisans. British Major Owens helped them send a telegram with their location to Bari. They also made the acquaintance of Bob Plan, a member of the Grady-Mansion team. The very next day an order was dispatched from Bari to return there as soon as possible. However, for the moment it was impossible. In their base reports they described skirmishes with the Germans, as well as the difficulties of getting through numerous communications.

Aided by the Partisans, they reached Ljubljana on May 10, 1945, and later Trieste, where they reported to members of OSS. From Trieste, Gerbner and Rosenthal, together with the British flying corps, flew to Udine on May 15 and from there to Foggia and to Bari.[36]

Gerbner and Rosenthal sent information pertaining to the enemy and Partisan armies, as well as to Home Guard propaganda. They also commended the high Partisan morale and the courageous Partisan fighters. Nevertheless, they were also critical, Gerbner being disappointed by the lack of democracy among the Partisans. Officers, for example, had certain perquisites, such as better clothing, lodgings, and food. Rosenthal on the other hand was less critical when it came to the differences in the treatment of officers and common soldiers, seeing this as merely an extension of Yugoslav military habits. Officers were entitled to privileges and more luxury because they had greater responsibilities, despite the scarcity of food, clothing, and weapons.

The two team members judged the Partisans' relations with the Home Guard as being very hostile. The Partisans feared the Home Guard because of their good knowledge of the countryside. In addition, they despised them because of their fascist ideology. To be captured by the Home Guard meant torture and certain death. The Partisans shot some of the captured members of the Home Guard, and others they either accepted among their ranks or sent them home without weapons and equipment. The Home Guard's political strength was directly bound to the strength of the German military apparatus. In larger villages, they strengthened their influence among the local population with the support of a large portion of the Catholic clergy, which feared the radical changes that Partisan rule would bring. Home Guard units were made up of men selected during the German mobilization in Slovenia, as well as Partisan deserters.

Gerbner and Rosenthal detected conflicting political views among the Slovenian farmers. On the one hand, they were proud of the Partisans' achievements. On the other, they were uncertain about future political and military events in Yugoslavia. On the whole, the peasants were friendly and generous in supplying the Partisans with food. The Partisans continually posed questions to the two Dania team members regarding American political goals in Yugoslavia. Rumors started circulating in the territory held by the Home Guard that Anglo-American forces had declared war on the Soviet Union.

The Partisans, in contrast to the peasants, were more specific about the future Yugoslav authorities. They emphasized they did not want the prewar form of government and claimed they would fight any external or internal power that would seek to reestablish the old regime. According to the opinion of both Dania teammates, the Home Guard were hopefully asking for an Anglo-American occupation to counteract the Partisans. Dania teammates saw the Partisans as a successful military force that also wanted to implement radical changes in the economic, societal, and political spheres. Everyone feared the changes that Josip Broz Tito, working under the tutelage of the Soviet Union, could implement. It was also hoped that an Anglo-American occupation would pave the way for the development of a "democratic" form of government in their country. In contrast to other OSS mission members, Gerbner and Rosenthal had unfettered access to Partisan officers, soldiers, and the local population.[37]

The two members of the Dania team encountered strong, unrelenting, and unanimous demands to annex Klagenfurt and Trieste to postwar Yugoslavia among the Partisans and in all Slovenian circles. They judged this irredentist thinking strong enough as to compel Tito to staunchly demand the annexation of these two cities lest he lose his political reputation among his ranks. They reported on how the Partisans considered Klagenfurt and Trieste to be their towns and how they were prepared to fight for them. The Partisans were completely taken by surprise when Anglo-American forces occupied Trieste and thus saw the arrival of New Zealand troops as unnecessary meddling. By talking to the Partisans, they ascertained that the Yugoslav territorial claims for Trieste and Klagenfurt were based on the nationalist principle, on historical rights, and on the idea that the Yugoslavs had gained the right to occupy the two cities because of their liberation efforts on the battlefield.[38]

George Mitchell jumped a few minutes before the other two members and was certain he had landed in Austria. He landed in a tree somewhere in the Drava Valley. He was slightly injured and failed to transmit the light signal to the remaining two. Gerbner and Rosenthal thus followed the wrong signal, and ended up elsewhere on the ground, jumping over an entirely different part of the landscape. After landing, Mitchell came to a village on the northern bank of the Drava River. Dressed as a German soldier, he soon drew suspicion. He was arrested and subsequently released. Soon after, he was arrested by two members of the Gestapo, who had been misled by the insignia on his uniform. However, after a meticulous background check of his documents, the Gestapo discovered that the name of the city clerk purported to have issued the documents had been faked. He was charged as a spy, but nevertheless successfully defended himself and had a good alibi. He was given a more lenient sentence and sent to the artillery barracks in Maribor.

After eight days, Mitchell managed to escape from prison because the Allied bombing of Maribor also damaged the artillery barracks. Two days later, he made his way home to his wife, where he also hid. The home of his strongly pro–Nazi parents served as a hiding place as well. On April 14, Mitchell's father came home with the news of President Roosevelt's death, thanking God for the demise of the most notorious of war criminals. The statement sparked a heated row between father and son. The father consequently betrayed his son to the German secret police and to members of the SS. Mitchell managed a timely escape, spraining his ankle in the process. He spent the next couple of days hiding out at the homes of his acquaintances. Meanwhile, his wife contacted a bishop in Graz, who provided shelter and financial support for him. It was at this time that he contacted Franz Weber from OSS Greenup mission.[39] Mitchell spent the remaining days of the war in his hiding place, which had fallen under the Soviet Occupation Zone. He never left his hiding place for fear of a Red Army soldier raping his wife. In the end, Captain Jules Konig made it possible for Mitchell and his wife to safely move to the British Occupation Zone. In June 1945, Captain Konig conducted an interview with him in Carinthia, which served as the basis for Mitchell's report.[40]

The Dania team was one of the most promising missions organized by the Austrian branch of OSS. The landing, which took place far from the arranged target and in another country's territory, made it impossible for the team to complete any goals linked to gathering intelligence in Austria. The intelligence reports were nevertheless valuable for OSS analysts because they contained useful information on the Partisan movement and its goals. For the first few days after landing, the men had no equipment, food, or additional clothing. They only survived and were later evacuated with the help of the local population and the Partisans. OSS analysts were of the opinion that the blame for the Dania team's lack of success cannot be attributed to Gerbner and Rosenthal. The end of the report thus reads: "After finding themselves in a situation in which they were unable to complete the mission, they decided to try and return to base. The fact that they managed to make their way through hostile territory in extremely difficult conditions only confirms their intelligence, their sangfroid in the face of difficult circumstances, and their moral and physical durability."[41]

The Guthrie Mission, and Other Teams and Individuals

On April 2, 1945, Jože Stante and Vladimir Kumar, who had already functioned as members of the Alum mission at the Slovenian Partisan headquarters, landed in Carinthia. Upon returning to the base, they had been sent back to the Slovenian territory as members of the Guthrie mission, which was tasked with providing information on enemy communications and company movements. Due to constant risks and numerous SS units, they soon left the dangerous area and established contact with the Slovenian Partisans.[42] OSS reports mentioned that Guthrie reported a successful landing on April 5, 1945, although its two members could not approach Klagenfurt. They were ordered to set up air signalization in a predetermined emergency location on the ground in case of a wireless communication breakdown.[43]

Archival documents also contain information about two Austrians that had been recruited in prisoner-of-war camps for German prisoners of war. They were given the cover names Smith and Black, and they joined the Partisans without announcement, who made arrangements for their departure to the Partisan Carinthian Detachment, where British Lieutenant Colonel Villiers and his team were also located. Their behavior probably did not earn them trust with Villers and the Partisans, who refused to cooperate with them. On their way to Italy they ran into an SS patrol; Smith escaped, but Black did not even try and surrendered to Germans. He betrayed the location of the Carinthian Detachment and the British team, and an attack followed within hours. This event additionally increased the distrust of Partisans in Austrians, and made the penetration of Allied missions north even more difficult.[44]

Another example of a bad ending was the mission of an Austrian that joined the Carinthian Partisans claiming that he was representing a group of Austrians from Graz that had established a resistance cell and sought contact with Americans. They wanted to have a wireless operator in order to communicate and, possibly, to set up a drop area for delivering help. Lindsay thus informed the base to send in a German-speaking wireless operator. OSS base responded that they would require two to three weeks to prepare a wireless operator and a radiotelegraph device for the drop. The Austrian decided to return and to send someone else to receive the wireless operator. Soon another Austrian from Graz arrived, explaining to the Partisans that the Graz group had already set off for the mountains to set up a resistance group. The Partisans soon received information that the Austrian was a Gestapo agent and learned through questioning that the Gestapo caught the first Austrian on his way back and sent their agent, who would eventually receive the Gestapo wireless operator.[45]

The historian Linasi also mentions that the couriers of the Slovenian Partisans in the Karawanks ran into two British that supposedly belonged to SOE. Documents often refer to them as two OSS agents, First Lieutenant Georg Charles Pump and Non-Commissioned Officer Henry Neuman. They brought them to the Partisans' Zilje Company and they talked about being released to a Partisan group in Tolmezzo and being in the company of a certain OSS mission. They said that they had a contract with the Partisans to send agents to Austria with help of the Partisans and that they had several problems. Two colleagues were caught during the pursuit, and Pump and Neuman separated from the Italian Partisans and traveled across South Tyrol to the Gail Valley, and joined the Slovenian Partisans there. They had a large amount of money, which they secretly distributed to the Partisans in order to win colleagues among them to help them land in Austria with a parachute, which eventually did not happen. They also told the Partisans that after the war Austria was to be restored within its old borders.[46]

A happy ending is connected with the mission of a young courier that joined the Partisans with safe clothes and addresses because his intention was to visit Cardinal Innitzer in Vienna, where he arrived dressed as a priest. OSS bases in southern Italy also intended to send Lieutenant Le Goff to Slovenia, who would be in charge of infiltration into Austria at the Slovenian Partisan headquarters. OSS planned the landing of several missions directly in Austria, without any help from the Slovenian Partisans and an infiltration attempt from Slovenian territory. One of them was the Dillon mission,[47] which consisted of Lieutenant Milos Pavlovich, Julio Prester, and three Austrian deserters, Ernst Fiechter, Karl Steinwender, and Helmut Kinzian, who landed in Carinthia on December 27. The network of collaborators was quickly broken and closed, with Pavlovich being killed during attempted apprehension, and Steinwender was killed for lack of discipline and reliability, and lying.

The Partisan leadership soon found that it was not effective in organizing resistance in Austria, and it resorted to new tactics. After the German surrender they planned to occupy and annex parts of the Drava Valley, for which they issued an order on the reduction of the number of Partisans in Carinthian Detachment, which was operating on the northern side of the Karawanks.[48]

6

Sabotage on the Dalmatian Islands

On September 9, 1943, American General George Marshall was of the opinion that the British plan for landing in Dalmatia and advancing across Yugoslavia to Austria was unworkable because it would result in the dissolution of the Anglo-American forces. At a meeting between British and American generals at the White House, and in particular between Churchill and Roosevelt, the decision was made to develop the advance of Anglo-American forces in Italy. However, the Balkan front had to be developed only if combat with Italy developed gradually and a favorable opportunity arose. Churchill's plans failed, and Joint Chiefs of Staff and Field Marshal Harold Alexander supported the advance through the territory of Italy.

Tito and the entire Partisan political leadership were concerned about a possible Anglo-American landing or interventions in Yugoslavia and therefore opposed the idea of Anglo-American landing. Tito advocated the idea that a possible landing should be only carried out by smaller units that would disembark in the sector of Istria and Dalmatia. Nevertheless, he would accept neither any Anglo-American civilian or military authority nor Anglo-American command over any of the Partisan units.[1] Conflicts, suspicions, and disagreements among the Partisans as well as in the relations with the United Kingdom and the United States increased in 1944, especially regarding issues such as the Anglo-American landing, international recognition of the Partisan movement, the position of King Peter II and the monarchy, the Tito–Šubašić Agreement, and the establishment of a common Yugoslav government.

On February 13, 1944, Churchill sent an official letter to Tito regarding British amphibious forces assisting the Yugoslav Partisans in liberating certain Dalmatian islands. In an official letter to Supreme Allied Com-

6. Sabotage on the Dalmatian Islands

mander Mediterranean General Wilson, Churchill requested the immediate establishment of amphibious commandos that were supported by air and sea. These units would help the Partisans crush units that had been left by the Germans on the Dalmatian islands.

In April 1944, the island of Vis was organized as an Allied base for British units and also for OSS / Operational Groups. The island of Vis was a great location for the further supply of Tito's forces by sea. Wilson informed Churchill that the defense measures had developed intensively and that time was needed to complete an airstrip on the island. In addition to the Partisans, a unit included British combat batteries, antiaircraft artillery, an infantry battalion, and signals and logistics detachments. Wilson wrote that Partisan forces together with British commandos were attacking German units on the Dalmatian coast and islands. He also informed Churchill that four British units had been joined by a Belgian unit and OSS units for special operations and operational groups.[2]

OSS / Operational Groups were composed of volunteers, such as parachutists and members trained for sabotage operations. They began to operate in the Balkans in October 1943, when fifteen OSS officers and 110 soldiers were sent to the Dalmatian islands. These units were followed by other groups in January 1944. They cooperated with British commandos in operations in which they were to gain experience before joining campaigns elsewhere in Europe. The Anglo-American forces on the island of Vis were under the command of Land Forces Adriatic and were composed of 2 Commando, 43 Royal Marines Commando, 40 Royal Marines Commando, Highland Light Infantry, Royal Artillery Ack Ack Battery 75mm, 111 Field Regiment and parts of No. 10 Inter-Allied Commando.[3] Thus, British units as well as OSS / Operational groups participated in supplying Tito's Partisans, defended the island of Vis against German attacks, and performed landings and attacks on German garrisons on the Dalmatian islands of Šolta, Brač, Hvar, Mljet, and Korčula, and the Pelješac Peninsula. Other significant tasks were also reconnaissance patrols on other islands with the aim of determining the location of German forces.[4]

It is an interesting fact that the British and the Americans set up sabotage schools in Yugoslavia. On the island of Vis a sabotage school operated between March 15 and July 15, 1944. The school was led by Anglo-American forces and included OSS instructors that trained 126 agents for sabotage operations and twelve agents for sector intelligence operations. The school was then passed over to the Partisans; however, training was still carried out by instructors.[5]

6. Sabotage on the Dalmatian Islands

OSS / Operational Groups, British commandos, and the Partisans conducted a range of successful operations on the Dalmatian islands, including the island of Hvar. Between January 26 and January 27, 1944, thirty-three members of operational groups, 150 British commandos, and seventy-five Partisans transported by fishing boats planned a military campaign on Hvar. However, due to high waves, some of the units had to return. The other part was surprised by German units that destroyed them and captured some of its members. However, a successful campaign on Hvar was carried out between February 20 and March 1, 1944, by eight members of operational groups and seven members of the Partisans. These successfully ambushed a German patrol, but suffered a wounded soldier. After several days of poor weather, they had to return to Vis. Nevertheless, this did not disturb the successful campaigns conducted on Hvar because new operations had been planned for Hvar on February 11 as well on March 22 and 23, 1944. The British commandos and the operational groups succeeded in destroying a German garrison. The operational groups were also participating in pre-reconnaissance operations. Later, the operational groups again participated in successful campaigns on Hvar. This is evident from documents that include several reports stating a successful operation between August 25 and 27, 1944, and other minor campaigns.

Anglo-Americans forces were also active on the island of Šolta. One such campaign took place on March 19, 1944, when British and American groups captured and destroyed an entire German garrison. This operation involved around 150 members of operational groups, who, in particular, carried out reconnaissance tasks, and around 450 British commandos. This was one of the operations that had been carried out from the island of Vis. The attack plan had been prepared by Mayor Fynn. These groups were tasked with establishing secure lines of communication for the Partisans and making supply deliveries possible from Bari to the Yugoslav coast. The island of Šolta was later attacked several times. These attacks were all combined because the five officers and fifty-five soldiers that had landed on Šolta were supported by a 75 mm gun crew.[6]

OSS / Operational Groups and British commandos participated several times in joint operations with Partisan units on the island of Korčula. One such operation took place between April 12 and April 19, 1944, when an eight-member operational group entered the island of Korčula. This group did not include a medic, which was later very much regretted by the commander of the group, OSS First Lieutenant Dobrinski. After a two-hour voyage by boat from the nearby island of Lastovo, the group

6. Sabotage on the Dalmatian Islands

met with the Partisans, who took them to a cave where they could sleep overnight. The next day they decided to ambush a German infantry patrol. However, the plan failed from the very beginning. The group had only just gathered on the slope of the hill, when suddenly a vanguard of a German infantry patrol showed up. The surprise was mutual. As soon as they spotted each other, fire was opened. The Germans jumped down from their motorcycles and began to run for cover. However, three of them were shot. While firing at the other two Germans, Dobrinski was wounded in the leg. However, both of the Germans were finally shot. The groups subsequently withdrew before the remaining infantry patrol arrived and managed to get back to their base.[7]

OSS / Operational Groups and the British commandos also participated in operations on the island of Mljet between May 22 and May 24, 1944, where they were not successful, as well as on the island of Brač, where, together with Partisan units, they carried out Operation Flounced between June 2 and June 4, 1944. Furthermore, the whole Partisan division and around one thousand Anglo-American soldiers, the Royal Marines, participated in this operation. Among these were around 140 members of operational groups that had been tasked with protecting the artillery. Between June 22 and June 25, 1944, as well as between July 31 and August 3, 1944, operational groups participated in an ambush of a German naval convoy along the cost of the Pelješac Peninsula.[8]

Anglo-Americans forces carried out campaigns in Yugoslavia more or less successfully in line with the British and American plans in close cooperation with the Partisans, who were constantly supervising them. Their assistance, which supplied Partisan units with weapons and ammunition and also established Partisan sabotage schools and built military air fields, had been more or less successful. With the progress of the war and the transfer of the main campaigns to northern Yugoslavia, to Slovenian and Croatian territory, operational groups and commandos were no longer necessary in operations in the southern Adriatic. The activity of operational groups and commandos on the Yugoslav coast complied with the strategy of the British and the United States, which was limited to reconnaissance and sabotage operations of smaller groups on the Dalmatian islands. These campaigns were considered an antecedent to the subsequent landing of Anglo-American forces in the Balkans—which, however, never happened despite the fears of the Partisan leadership in Yugoslavia.

7

Slovenians in the U.S. and Their Cooperation with OSS

The activities of the American Slovenians during the Second World War can be divided into two periods and two lines. The first period extends from the beginning of the Second World War to the end of 1942. During the first years, Slovenian immigrants and their leaders supported the Yugoslav nations' fight against the Axis powers by corresponding with important world leaders, members of the Yugoslav government in exile, and later its members in exile. The leaders of Slovenian fraternal benefit organizations in the United States founded the Slovenian Section of the Yugoslav Auxiliary Committee (*Jugoslovanski pomožni odbor-slovenska sekcija*, JPO-SS). With the help of the American-Slovenian Catholic Union, they established another auxiliary committee at the beginning of 1942, which was coordinated by Slovenian parishes in the United States. The activities were organized by Father Bernard Ambrožič, who, together with Father Kazimir Zakrajšek, endeavored to send funds to Yugoslavia as soon as possible. However, the Slovenian Section of the Yugoslav Auxiliary Committee disagreed, which was already indicative of disagreements among the American Slovenians, who remained united for the time being.[1]

The second period of Slovenian-American immigrant activities began in December 1942, after the Slovenian-American National Council (SANC) had been founded. The Congress deliberated on and adopted resolutions on the American Slovenians in war, the situation of the Slovenians in Yugoslavia and neighboring countries, the future of Yugoslavia, and political actions of the American Slovenians. The desire of the American Slovenians was to support the aspirations of the Slovenian nation toward the establishment of a united Slovenia at the end of the war,

7. Slovenians in the U.S. and Their Cooperation with OSS

and to provide material support to Slovenian compatriots in their homeland. The Congress also adopted a special resolution against the efforts of Otto von Habsburg to establish an Austrian battalion within the United States Army, which would be formed of emigrants from former lands of the Habsburg Monarchy. The controversial battalion was disbanded in March 1943 due to protests by emigrant leaders from countries of the former Habsburg nations. In addition, numerous ideas emerged on founding new federations in central Europe. Some of them did not envisage the re-establishment of Yugoslavia, and nearly none proposed a satisfactory solution to the issue of the Slovenians, whose goal was to unite the territory regarded by them as their ethnic territory. The exception was a proposal to establish a Danubian Catholic Federation under the leadership of a descendant of the Habsburg dynasty.

The American Slovenians were thus actively involved in raising funds to help their homeland. The action was initially led by the Slovenian Section of the Yugoslav Auxiliary Committee, and later by the Slovenian American National Council within the War Relief Fund of the Americans of South Slavic Descent. Meanwhile, other American Slovenians focused on political action in support of their homeland, which was initially discussed at the Slovenian Section of the Yugoslav Auxiliary Committee meetings, with initiatives also coming from the Slovenian members of the Yugoslav government in exile. On the basis of all the initiatives and counterinitiatives, the Slovenian American National Council was formed, later followed by the United Committee of South Slavic Americans at the Slovenian initiative. Upon receiving information about the Partisan battles in Yugoslavia, the Slovenian American community became polarized into those that supported the Partisan movement and those that still opposed it.

In addition to the American Slovenians, some important individuals that had emigrated to the United States after the initial attack on Yugoslavia were active there. OSS monitored the political activities of the leaders of the Slovenian People's Party, Franc Snoj and Miha Krek, as well as their party colleagues. Among them were Msgr. Franc Gabrovšek, who had had a long party career that included frequent travel to France, and Alojzij Kuhar, a graduate of the Paris Institute of Political Studies, who was regarded as an expert on international politics. In addition to the four exponents in exile, OSS monitored a liberal professor from the University of Ljubljana, Boris Furlan, and the liberal politician Ivan Matija Čok. OSS not only monitored the activities of certain important Slovenians, but also kept a list of all other political and military figures from Yugoslavia and Slovenia. Some Slovenians that were active in the United States during the war were actively involved in OSS, mostly cooperating with OSS / Secret Intelligence, Special Operations, and Foreign Nationalities Branches. It should be noted that they were not typical agents or trusted associates of secret services because the available documentation reveals that they did not secretly search for or inquire about confidential information. Some of them could be classified as OSS associates, and others as employees that provided information to OSS about the situation in Yugoslavia via various reports, memorandums, brochures, and other initiatives. Among the notable Slovenians that worked for or closely cooperated with OSS in the United States and its overseas bases were Franc Snoj, Ivan Marija Čok, Louis Adamic, Captain Andrej Kobal, Lieutenant Ilyja Bratina, and Captain John Blatnik. Of those mentioned here, Blatnik was the only one that was sent to Yugoslavia as the head of OSS mission. Some Slovenians—for example, Franc Gabrovšek, Father Kazimir Zakrajšek and Father Bernard Ambrožič, Izidor Cankar, Etbin Kristan, Janko Rogelj, the brothers Anton and Joe Grdina, and others—were welcome informants delivering information on the assessment of the situation in Yugoslavia. The Research and Analysis Branch conducted several interviews with them, analyzed their brochures, or simply gathered opinions on certain political affairs in Yugoslavia and among the American Slovenians. Other Yugoslav politicians also cooperated with OSS; for instance Ivan Šubašić, and Sava Kosanović, the Federal People's Republic of Yugoslavia's postwar ambassador in Washington, as well as the notable Croatian lawyer Josip Smodlaka, who was the Commissioner for Foreign Affairs at the National Committee for the Liberation of Yugoslavia (NKOJ) in 1944 in Bari.[2]

Research on Slovenian expats in the United States was made possible particularly by OSS reports collected and analyzed by OSS / Foreign Nationalities Branch. The branch helped OSS to receive information on developments in Yugoslavia. However, it did not have the autonomy to make decisions on political issues. The Foreign Nationalities Branch closely monitored the activities and political orientation of Slovenian expatriate organizations in the United States. By maintaining contacts with important individuals among immigrants and political refugees, the branch broadened its understanding of political potentials in Yugoslavia.

The Foreign Nationalities Branch also published a handbook on Yugoslavia, which stated that in the United States census 161,093 residents indicated Yugoslavia as their country of birth. The strongest Slovenian center was Cleveland, the Croatian centers were Pittsburgh and Chicago, and the strongest Serbian centers were Detroit, Pittsburgh, and Chicago. The handbook explains international disputes in Yugoslavia, particularly the conflicts between Serbian and Croatian nationalists. Serbian nationalists from the United States were particularly ardent supporters of the fight against Tito and the Croats, their hero being General Draža Mihailović. Under "clerical" leadership, Croatian separatists from the United States also initially opposed Tito and the Partisans, but the majority of Croatian émigrés soon took Tito's side. Ever since its foundation in August 1943, the United Committee of South Slavic Americans supported the Partisan movement in Yugoslavia, including renowned Americans of South Slavic descent, the writer Louis Adamic and the violinist Zlatko Baloković, as well as Sava Kosanović, who later joined the Šubašić government.[3]

After the meeting of the Slovenian American Congress in Cleveland on August 9, 1942, the attendees emphasized the demand for the reconstruction of Yugoslavia in the spirit of American democracy, including the Slovenians and the Croats living in the territories that had been awarded to Italy, Austria, and Hungary after the First World War. At the December meeting of the Slovenian American Congress, Krek and Snoj were not welcome to speak because a number of attendees were in favor of a republican or federal Yugoslavia, whereas left-wing members favored a united Slovenia in a postwar Balkan federation. The head of the OSS / Foreign Nationalities Branch, DeWitt C. Poole, also spoke to the congress delegation. He was told that first a Slovenian state should be formed, able to enter, on its own initiative and by consensus, a federation that would not be governed by the Serbs. Poole was also told that it would be a good idea for Bulgaria to join the federation as well. A special memorandum was addressed to the State Department by the Union of Slovenian Parishes, expressing a demand for a democratic Slovenia in a federation with the Croats and the Serbs.[4]

Being interested in information on Yugoslavia, the Foreign Nationalities Branch made contact with many Yugoslav politicians that had found refuge in the United States. OSS received the first news on the situation in Yugoslavia from Yugoslav refugees, several British agents, information and evidence submitted by the Soviet Union, and finally OSS agents. DeWitt C. Poole was thoroughly briefed on the political and military situation in Yugoslavia because his branch, together with the Research and Analysis Branch, came to the conclusion already in November 1942 that Mihailović was collaborating with the Axis forces.

A report dated August 17, 1943, stated that the Yugoslav nations were fighting a brave fight against enemy units and the cruel and dictatorial regime established in Yugoslavia by the enemy. It continued by saying that the Yugoslav government in exile and the Yugoslav Army were plagued by numerous ethnic conflicts. What is more, the government had a negative attitude toward the Partisan National Liberation Movement in Yugoslavia and cultivated a myth surrounding Mihailović, who was in fact collaborating with the Axis powers.[5] In May 1944, DeWitt C. Poole sent a memorandum to Donovan, informing him on the political situation in Yugoslavia. He noted that fierce Soviet propaganda had been launched in Yugoslavia against the leader of the Croatian Peasant Party, Vlatko Maček, which was damaging to Ivan Šubašić's reputation, who had been selected by British Prime Minister Churchill to be the new Yugoslav Prime Minister. DeWitt C. Poole stated that Šubašić was a *persona non grata* to the Soviets, but Šubašić assessed the attack as not serious. He also warned Donovan of the fact that, despite criticism, Šubašić was considered a Russophile, and that the Soviet campaign against Maček led Šubašić into seeking support from the British and the Americans.

One of the drawbacks of the Slovenians that cooperated with OSS was that they were not considered a sufficiently objective source of information by some high-ranking OSS officials because most Slovenians as well as other Yugoslavs in the United States were distinctly politically oriented.[6] Representatives of Yugoslav emigrant groups and societies were markedly ethnically and politically divided, a trait also displayed by the Slovenians in the United States.

Ivan Marija Čok

Ivan Marija Čok, a lawyer and politician from Trieste and president of the Yugoslav Committee from Italy, worked for OSS first in the Special Operations Branch and later in the Secret Intelligence Branch. Čok wrote a series of political analyses reporting on Axis-controlled Yugoslavia and its political figures, and strove for the establishment of closer links between OSS and the Royal Yugoslav Army in the Middle East. At the beginning of 1944, he invited members of the Royal Yugoslav Army to join Tito's Partisans. After British complaints against him, he agreed to leave OSS.[7]

OSS considered Čok a liberal democrat with an anti-clerical, anti–

Italian, and anti–German stance, and simultaneously a dreamer with an artistic temperament that was, above all, ambitious because he wanted to become a member of the Yugoslav government in exile by any means. He received good reviews from the British ISLD, who did not oppose his links with OSS and commended his work to the Yugoslav Committee in Italy, emphasizing his connections with the Partisans.[8] In his personal files, Čok was labeled a leader of Yugoslav underground movements, with whom he maintained close contact, and an expert on Yugoslavia and northern Italy, whose goal was the liberation of Yugoslavia. It was also noted that he was in conflict with the Yugoslav government in exile, and would be ready to leave for Yugoslavia at any time.[9] Čok showed great interest in Yugoslav politics, and so some of his publications put OSS in the Middle East in a predicament. He also concealed the fact that he received monthly payments of £125 from the Yugoslav government in exile, which was a considerable sum at the time. In McBaine's opinion, Čok did not have any useful value for OSS because relations between OSS and the Yugoslav government in exile were not good, whereas relations with the Partisans in Bari were productive, and hence there was no need for an intermediary.[10] During the war, much was also written about Čok and his political activity and work by OSS Captain Andrej Kobal of Slovenian descent that worked for OSS in Cairo and Bari. He was originally based in the American Military Intelligence Service (G-2), but his services were "borrowed" by OSS. Initially, Kobal gave a favorable review of Čok and his work. He provided a particularly thorough description of Čok's past activities, and proposed him as an appropriate candidate for dealing with certain strategic issues. The two men later met in New York, with a view to including Čok in Special Operations Branch. That time, however, Kobal's review of Čok was negative. In his opinion, Čok was too involved in Yugoslav political intrigues to be impartial, and might therefore prove to be a biased OSS employee. On those grounds, OSS included Čok in the Secret Intelligence Branch. Kobal sent his review of Čok in a letter addressed to McBaine. He stated that Čok's main issues were his intense individualism, unyielding position regarding Yugoslav politics, burning desire to participate in the Yugoslav government in exile, constant wavering between different groups, full commitment to the Partisan movement, and denials of his anti-government statements. Kobal suggested that OSS cut links with Čok on the grounds that his reports were overly biased, with the main argument against him being that he had been receiving payment from a foreign government.[11]

Ivan Marija Čok

The Foreign Nationalities Branch also invited Čok into its ranks with the help of Louis Adamic, an American writer of Slovenian descent. Čok was one of the first to draw Adamic's attention to the Yugoslav Partisan movement. Extensive notes have been written on Čok's life and activities, also mentioning that he began cooperating with representatives of the Greater Serbia group in London, who used him to exert pressure on the Slovenian representatives in the Yugoslav government in exile, Krek and Snoj. After numerous complaints from Slovenia, which indicated the people's dissatisfaction with his propaganda, the British dismissed him, and so Čok decided to leave the United Kingdom for the United States. All of the groups within the Yugoslav government welcomed his resolution, but others wanted to get rid of him. The Greater Serbia circles believed him to be the right person to work among the American Slovenians against Slovenian ministers in the government in exile, who at the time were cooperating closely with the pro–Yugoslav Croatians in the government. Thus, Čok continuously maintained close contacts with the Yugoslav Ambassador in Washington, Konstantin Fotić, who used him to discredit the Slovenian minister Franc Snoj. In addition to Snoj, Boris Furlan was in a dispute with Čok, and he refused to even speak to him. In the United States, Čok was brought into the public eye via his articles, and he also tried to establish a new committee of Yugoslavs from Istria.[12]

In February 1943, Čok complained to Adamic, who reported to the head of the Foreign Nationalities Branch DeWitt C. Poole, that he was concerned about the fate of Yugoslav troops under British command stationed in Egypt. He feared that they might be used for the Allied invasion of Yugoslavia, where they would come into contact with Draža Mihailović's Chetniks. OSS official later spoke to Čok, who began striving for Yugoslav troops to participate in the invasion of Yugoslavia, and realized that the issue with Yugoslav troops was that they were losing faith in the Yugoslav government in exile and its policy, and were unwilling to sacrifice their lives for a future Greater Serbia.[13]

In 1943, there was constant tension between Serbian officers, the Yugoslav government in exile, and Slovenian soldiers, who grew increasingly unsettled—all during the time when a Partisan military mission arrived in their midst, agitating for participation in the Partisan National Liberation Movement. Moreover, official one-sided information on the situation in Yugoslavia issued by the government in exile was circulating among Yugoslav soldiers in the Yugoslav Royal Guard Battalion in Palestine, with the only other source of information being Radio Free Yugoslavia (*Radio*

Svobodna Jugoslavija). This led to growing opposition among the soldiers to the official propaganda broadcast by the Yugoslav government in exile. The majority of soldiers in the battalion resisted and wanted to join Tito's newly-formed Overseas Brigades. On January 7, 1944, Čok wrote a letter relating the events to the Yugoslav soldiers stationed in the Middle East, in which he defended the Partisan Liberation Front and reported on the Serbo-Croatian conflict and the fact that eighty to ninety percent of the soldiers in the Yugoslav Royal Guard Battalion were Slovenians, who wanted to fight for Tito. Despite Čok's efforts, the British General Beaumont-Nesbitt made it clear that Čok was not allowed to interfere in the Yugoslav Army operations in the Middle East. On January 29, 1944, Čok published a letter in *Bazovica*, a newsletter issued by the Yugoslav Committee in Italy, calling on all Yugoslav volunteers in the Middle East to join the Partisan National Liberation Army in a disciplined manner and as one whole. The British were disturbed by Čok's publication, and he paid for it by being issued with a reprimand from British General Beaumont-Nesbitt, and OSS dismissed him from the Secret Intelligence Branch as a result of the British complaints against him.[14]

Despite his dismissal, Čok remained politically active and strove to resolve the issue of Venezia Giulia for the benefit of Yugoslavia. Until the end of the war, he focused on promoting the Partisan movement, supported the Tito–Šubašić Agreement, and expected liberation in the hope that he would be able to assist with the postwar demarcation of the Slovenian Littoral. It soon became evident, however, that he was unwanted due to his wartime activities and, after remaining in Trieste for a while, he eventually moved to the United States, where he died in 1948.

Louis Adamic

A great supporter of the Yugoslav nations in the United States was also the renowned writer, translator, publicist, and political worker of Slovenian descent, Louis Adamic (born Alojz Adamič). He was not only active among the Yugoslav Americans, but was also a leading member of the Common Council for American Unity, which stood for the social and ethnic rights of U.S. immigrants. In 1940, he became an advisor for the National Defense Research Committee, which was created as part of the Council of National Defense in the United States. He played an important role in organizing Slovenian Americans during the Second World War, and he had strong connections with government authorities and President Roosevelt's wife Eleanor. Adamic was also the president of the United Committee of South Slavic Americans and honorary chairman of the Slovenian American National Council. Until the end of 1942, he worked as an individual, supporting the Yugoslav nations' fight against the Axis forces and writing letters to important leaders. After 1942, as honorary chairman of the Slovenian American National Council, he was a legal representative of the American Slovenians. He also started cooperating with OSS, predominantly with the Foreign Nationalities Branch. For some time, he believed in the idea of an Allied Committee that would take over the command of the resistance movements in Yugoslavia. However, the idea was not feasible on account of profound opposition between the Chetnik and Partisan movements.[15]

Up until the second half of 1942, according to Adamic as well as the rest of the Americans, Draža Mihailović was the main leader of the Yugoslav resistance movement. As early as in 1941, newspapers published by Yugoslav emigrants in the United States featured articles on communist attacks on the Axis powers in their homeland.[16] Adamic sent a letter to Roosevelt in February 1942, proposing the establishment of the American Legion of Freedom, which would consist of small and mobile units comprised of the Yugoslavs, Greeks, Bulgarians, Italians, Jews and Albanians, and would fight as commandos against the Axis powers under the command of American officers. In the letter, Adamic still spoke in favor of Mihailović and asked for help to be sent his way. Roosevelt replied on March 3rd that he found Adamic's letter very useful, and that government agencies and departments were analyzing his proposal.[17] After long discussions with OSS representatives spanning over several weeks, Adamic published an article in *The Saturday Evening Post* on December 19, 1942, in support of the Partisan National Liberation Movement. The publication of the article signaled the beginning of a propaganda war in the American press between the supporters of Mihailović on the one hand and Tito on the other. DeWitt C. Poole wrote to Donovan in January 1943, saying that Adamic's philosophy was "left-wing" but moderate because he was not a communist. He characterized Adamic as being deeply devoted to the United States and the American idea, although in his essence he remained a peasant and an individualist.[18]

Adamic also published a pamphlet entitled *Inside Yugoslavia*, which was assessed by OSS analysts as being appropriate, with the exception of his arguments often being unclear and the lack of evidence relating to the dispute between Mihailović and Tito. According to OSS analysts, Adamic failed to provide sufficient information on where the necessary documentary justifications could be found on certain subjects he discussed in the article. He failed to state clearly enough that war was being fought in Yugoslavia between the Soviet Union, the United Kingdom, and the Yugoslav government in exile, making it the "new Spanish War." Adamic portrayed the Partisans as "angels," even though many of them were thieves, some were idealists, and their leaders were all communists. As early as in February 1943, Adamic advocated that the Americans send a committee to the Partisans, with a view to examining the situation in both resistance movements.[19]

Adamic strove for the United States to issue a declaration on Yugoslavia. In April 1943, he wrote to Donovan, urging him to pay attention to the book *The Serbs Choose War* (and the chapter "Ready, My Chetnik Brothers") by Ruth Mitchell, which had compromised a united Yugoslavia and the Yugoslav fight against the Axis powers, and further aggravated and worsened the relations between the Serbs, Croats, and Slovenians. At the same time, he asked Donovan to ban the book. However, it remains unclear whether that actually happened.[20] On October 1, 1943, Adamic and Etbin Kristan visited Malcolm W. Davis from the Foreign Nationalities Branch and strongly objected to the Italian anti–Fascist politician in exile, Count Carlo Sforza, who argued that territories that came under the Italian jurisdiction following the dissolution of Austria-Hungary should remain Italian in the future. They criticized the Yugoslav government in exile and advocated the Partisan National Liberation Movement. Adamic continued his correspondence with Roosevelt, sending him a letter in February 1944 to point out the need for the formation of a bridgehead on the Adriatic coast that would extend far enough to reach the first mountain ranges, thus securing supplies of weapons and military equipment.

By utilizing his contacts in Washington, he managed to arrange an audience with DeWitt C. Poole and Under Secretary of State Sumner Welles on January 15, 1943. A delegation from the Slovenian American National Council headed by Adamic delivered a memorandum to U.S. officials describing the situation in Slovenia and drawing attention to the demand for a united Slovenia with broad autonomy in a federal democratic Yugoslavia. Prior to the meeting with Sumner Welles, there was a meeting with Father Kazimir Zakrajšek, who resigned as secretary of the Slovenian American National Council because he disagreed with the council's positive attitude toward the Partisan movement. Kazimir Zakrajšek, a priest, expatriate organizer, journalist, publicist, and religious writer, is also mentioned in several documents relating to the Foreign Nationalities Branch, and was mostly known for his anti–Yugoslav propaganda because he stood for a united Slovenia.[21] On January 15, 1943, Zakrajšek visited DeWitt C. Poole together with the aforementioned delegation from the Slovenian American National Council and reminded him during their conversation that certain groups of Serbs in exile had accused him of espionage in the newspaper *Srpsko Jedinstvo.* According to the Serbian newspaper, Zakrajšek was a Vatican agent that was striving in the United States for the formation of a Catholic state in central Europe. He was also accused of espionage by several representatives of the Yugoslav government in exile in the United States, who had asked Louis Adamic for his opinion on whether Zakrajšek was a Vatican or Italian agent. Zakrajšek explained his activities and the background of the accusations to DeWitt C. Poole, labeling the accusations absurd and unjust.[22] On the basis of research on OSS archival documents, it is impossible to claim that Zakrajšek was either a Vatican or Italian agent because the archival documentation portrays him in a positive light, as someone that had done much for the Slovenian expatriate community.

Adamic continued to actively support the Partisan National Liberation Movement. In February 1944, he strove for the United States to prevent the king's return to Yugoslavia and to help the Partisans because all help had been coming from the British, who only had their economic interests at heart and were therefore not to be trusted. The United States, he felt, should present itself as a friendly country.[23] In July 1944, Adamic was offered a post as an adviser, which he promised to accept on condition that the United States accept his views on Tito and Yugoslavia. He ended up refusing the offer, but he continued to cooperate with the Foreign Nationalities Branch as an external associate and informant.[24] Adamic's knowledge of the situation in Yugoslavia was useful to OSS and the Foreign Nationalities Branch, even though he was considered a man with left-wing ideas. He was a strong advocate for the support of the Partisans, and he remained loyal to Tito after the war and sided with him after the Tito–Stalin Split. He died under suspicious circumstances in 1951.

Franc Snoj

Franc Snoj, a Slovenian representative in the Yugoslav government in exile and an exponent of the Slovenian People's Party, emigrated in April

7. Slovenians in the U.S. and Their Cooperation with OSS

1941 with other members of the Yugoslav government in exile to Jerusalem and Cairo and later to the United States. He was sent there with a view to organize the political action of the American Slovenians in support of the Yugoslav government in exile. Snoj, who operated in OSS under the code name Lambda, kept in touch with influential OSS officers, particularly the Foreign Nationalities Branch and the head of OSS, General Donovan. OSS planned to train him and send him to Yugoslavia, but soon deemed it inappropriate, whereas Snoj himself offered his help in recruiting Slovenians for OSS in Cairo and Bari, which never came to fruition. He was actively involved in initiatives regarding the future political regime of the Yugoslavia that were circulating in the United States. On October 23, 1941, he wrote to Izidor Cankar in Argentina, informing him of three currents among the American Slovenians: Yugoslavia as a monarchy, Yugoslavia as a republic, and Zakrajšek's free state of Slovenia, although Zakrajšek kept the option of forming a central European union open in his discussions with foreign politicians.[25]

Throughout his stay in the United States, Snoj advocated the idea of reconstructing the Kingdom of Yugoslavia and a special position of Slovenia within it. He mostly provided OSS with information on the situation in Slovenia. Snoj's assessment of the aforementioned December meeting of the Slovenian American Congress was that everyone agreed on the necessity for a federal Yugoslavia. The majority of attendees opposed the Karadjordjević dynasty, but they were not very united in their opposition to the Habsburg Monarchy. The prevailing opinion at the congress was that a Slovenian state should be formed first, which would be able, on its own initiative and by consensus, to enter a genuine federation that would not be governed by the Serbs, and that it would be a good idea for Bulgaria to join the federation as well.[26]

In their political propaganda they endeavored to create the deepest possible distrust of the Partisans and the Liberation Front. Members of the Slovenian People's Party often claimed in their official contacts with the Allies that the Slovenian communists were actually Trotskyists, who were being given directions from Vienna and Berlin to try to establish a Slovenian Soviet Republic within a central European communist Soviet republic based in Berlin, which was all supposedly a Nazi conspiracy against the Slovenian nation. Snoj, for example, told OSS representatives in New York as early as in 1942 that Slovenian communist leader Boris Kidrič was a Trotskyist collaborating with the Germans, and that the American Slovenians were united in their opposition to Otto von

Habsburg and the potential restoration of the Habsburg Monarchy. Snoj favored the reconstruction of the Kingdom of Yugoslavia, but he also believed at the beginning of March 1943 that a Balkan federation including Yugoslavia, Bulgaria, Greece, and Romania would be formed, and that a central European confederation would encompass Poland, Austria, and Czechoslovakia. In March 1943, Snoj met with Donovan, who promised him that information on the situation in Slovenian territory would be passed to him via Dulles in Bern. This, however, does not necessarily mean that he in fact received the information because it is not evident from the archival documentation.[27]

Meanwhile, the archival documents pertaining to OSS reveal that Snoj always advocated the idea of a renewal of the Kingdom of Yugoslavia, whereas he did not speak of a special position for the Slovenians, except that Yugoslavia would be a federal state. In the spring of 1943, he rejected the idea of establishing a Catholic federation, but he was in favor of dividing Austria between Yugoslavia and Czechoslovakia. His activity also included spreading anti-communist propaganda maintaining that Slovenian communists were Trotskyists striving for a formation of a Central European Soviet Republic under Austrian rule. In April 1944, Snoj wrote a Memorandum entitled "The Slovenes and the Partisans." It describes the cooperation between the Partisans and the Italians in Slovenian territory, and the agreement between the Italians and the Partisans in the village of Vavta Vas, where the Partisans obtained territory around Novo Mesto and were allowed to move freely. He wrote that, after defeating Nazism, the Americans and the British would not permit communism to conquer Europe.[28] Throughout his active years in the United States, Snoj maintained contacts with OSS representatives, who valued his endeavors to help his Axis-controlled homeland, analyzing his contributions on political and military developments in Slovenia and taking them into consideration. To OSS officers, Snoj represented a certain authority because he was a member of the Yugoslav government in exile and later Šubašić's government after the Tito–Šubašić Agreement had been signed. Following the signing of the agreement and the rift within the Slovenian People's Party, Snoj began supporting the Partisan National Liberation Movement in August 1944. He came to Yugoslavia and unsuccessfully urged members of the Slovenian Home Guard to join the Partisans. After the war, he was elected to the Slovenian National Assembly and became Minister of transportation in the Slovenian government. He was later convicted during the Nagode Trial, but was released after four years. He died in Ljubljana in 1962.

7. Slovenians in the U.S. and Their Cooperation with OSS

Ily Bratina

Ily Bratina was a Slovenian from a well-off Slovenian family in Italy, a representative of the Yugoslav minority. Soon after graduating from high school, he left for the United States, where he graduated from New York University. He was single, around forty years old, and he traveled abroad a lot and learned numerous European languages. In February 1942, SOE contacted Bratina and regarded him as a suitable candidate for departure to Yugoslavia due to his supposed experience with subversive actions in Istria and Carinthia. However, later SOE in London was not interested in Bratina because he did not wish to return to Yugoslavia.[29]

Eventually Bratina joined OSS and worked in the Yugoslav Section in Bari as an administrative assistant. Bratina is mentioned in OSS documents as a financier that pointed out mistakes made in regular monthly payments to the Yugoslav agents in OSS because their salaries were not indexed in accordance with the type of work being performed, and payments were often late. He tried very hard to go to Italy, where he wanted to work for the OSS office in Rome, which questioned him for more information on the interview with three leaders of the Yugoslav anti-fascist underground movement in Italy.[30] Any specific information on who the representatives of the underground movement might have been could not be located in the archival documentation. Information on Bratina working in Rome during the war, or on him being sent as head of an OSS mission to Yugoslavia, could not be found either.

Andrej Kobal

One of the prominent American Slovenians to join OSS was also Captain Andrej Kobal. In March 1943, he applied for the Yugoslav project, which also recruited Yugoslavs that were prepared to cooperate with OSS. OSS described him as a Slovenian from a Yugoslav family in Italy, specifically from Cerkno, a psychologist, and a married man. He graduated from Northwestern University in Chicago and Columbia University in New York, where he studied multiple disciplines, from history, psychology, literature, and linguistics to economics. He received his doctorate from Columbia University in New York. He worked for a while for the Colt Ammunition Factory as a personnel director. He was a Slovenian instructor at Columbia and taught Yugoslav literature. After the Second World War began, he received an offer from the Pentagon to work as a psychologist and began working for the American Military Intelligence Service (G-2) and later for OSS. He performed various types of psychological examinations and tests for Military Intelligence Service, where he checked the soldiers' ability to perform military service. After completing a three-month course conducted by OSS by the Potomac River, he had the opportunity to find a more interesting position within OSS. He was first assigned the task of recruiting new candidates for work in OSS, and so he visited infantry and air bases across Virginia, North Carolina, South Carolina, Alabama, and Texas. He had to refuse entry into OSS to people from questionable expatriate organizations as well as members of the largest Slovenian organization in the United States, the Slovenian National Benefit Society. In the second half of 1944, Kobal traveled to Egypt and agreed to Military Intelligence Service lending his services to OSS in Cairo, where he worked for the Yugoslav Section in Cairo, helping recruit the Yugoslav agents that were to be sent on OSS missions to Yugoslavia. As mentioned above, he strove hard for OSS to refuse cooperation with the president of the Yugoslav Committee in Italy, Ivan Marija Čok.[31]

Kobal, who was "on loan" by Military Intelligence Service, worked for OSS / Secret Intelligence Branch. In his memoirs *Svetovni popotnik pripoveduje* (Tales of a World Traveler), published in two parts, he states that it was absolutely essential to recruit and train new agents, which was no easy task because the extremely perilous job was completely voluntary and many could not see themselves applying for it. During his work in Cairo, Kobal established contacts with the Yugoslav government in exile, which were mainly unofficial. Soon afterward, in March 1944, he had to leave Cairo, and OSS negotiated an extension of his services from the Military Intelligence Service. In March 1944, he was transferred from Cairo to the newly established base in Bari, where, owing to his anti-communist views, he refused to cooperate with the Partisans stationed there. He was also one of the instigators promoting the deposition of the head of the Yugoslav Section in Bari, Major Arnoldy, because he regarded him as a pro–Partisan OSS officer. Kobal's assessment of Major Arnoldy, with whom he did not have good relations, is interesting. Kobal wrote that he was "an Americanized Russian, a capable officer, but one clearly more willing to meet the Partisans' demands rather than represent the interests and objectives of OSS and his team."[32]

Ever since his arrival in Bari, the relations between Kobal and the Partisans were constantly strained, predominantly due to the Partisans' opposition to agents being sent to Yugoslavia. The agents in question were not American citizens and the majority had origins in Yugoslavia. The base in Bari was therefore forced to transfer staff that had already been trained, all due to theoretical and ideological demands made by the Partisan representatives. Kobal believed that the Partisans were seeking to be in control of OSS. Kobal also wrote in a negative way about Wuchinich; namely, that his reports daily described Partisan units defeating entire German divisions in one area or another. Wuchinich exaggerated, and because the Americans knew of the existence of each regiment and battalion in Yugoslavia from Military Intelligence Service reports, it was extremely easy to distinguish between reality and fiction.[33] Kobal also took a strong stance against the writer Louis Adamic on account of his left-wing political orientation and his support of the Partisan movement. Kobal regretted the fact that the majority of the Yugoslav government in exile had gone over to the side of the Partisan movement. Kobal remained a proponent of Draža Mihailović and his Chetniks until the end of the war. He returned from Bari to Washington following the agreement with Military Intelligence Service. On the way, he stopped in Istanbul, where he performed tasks for the Military Intelligence Service department of politics. After the war, he was a member of the Allied Control Commission for Bulgaria. He died in 1988 in Murnau, Bavaria.

8

Vladimir Vauhnik and Connections with OSS

Colonel Vladimir Vauhnik, the last military attaché of the Kingdom of Yugoslavia in Berlin, also cooperated with OSS. Several days prior to the German attack on Yugoslavia, Vauhnik notified the General Staff of the Kingdom of Yugoslavia of the planned German attack on Yugoslavia on April 6, 1941. Shortly after the attack on Yugoslavia, he was expelled from Germany and imprisoned in a Gestapo prison, and later released. With the help of the Germans, he obtained a job at the General Headquarters of the Independent State of Croatia. He was supposedly also in contact with General Glaise von Horstenau. At the beginning of 1942, he was dismissed from the Croatian Home Guard, at least according to the message delivered by the Independent State of Croatia Consulate in Ljubljana. Between 1942 and 1944, he and Ante Anić were active in the intelligence network under a code (*Berliner Börsen-Zeitung*, BBZ). The network was operated by the British and also covered the intelligence network across Slovenian territory, Croatia, and even further into central Europe. During his stay in Ljubljana, he made contact with the Italian headquarters in Ljubljana because he was allegedly familiar with the British underground plans for how to win Italy over to their side and convince it to terminate its obligations to the Axis powers. The intelligence agencies of the Axis powers were active not only in their fight against the Partisan movement, but also in their search for connections such as those Vauhnik had. In June 1944, the Gestapo exposed the intelligence organization, and Vauhnik emigrated to Switzerland, where his cooperation with OSS commenced.[1]

On the basis of OSS archival documents, Dulles was informed about a former Swiss military attaché in Berlin facilitating Vauhnik's entry into Switzerland in the summer of 1944. OSS Captain Charles T. Katsainos included a summary of Vauhnik's biography in his memorandum to Dulles,

8. Vladimir Vauhnik and Connections with OSS

in which he stated that Vauhnik was a personal friend of the German General in the Independent State of Croatia, Glaise von Horstenau. Katsainos wrote that in December 1941 the Germans sent Vauhnik to Ljubljana, where he later formed the Slovenian Home Guard under German command. Vauhnik was allegedly sent to Switzerland by the Gestapo in order to spy on Yugoslav activities and accelerate work on shattering Yugoslav unity. He noted that Vauhnik was an intelligent man, a born conspirator, an exemplary member of the Roman Catholic Church, and an Austrian that intended to separate Slovenia from Yugoslavia and then annex it to Austria, while he himself would, of course, become the ruler or military leader of Slovenia. Katsainos also stated that Vauhnik often claimed to have been working for the British intelligence service, which was also possible. However, he remained a Gestapo agent. Katsainos concluded in the memorandum that Vauhnik could be used by OSS, although he was never to be trusted.[2] To sum up, OSS did not actively include Vauhnik in its ranks because it distrusted him. A detailed analysis of American and British archival documents does not reveal any concrete evidence of Vauhnik's links to the Gestapo either, and the same holds true for his cooperation with the British intelligence agencies.

During his departure for Switzerland in the summer of 1944, Vauhnik strove for a united Slovenia within a non-communist Yugoslavia, but after his arrival in Switzerland he was already developing ideas about an independent Slovenian state including Trieste. He endeavored to establish a Roman Catholic state in central Europe, which would include Slovenia with Vauhnik as head of state, Bavaria, Austria, Hungary, and possibly even Croatia. Slovenia would represent an important part of this federal country because the Port of Trieste allowed access to the sea. Vauhnik supposedly drafted a memorandum and sent it out to other agencies. The memorandum was allegedly written on November 10, 1944, in Ljubljana, bearing the subtitle *O položaju slovenskega naroda in njegovi osvoboditvi z ustanovitvijo svobodne slovenske države* (On the Situation of the Slovenian Nation and its Liberation by Forming a Free Slovenian State). Vauhnik sent it to Dulles. The memorandum mentioned a so-called National Committee, which sent its delegation to Rome under the aegis of Vatican. After the liberation of Rome, contact with the delegation was prevented, and the former Yugoslav government in London lost all its influence, especially after the Soviet armed forces' invasion of Serbia. The memorandum also rejected the efforts of Tito's National Liberation Movement to include Slovenia in a new Yugoslavia because that would mean a horrible civil war.

8. Vladimir Vauhnik and Connections with OSS

He strove for Slovenia to gain permission to become a member of a larger union of states within a Danubian Catholic federation including Czechoslovakia and Austria, or an Adriatic union with Croatia and Hungary, or a new Yugoslavia within a western Balkan union. The Slovenian state was to regain the territories awarded to other countries in 1919, such as Trieste, Gorizia, Istria, and southern Carinthia. The Allied Command in Italy was requested to allow a disembarkation in Istria or a quick march across Venetia, and it would be supplied with a secret army consisting of six brigades. There is no trace of Dulles confirming receipt of the memorandum and the enclosed letters.[3]

One of the reports written by Vauhnik says that the Partisan movement in Slovenia followed the Bolshevization of Slovenia. The author also states that the Anglo-American forces would hand over to the Slovenian Democrats authority over a free and united Slovenia, extending from Trieste to the High Tauern and Lake Balaton, and that the Partisans were planning to slaughter forty thousand Slovenians. In January 1945, on behalf of politicians and economists in exile from ten different countries, a new memorandum from Vauhnik explained the idea of founding a union of European countries or United States of Europe, which would encompass twenty-five to thirty individual countries. The central government would be located in Vienna, Prague, and Geneva, and comprised of an elected president, a general secretariat, and five general federal departments for foreign and domestic policy, economics, transport, social affairs, and defense. The author mentioned that each state should have five representatives for these sectors, with approximately 150 delegates in a European Federal Congress.[4]

Many questions have arisen regarding Vauhnik because it is difficult to prove, on the basis of written sources, his links with the British or German intelligence agencies. He probably worked for both intelligence agencies, which also raises the question of which intelligence agency he informed correctly and which one incorrectly. As mentioned by Makso Šnuderl in his foreword to Vauhnik's memoirs *Nevidna fronta* (The Invisible Front), SS functionary Walter Schellenberg stated in his memoirs that Vauhnik was ready to work for the Gestapo and that he did invaluable favors for him in Italy as well. In Yugoslav journalism, Schellenberg's record was for a long time the reason for labeling Vauhnik a traitor to his country, which at present cannot be confirmed because there are no sufficient archival documents available.[5] After the war, he emigrated to Argentina, where he died in 1955.

9

Allen Dulles
and Connections
with Yugoslavia

The work done by the Bern station chief and later head of the CIA, Allen Dulles, was highly significant for the United States. He reported vital information on German air defense, German submarines, V-1 and V-2 missiles, and the state of the German war industry. He obtained intelligence information from Germany, Austria, Hungary, and the Balkans. There were five OSS officers in Bern and twelve cryptographers, several translators, and at least one hundred agents that were connected to field operations. Dulles submitted many reports on the situation in Germany and enemy-held territories. He initially opposed the German unconditional surrender, but later achieved his greatest success, namely the surrender of German forces in Italy, better known under the name Operation Sunrise.[1] The operation involved secret negotiations between Allen Dulles and the representatives of the German armed forces in Italy. The negotiations resulted in a separate capitulation of German forces in the territory stretching to the eastern bank of the Isonzo River, and allowed the Anglo-American forces a rapid breakthrough to Trieste. On March 1945, the head of the police and SS General Karl Wolff attended a secret meeting with Dulles in Locarno, Switzerland, where he submitted a folder containing German information on the Partisan battle formation and positions to the American intelligence officer. Wolff also mentioned that the Serbs and Slovenians under his command had gathered around Gorizia, by which he meant the quisling Slovenian National Defense Corps in the Adriatic Littoral, the Serbian Volunteer Corps (also known as the *Ljotićevci*), Nedić's Serbian State Guard, and Chetnik squads under General Miodrag Damjanović's command. Even though Dulles met with Tito's agents, he was distinctly anti-communist oriented and believed that the Allies should stick with Mihailović rather than fall into the trap set by the communist propagandists.[2]

OSS Bern was not the main intelligence base for the territory of Yugoslavia and it therefore played a secondary role in Yugoslav matters. Nonetheless, Dulles occasionally reported on the situation in Yugoslavia, mostly on the basis of contacts he maintained with Yugoslav emigrants in Switzerland. One of Dulles's assistant informants reporting on developments in Yugoslavia was Agent no. 663, known under the nickname Beki, with whom Čok and Snoj also had contacts.[3] Another important agent was Agent no. 476, who was close to the Nazi intelligence service. He supposedly provided Dulles with information, which Dulles used as proof of Mihailović's collaboration with the Axis powers. On December 1, 1943, the agent informed Dulles that, as far as the fight against the communists was concerned, Mihailović always collaborated with the Nazis, and that the collaboration was becoming increasingly intimate, especially after relations with the British had become more distant.[4]

Via Dulles's correspondence, increasingly more information was coming to Bern on the agreement between Mihailović and the Germans. On December 13, 1943, Agent no. 819 informed Dulles that the Chetnik leader had signed a non-aggression treaty with the Germans, and that pre-war leader of Croatian Peasant Party, Vlatko Maček, was still holding strong, especially in Croatia, which was the reason for the negotiations underway between Maček and Tito. Dulles was also informed of the situation in Slovenian territory by Snoj. On October 8, 1942, Snoj sent him a booklet regarding the history of the Italian occupation of Slovenian territory, together with the latest information on developments in Yugoslavia. In addition to Snoj, Colonel Vladimir Vauhnik was also in contact with Dulles.[5]

10

Department of National Security and the Supervision of OSS Agents

The analysis of Anglo-American missions in the Department of National Security (later after the war the State Security Administration) archive materials were rather superficial and simplified. The Yugoslav security agency bodies were tasked with uncovering infiltrated (inserted) agent organizations and with halting destructive activity in Partisan units, and particular attention was dedicated to suspicious Anglo-American missions. Conflicts, suspicions, and misunderstanding between the Partisans and Anglo-Americans became even more intense in 1944 for various reasons. The most important reasons were international recognition of the Partisan National Liberation Movement, the possibility of Anglo-American landing and (non)intervention in Yugoslavia, the Tito–Šubašić agreement, and deployment of the Ranger mission to the headquarters of Draža Mihailović. The situation worsened after the Tito–Šubašić agreement in June 1944, when the leading member of Yugoslav communists Edvard Kardelj issued instructions that the political role of the Anglo-American missions should be given less attention and that their involvement in various gatherings and rallies was no longer necessary and useful. This of course indicated that in former times the Anglo-American missions were important for the Partisans also due to their political support for the Partisans, which represented a very important means of propaganda in the search for international legitimacy. A sharp response also followed sending the Ranger mission to the Chetniks, when Tito protested to Wilson and ordered the missions to remain only with Partisan headquarters and removed the right to use special channels and insight into the plans and moves of Partisan units.[1]

10. Department of National Security and Supervision of OSS Agents

The archives of the postwar State Security Administration also include a detailed report on the activity of OSS and British intelligence agencies. One of the reports concludes that Allied missions operated both in the military and among the civilian population and they arrived in Yugoslavia in increasingly larger numbers and often without the permission of Tito's Supreme Headquarters. According to the assessments of the State Security Administration, they were not able to provide all of the help promised, which only increased suspicions and supervision.

A detailed postwar report of the State Security Administration concluded that the supervision of the British missions revealed that those missions "were involved in gathering information of a political and military nature, gathering information on the location, strength, and movements of enemy units, and gathering information on the development and activity of domestic counter-revolutionary forces."[2]

The archives also contain many documents about the supervision of Yugoslav agents that worked for OSS, especially those agents that joined the Partisans. The Department of National Security warned the Partisan leadership about joining Yugoslav agents from Anglo-American missions to Partisan troops: "Due to the lack of understanding and wisdom of our headquarters, they were immediately integrated into National Liberation Movement without being given any further attention."[3] It should be clarified that the Department of National Security generalized transfers to Partisan troops for all Anglo-American agents, although the Partisan movement was joined only by Yugoslav agents from British missions, with the exception of one operating in American missions. Similarly, the Yugoslav security agency noted in its conclusions the aspirations of Yugoslav agents from Anglo-American missions for admission to the Communist Party, where there are again references to Yugoslav agents in British missions. The Communist Party had the opinion that, according to the document, Yugoslav agents made every effort to become members of the Communist Party, which they eventually succeeded in to a great extent because the document says that they managed to fully integrate into the Partisan National Liberation Movement and establish contacts with the Partisans and officials, and, on the other hand, to maintain contact with Anglo-American missions and inform them about everything. An interesting conclusion refers to the fact that all Yugoslav agents tried to make acquaintances in the civilian population, especially to establish relations with women. They had love affairs, sometimes even with two, three, or even more women.

10. Department of National Security and Supervision of OSS Agents

In all instances they sought a wife, preferably in the Partisan National Liberation Movement or a naive country girl.[4]

The Yugoslav security agency was also convinced that to establish connections in the field the Yugoslav agents of Anglo-American missions should look for all former emigrants from the United Kingdom and the United States that had mastered English, whereas fewer contacts were sought with intellectuals proficient in English. The Department of National Security noted that Yugoslav agents favored contacts with people that were politically not in favor of or even opposed the Partisan political leadership.[5] In this way, the Yugoslav Secret Police controlled all members of the Anglo-American missions, whose movement became increasingly restricted and communication even harder. It also realized that the relationships within the Anglo-American missions had lately become increasingly businesslike and official, they demanded more autonomy, and when they failed they often had a negative approach toward the Partisan leadership and its struggle. This remark also refers to the conclusion about a growing opposition between the British and American missions.[6]

The detailed report on the activity of so called "American mission" pointed out that it processed three major subjects: American missions at the Partisan headquarters, the relevant subordinate American mission at the Ninth Corps, and the Fourth Operational Zone. The missions also included a meteorology group, a group for receiving help, and teams and groups for Austrian infiltration. The reconstruction placed special emphasis on Slovenians involved in American missions. The report mentions that, in addition to mission members, rescued Allied airmen, and Yugoslav agents of Anglo-American missions came to Slovenian territory. Almost all of them were wireless operators, who were scarce in Partisan troops, and a great portion of them joined the Partisans. The Department of National Security was convinced that they had regular contacts with OSS agents and were paid by the United States for a long time. In reality, Yugoslav agents already demanded better pay or were promised unpaid salaries during their training. One of the documents of the Department of National Security states:

> The American missions came with the goal of carrying out intelligence activity to register the deployment of German divisions. Later on there was some talk about joint actions with Partisans, where they would participate with air raids on communication lines for transporting troops, weapons, and rations to the front. Mission members soon established contact with their families, civilians, and Partisans. Various material also indicates the likelihood of contacts with Be-ga.[7]

10. Department of National Security and Supervision of OSS Agents

The Department of National Security closely monitored every OSS mission and was at the same time specifically interested in the political situation at the OSS base in Bari because the base had allegedly intensified its cooperation with the Chetnik movement in August 1944. The Yugoslav security agency condemned the activity for Yugoslavia by OSS representatives in Bari, who supposedly provided material support to the Chetnik movement and sent OSS missions to Mihailović's Chetniks. In the opinion of Partisan intelligence staff, the head of OSS Bari, Robert P. Joyce, and the head of the Yugoslav Section, Lieutenant Holt Green, were particularly in favor of the Chetniks. The document quite rightly noticed that OSS agents were also sending assistance and missions to the Chetniks despite the Anglo-American decision to support Tito's Partisan movement in Yugoslavia,[8] but "forgot" the active cooperation between the Partisan representatives and OSS in Bari, and support for the Partisan movement provided by OSS Bari already since October 1943. It is true that Arnoldy was replaced by Green on account of his excessive pro–Partisan approach, but this did not mean that after this change the entire OSS Bari base would stop supporting the Partisan movement.

The arrival of Yugoslav agents of Anglo-American missions presented an inevitable evil for the communist leadership: on the one hand, it indicated the political/moral victory of the Partisan movement and the arrival of specific material aid, but on the other hand it worried the Communist Party that someone else would prevent it from taking power and threaten its monopoly. In the search of a necessary compromise, the Communist Party emerged as the big winner with the obvious help of the Department of National Security. Everybody that cooperated or had contacts with the Anglo-American intelligence agencies became suspicious. This postwar prejudice, to a greater or lesser extent, persisted for quite some time.

11

The Postwar Role of Slovenia Inside the Yugoslav State

Toward the end of the war, the principal task of Anglo-American missions was to report from areas of territorial dispute between Yugoslavia and the neighboring countries. There was no consensus between the British and the Americans regarding the kind of policy that should be followed with regard to the Yugoslav territorial claims. OSS was actively involved in analyzing the problem of the Yugoslav borders, especially its Research and Analysis Branch, which was in charge of gathering and conducting analyses, and assessing intelligence information coming from Yugoslavia. Within the branch, the brothers Wayne and Alexander Vuchinich were particularly active, working as analysts and experts on Yugoslavia. They were both professors at Stanford University and descendants of Serbian parents. Wayne had already started working for OSS at the end of 1941, and Alexander started in March 1942. Before the war, they both lived in Yugoslavia for some time. The majority of analyses and memorandums regarding the situation in Yugoslavia were written by Alexander, who also worked at OSS bases in Bari, Cairo, and Belgrade.[1]

OSS / Research and Analysis Branch received a fair number of proposals concerning the postwar political regime of Yugoslavia and Yugoslav territorial claims submitted by Yugoslav politicians in emigration. The Yugoslavs at home and abroad spent a considerable amount of time preparing memorandums and plans for the postwar Yugoslav borders. Proposals and memorandums were even superfluous because the multitude of memorandums led to confusion and made a bad impression in OSS and other circles abroad, making it seem that Yugoslavs did not know what they wanted. This poor impression was compounded by numerous disagreements within the Yugoslav government in exile. OSS also received information that, particularly in anti-communist emigration circles in the United States, ideas about an independent Slovenia had spread. On September 8, 1941, Krek sent a letter to Snoj in which he explained how Slovenian members of the Yugoslav government in exile imagined the future of the Slovenians and mentioned three solutions. The most desired solution was to keep Slovenia within Yugoslavia. If that was not possible, a union with the Croats in the same country would be the next best option, and the least desired idea was Slovenia with Trieste as an individual country under British protection. During the war, numerous alternative proposals were developed, each of them defining in its own way the role and size of Slovenia within Yugoslavia after the end of the war.[2]

The Research and Analysis Branch also registered a report sent by the Slovenian Covenant to Franc Snoj on May 20, 1942. According to the report, the Slovenian Covenant had been established at the initiative of Draža Mihailović in May 1942. It stood for a complete union of the Slovenian nation in a free Slovenia as a constituent and equal part of the national state of Yugoslavia. Any separatism was considered detrimental to the Slovenian nation.[3] In December 1942, the American Slovenian Congress was organized in the United States, which sent its delegation to the head of the Foreign Nationalities Branch, DeWitt C. Poole. In their talks, Poole observed that, first, a Slovenian state should be formed. On its own initiative and by consensus, it should be able to enter a federation that would not be governed by the Serbs. It would be a good idea for Bulgaria to join the federation as well.[4] In April 1943, the Research and Analysis Branch received another report from the Slovenian Covenant, which said that the organization strove for any type of solution to the Slovenian question: Yugoslavia, Slovenia plus Croatia, or independent Slovenia. However, it was perfectly clear that no one wanted to remain under the rule of Austria, Italy, or Germany. According to Krek, all Slovenian politicians in exile should be active in spreading propaganda, particularly in Washington and London. In both capitals, they should propagate the restoration and extension of Yugoslavia to encompass all of Slovenian ethnic territory, or the incorporation of all Yugoslavs into some type of Danubian or Balkan federation or union in the event that the United Kingdom no longer favored small nation-states.[5] Letters by the Slovenian Covenant thus reveal that Krek and his associates developed ideas of an independent Yugoslavia and Slovenia as early as the spring of 1943, when disputes concerning Bosnia and regarding Croatian borders escalated. Krek envisaged an independent Slovenia with Trieste, Rijeka, the Kvarner Bay islands, and Carinthia. The ideas were rejected by the British on the grounds that their intention was to rebuild Yugoslavia.

As mentioned above, Roosevelt questioned whether rebuilding Yugoslavia was reasonable, and was also skeptical of Ivan Šubašić's success as the new Yugoslav mandatary after the removal of the Purić government. Although Roosevelt preferred Yugoslavia, he thought that three separate states with three separate governments within a Balkan confederation would solve many problems. In May 1943, the OSS special Foreign Language Division also prepared a Memorandum for Donovan, setting out all options regarding the federation and presenting them in the manner in which ethnic immigrant newspapers in the United States discussed them. The document also discussed an idea of a Catholic federation, where, after the war, all Slovenians would be united on their ethnic territory. Behind the Catholic federation was the Vatican, and a map of Slovenia, Croatia, Czechoslovakia, Austria, Hungary, and Romania was added to the memorandum.[6]

Toward the end of 1943, liberally oriented Slovenians in the Middle East that intended to establish a Slovenian Littoral legion advocated an autonomous Slovenia within Yugoslavia. Ivan Rudolf also provided detailed information to the Research and Analysis Branch on the problems encountered by the Slovenians and Croats under Italian rule. On behalf of the Yugoslav Committee in Italy, he wrote a brief document concerning the committee's efforts and the political situation in Yugoslavia. He wrote about the difficult situation of the Slovenians and Croats under Italian rule and on volunteer recruitment for the Yugoslav Army in Exile. Members of contingents in prisoner-of-war camps would form a Slovenian Littoral Legion, which would consist of two battalions and operate under the aegis of the American Army.[7]

The Americans did not support Rudolf's plan, whereas during the first years the British assisted the Yugoslav Committee in Italy a great deal because the majority of Yugoslav agents sent to Yugoslavia as part of SOE and ISLD missions were selected from the ranks of inhabitants of the Slovenian Littoral, Istria and Dalmatia and recruited by Rudolf and his associates from Africa and elsewhere. After the Tito–Šubašić Agreement was signed on Vis in June 1944, Krek strove for the Allied forces to occupy Yugoslavia, as opposed to Soviet forces or only Tito's Partisan forces. He believed that the Soviet Union was not directly interested in Slovenian territory and would therefore not oppose the Anglo-American

Assembly of the Slovenian civilians, Partisans and the Allies in the Vipava Valley, July 25, 1944 (National Museum of Contemporary History).

occupation of Slovenian territory. The Slovenian Home Guard units were to join the Anglo-Americans forces and, in Krek's opinion, the majority of the Slovenian Partisans, who would be reorganized, would do the same.[8] In the second half of 1944, he delivered a letter to American Colonel Torielli, in which he claimed that the only goal pursued by the Partisan movement in Slovenia was a violent bolshevization of Slovenia as one of the most important geopolitical parts of Europe. He also recommended that the Anglo-American Allies hand over authority over a free and united Slovenia extending from Trieste to the High Tauern and Lake Balaton to the "Slovenian Democrats" because the Partisans were planning to slaughter another forty thousand Slovenians.[9]

After the signing of the Tito–Šubašić Agreement on Vis in June 1944, a rift opened up among Slovenian politicians in exile in August 1944 over the proposal that the Slovenian Home Guard units should join the Partisans and cease their collaboration with the German forces. As a result, the Slovenian emigrant politicians in the Slovenian People's Party Snoj, Kuhar, and Cankar deserted Krek and opted to support the Partisans. According to OSS reports, in August 1944 in Bari, the Slovenian mission, which was comprised of Milko Brezigar, Fran Mačkovšek, and Josip Germ, made a stand on behalf of the Slovenian Covenant for a democratic federal kingdom of Yugoslavia including Trieste, Istria, and the Adriatic islands, which would border Italy all the way up to the 1914 Austrian-Italian border and include Carinthia, Klagenfurt, Villach, and Slovenian ethnic territory.

At the end of August 1944, the Research and Analysis Branch received a report about the representatives of the Slovenian People's Party and the Croatian Peasant Party proposing the establishment of Catholic states to Pope Pius XII. The Slovenian idea was to found a Catholic country consisting of Slovenia, Croatia, Austria, and Bavaria, and the Croats also wanted to include Hungary and Slovakia in the country. From sources available to date, the reaction of OSS to the report remains unclear. It is known, however, that the majority of memorandums and other proposals by Slovenian emigrants were not taken seriously by OSS.[10]

Less promising for the Yugoslavs was the American standpoint, which was based on the request made by the State Department in September 1944, that the Anglo-American military authority should be extended to the entire territory of the Kingdom of Italy from 1939. Consequently, American diplomats rejected all propositions regarding a temporary demarcation line. In accordance with the resolution endorsed by President Roosevelt, Supreme Allied Commander Mediterranean Field Marshal Harold Alexander decided in November 1944 to extend its control to all of Italy, including Venezia Giulia, not for military but political reasons. Because the area was a disputed territory, it had to be proven that its fate could not be decided by anyone on their own. In November 1944, Alexander reported to OSS commanders in the same context, although he simultaneously emphasized that negotiations with the Yugoslavs had to be opened with a view to reaching an agreement. Alexander maintained that he needed Trieste and Rijeka as important ports for the control over port and railway transport, which would ensure transport links between the British forces in Italy and those in Austria.[11]

The Liberation Front and Yugoslav communists never recognized the partition of Yugoslavia because it stood for unity and understanding among its nations and the territorial expansion of Yugoslavia within its ethnic borders. At the time of Tito's speech on Vis on September 12, 1944, in which he clearly expressed Yugoslav demands for the liberation of Carinthia, the Slovenian Littoral, and Istria, the Research and Analysis Branch drafted a document entitled "Territorial Aspirations of Partisan Yugoslavia," which was based on two criteria. The first criterion covered the territories that were assigned to Yugoslavia by the Treaty of Versailles and should remain under Yugoslav rule; the second one was territories claimed by Yugoslavia on the grounds that they were ethnic Yugoslav areas and should be incorporated into the new Yugoslavia. All requested Yugoslav territories were based on the two criteria, with the exception of Trieste, which Yugoslavia claimed predominantly for economic reasons. In addition to Trieste, Yugoslav aspirations in Italy included the Slovenian Littoral, Istria, and Dalmatia with the city of Zadar. The Research and Analysis Branch proposed that the Italian minority issue be resolved by means of a population exchange. The Partisans also had territorial aspirations for parts of Austria, namely Carinthia and Styria, where the population was more mixed than in Italy (the Slovenian Littoral and Istria).[12] On November 22, 1944, Kardelj, accompanied by Šubašić, traveled to Moscow, followed by Andrija Hebrang and Arso Jovanović in January 1945. In both talks, they opened the topic of new Yugoslav borders and their claims to the neighboring countries, including the issue of Trieste. Stalin expressed scruples regarding bold Yugoslav claims in his talks with Jovanović and Hebrang. Nevertheless, Tito and his associates counted on Stalin's unconditional help.[13] Due to increasingly large Partisan aspirations for postwar border changes, the Research and Analysis Branch kept a vigilant eye on the activities of the Yugoslav Partisans because they were regarded as the only military force that could jeopardize the Anglo-American interests in Venezia Giulia and Carinthia. In January 1945, the Research and Analysis analysts received an analytical report written by an OSS representative on the Slovenian-Austrian border entitled "Slovenian Territorial Claims." He distinguished between the official policies of the National Committee for the Liberation of Yugoslavia (NKOJ) and the Slovenian National Liberation Committee (SNOOS). According to OSS assessments, the National Committee for the Liberation of Yugoslavia (NKOJ) was to take the British interests into consideration, and thus made such demands for border revision that were acceptable to the British. Unofficial propaganda in the Partisan Fourth Operational Zone, however, laid claim to territory extending to the Carnic Alps and north of Maribor, although the Partisans in charge in fact neither made nor supported such demands.

OSS representative estimated that the Partisans would take up military occupation of disputed military territories before an international agreement had been reached, thus presenting the Allies with a fait accompli. The occupation would be followed by a plebiscite, and the weak Austrian government would support the Yugoslav territorial claims. OSS considered the claims as a touchstone of reaction of the Anglo-American

11. The Postwar Role of Slovenia Inside the Yugoslav State

Session of the Slovenian National Liberation Committee in Črnomelj, February 19–20, 1944 (National Museum of Contemporary History).

missions. In their opinion, the Austrian Liberation Front (*Österreichische Freiheits Front*, ÖFF) was under the authority of the Slovenian Partisan leadership of the Liberation Front. The report estimated that both organizations would gain even greater significance, which would continue to increase in proportion to the Soviet speed of advance toward Vienna, and consequently the scope of Soviet control and influence in Austria. With the help of the Austrian Liberation Front, the Slovenian National Liberation Committee would secure the revision of the border with Austria and assistance with the establishment of a government in Vienna. All missions sent to Carinthia had been notified in advance of a substantial Slovenian minority in Klagenfurt and the region.[14]

In February 1945, Eden presented a document to his Soviet and American colleagues in Yalta. He pointed out the fact that the Partisans were already present in part of Venezia Giulia, and suggested that the Big Three draw a dividing line between the zone intended for the Anglo-Americans and the zone under Partisan occupation. For that purpose, a group of experts should be formed, who would set a temporary border, while taking into account the ethnic principle. The Soviet Foreign Minister and the U.S. Secretary of State promised to examine the proposal, but the matter was not pursued further. The United States remained true to its position—namely, that Anglo-American forces should occupy the entire area of Venezia Giulia—whereas the Soviet Union probably wanted to keep its options open to see whether the implementation of a "fifty-fifty" arrangement was possible in the case of Trieste as well. At the Yalta Conference, the British formulated a proposal relating to the occupation zones in postwar Austria, which U.S. Secretary of Foreign Affairs Edward Stettinius also agreed on. In their proposal, the British appealed to all three superpowers to persuade Tito that the Austrian borders should stay the way they were before the peace conference. The Allies conceded that Yugoslav territorial claims in Venezia Giulia were party justified because there was partial support of its population for Yugoslavia, whereas their opinion was different with regard to the northern borders; namely, they argued for the Austrian borders from 1937. The issue of Carinthia was decided at the Allied conference in Moscow in October 1943, when the Big Three resolved that all three superpowers would occupy Austria in joint cooperation and that Carinthia would fall into the British occupation zone.

An interesting report was received by the Research and Analysis Branch in March 1945, stating that the Vatican endeavored to incorporate Slovenia and Venezia Giulia into Austria.[15] Unfortunately, further data on the Vatican's efforts could not be located in the voluminous archival material. In April 1945, Tito entered into a twenty-year cooperation agreement with Stalin. By doing so, he clearly violated the agreement reached the previous year between Churchill and Stalin. This fact greatly alarmed the Anglo-Americans. During this time, Field Marshal Alexander also faced the dilemma of whether to occupy the entire region of Venezia Giulia, as the Americans wanted, or only its western part, as the British wanted. In mid–April 1945, he opted for the first option and notified the Joint Chiefs of Staff in Washington that he would demand that Tito order all Partisan troops in the area to be occupied by the Anglo-Americans to recognize his supreme command. He counted on Churchill's support because the British prime minister sent a telegram to the new American President Truman the very next day, trying to convince him that the time for action had come. He believed that Trieste should be occupied as soon as possible. Similarly, Roosevelt attributed great meaning to Trieste as a starting point for the Danube region.[16]

In the meantime, Lindsay, the head of the American diplomatic mission in Belgrade, submitted a report to American Ambassador Richard C. Patterson on the military situation and problems in Venezia Giulia and southern Austria. Lindsay stated that the Yugoslavs were planning to occupy and annex the Italian territory in Istria and Venezia Giulia extending to the Isonzo River, including the cities of Trieste and Rijeka. He reported that, for the time being, the Anglo-American policy toward all territorial revisions remained unchanged, and that they should be postponed until the peace conference after the war. Lindsay believed that, in case of Yugoslav occupation, it would be more difficult to reach a final fair agreement on borders. He also reported on the meeting of Alexander with Tito, where Alexander demanded that upon the Allied occupation of Austria control should be exercised over lines of communication to Trieste, as well as Trieste itself. Alexander hoped that the Allied forces would be able to occupy all Italian territory west of the 1939 borders. Tito agreed to the Allied control proposed by Alexander, but on the condition that the civil administration established in the disputed region be maintained. Alexander replied that the matter would be handed over to Combined Chiefs of Staff for examination.[17]

OSS had significant difficulties in the territory around Trieste, predominantly with the British, because OSS agents had been eliminated from the game, and so they strove for as many informants as possible to come into the city. OSS assigned the territory of Trieste to Lindsay, who arrived in Trieste from Belgrade in early May. Among the most active in Trieste were OSS / Counterintelligence Branch and the British Special Counter Intelligence Units, which competed with OSS. The counterintelligence agents interrogated persons coming to Trieste from the Balkans and heading for northern Italy. Among OSS staff in the city of Trieste were Captain Bruno Uberti, Captain Marcel, Corporal Valeri Melchiori, Sergeant Albin Perno, Lance Sergeant Sal Campore, Alfred Magone, Ego de Baseggio, Livio Corsi, and others that joined them later. On May 24, 1945, Trieste was incorporated into the command of the Allied Eighth Army, and Captain Blatnik, Lieutenant Edward Wells, Sergeant Arthur Kern, Theodore Korolchuk, and Theodore Zaloga also joined OSS Trieste.[18]

OSS agents in Trieste complained that the British officers had many agencies and plainclothes agents that were not recognizable. They reported on the British preparing an uprising in the city in order to force an armed Allied intervention, which was not in the United States' interest. On May 31, 1945, the British even refused to issue a mere temporary permit for an OSS group to visit Trieste, arguing that they themselves would provide the Americans with all the necessary intelligence information. OSS agents in Trieste also kept in touch with members of the national liberation committee (*Comitato di liberazione nazionale*) in Trieste. The British suspected the Americans of being biased in favor of the Italian side and, furthermore, they had plenty of American staff of Italian descent.[19]

In May 1945, the Joint Chiefs of Staff received a report about the Partisan units unexpectedly liberating Trieste, Gorizia, and Monfalcone, and so General Clark congratulated General Drapšin and simultaneously informed him that the Eighth Army was planning to occupy Trieste as well. Joint Chiefs of Staff also received information about the Yugoslav Army behaving badly toward the Anglo-American forces in disputed regions, and, what is more, the Partisans forbade the Anglo-American missions at the Partisan headquarters to send intelligence reports to their own bases. Conflicts were becoming increasingly evident in the disputed territories that Yugoslavia wanted to occupy. Therefore, Under Secretary of State Joseph C. Grew wrote a memorandum to Truman on May 10, 1945, saying that the United States had to decide whether to permit the Soviet government to operate in the Mediterranean Theatre via its satellite. The objective of Yugoslavia and the Soviet government was to establish states and borders that would best suit the Soviet Union. The occupation of Trieste would therefore have far-reaching consequences. Truman had no desire for a new conflict. On May 14, 1945, he therefore wrote to Churchill, maintaining that it was impossible for him to enter a new war unless Tito's forces attacked.[20]

On May 11, 1945, the issue of the northern Yugoslav borders gradually started to be tackled. Alexander sent an official letter to Tito that specified that Austria would remain within the borders from 1937 and that the French, American, Soviet, and British forces would divide it into occupation zones. Yugoslavia initially wanted its own occupation zone. Later, it demanded the participation of its forces in the Soviet zone, which the British and Americans adamantly opposed. This resulted in the Yugoslav Army's withdrawal from Carinthia.[21]

The animosity continued to escalate, causing relations between the Allies to grow increasingly strained. OSS documents, which report on the issue of dealing with Yugoslav territorial claims, also reveal the American views of the fate of Yugoslav collaborators. The United States also commented on Tito's statement dated September 15, 1944, in which he stated that all members of the Slovenian Home Guard units, Chetnik, and other forces fighting against the Partisan National Liberation Movement would be brought before a court martial as national traitors and punished with severe sentences. In their response to Tito's statement, the Americans

11. The Postwar Role of Slovenia Inside the Yugoslav State

clearly stated once more that they would not interfere in Yugoslav internal matters. They observed that Tito was less friendly to the Anglo-Americans due to the Soviet entry into Yugoslav territory, while at the same time more confident and having less appreciation for the Allied assistance.[22]

The United States regarded the Yugoslav demands concerning disputable territories in Friuli-Venezia Giulia and Carinthia as a Soviet attempt to break into their area of influence. In early May 1945, the Anglo-Americans demanded that the Yugoslav People's Army retreat from parts of Friuli-Venezia Giulia and Carinthia. On May 9, 1945, Colonel Charles Thayer wrote to Donovan, who in turn contacted President Truman. Donovan wrote that the dispute between Yugoslavia and Italy over Friuli-Venezia Giulia could be construed as a conflict between the Soviets and the Americans. It was mainly the question of how far into western Europe the areas under Soviet control should be allowed to extend. The British and American policies regarding the postwar Yugoslav borders differed in their views of the western Yugoslav border. The British were more open to Yugoslav territorial claims, whereas the American position was less favorable for the Yugoslavs. In contrast to the British, the Americans insisted that the Allied Military Government take control over all territories that were part of the Kingdom of Italy in 1939, and they consequently refused proposals for a demarcation line (the Robertson–Alexander Line). It can be concluded that OSS received numerous reports on Yugoslavia's unjust borders with its neighboring countries. The fate of the Austrian border was determined by the 1943 Moscow Declaration, whereas the amendment of the border between Yugoslavia and Italy was still a matter of great concern. OSS reports from ethnically disputed territories and various initiatives and memorandums by Yugoslav politicians of different political orientations relating to unjust borders between Yugoslavia and its neighboring countries did not affect the Allies' decision on postwar Yugoslav borders, which were subject to the peace conference after the war. Nevertheless, it was these sources of information that alerted the Allies to unjustly established borders and made them aware of the ethnic situation in the disputed territories demanded by Yugoslavia.[23]

Conclusion

Following the Teheran Conference, the Allies decided to support the resistance movement that was doing most harm to the Axis powers. The policies of Churchill, Stalin, and Roosevelt were responsible for prosecuting war on a global scale. The policies they adopted toward individual countries reflected the scope of their responsibility, the limits of their power, and a sense of their priorities. In Yugoslavia they supported Tito, and this decision was mostly pragmatic and not political. Tito's communist resistance movement was more active in fighting against the Axis powers, it was present in almost all parts of Yugoslavia, and it had the support of all Yugoslav nations. The Allies saw a problem in the collaboration of some Chetnik groups that were subordinated to Mihailović and in Chetnik passiveness in the struggle against the Axis powers. The Allies quickly realized that the Chetniks operated only in some parts of Yugoslavia and that they had pro–Serbian nationalistic ideas. The Allied liaison officers' intelligence reports were not key to the Allies' decision to support Tito's resistance movement. The key role in this regard was played by the German reports from the Balkans that the British intercepted using the Ultra decoding system. The OSS supporting role in the drama of events in Yugoslavia gave the agency little, if any, influence on the course of Allied policy in Yugoslavia. Yugoslavia lay within the theater of operations where British and Soviet interests predominated, which meant that British intelligence agencies had responsibility for implementing policy as it related to the resistance movements. Roosevelt's main concern with the Balkans throughout the war was how best to stay out. Military aid to the Partisans was important especially for holding Axis units back from anticipated targets of Allied action.[1]

Based on the analysis of the final reports of OSS liaison officers from Yugoslavia, it can be summarized that every officer favored and supported the movement he participated in, with some officers retaining a certain level of criticism, whereas the others operated under the impression of the movement to which they belonged. OSS liaison officers in the Yugoslav Army in the Fatherland (the Chetniks) favored and supported Mihailović's mostly inactive fight against the Axis powers and waiting for the final "D-Day." They also wrote about collaboration between the Chetniks in Herzegovina and Montenegro, but they never witnessed Mihailović personally collaborating with the Axis powers. In comparison to those with the Partisans, OSS agents in the Chetnik movement could move freely and carry out intelligence activity.

The true value of the OSS missions was that they supplied much important information about the military power and deployment of the Axis powers in Yugoslavia, the Partisan and Chetnik resistance movement, and the weather conditions in the Balkans. OSS missions also organized significant amounts of the Allied military aid that was sent specially to the Partisan movement and saved the lives of many Allied airmen. OSS intelligence reports from the Partisan National Liberation Movement assessed the Partisans on a positive level, particularly regarding tactics, guerrilla fighting, situational awareness, high morale, and great desire for the liberation of their homeland. It should not be forgotten, however, that OSS officers wrote several critical reports on the Partisan struggle and their communist orientation. Due to restricted gathering of intelligence messages, OSS believed at the end of the war that intelligence reports from Yugoslavia were not created on the basis of information secretly gathered by agents because they received information on the basis of extracts provided by the Partisans. In many cases the same intelligence extracts were received by the British, and therefore the information was unnecessarily duplicated and sent to the bases.

In the OSS reports the Partisan movement was evaluated as only capable of guerrilla and sabotage warfare and as unable to grow into a strong army capable of frontal attacks, major maneuvers, and conquest of territories. In analyzing the activity of all of the missions and groups responsible for the penetration into Austria, it can be concluded that the Partisans blocked every effort by the Anglo-American Allies to obtain intelligence reports from Austria, infiltrate agents, and organize an Austrian partisan movement against the German regime. The Allied personnel were not allowed any autonomous activity in gathering intelligence or questioning captives, fugitives, and similar persons that came from the territory under German control. The Yugoslav Partisans were afraid that the Allied efforts

Conclusion

in Austria would conflict with their territorial aspirations for Klagenfurt and Villach.[2]

Especially at the end of the war, OSS became actively involved in addressing the issue of postwar Yugoslavia and its borders, and it produced a number of intelligence analyses and reports concerning the military and political situation in Yugoslavia. A new theme in post–1991 Yugoslav history is the study of Yugoslav-born OSS agents. They entered OSS voluntarily, and their only wish was the liberation of their homeland. OSS recruited Yugoslavs into its ranks based on prior consent by the Yugoslav government in exile and, later on, the Partisan authorities. After OSS selected and trained Yugoslavs to become their agents, they were normally sent to the Partisan and Chetnik resistance movements. Some of the Yugoslav-born agents that worked for the British or American intelligence agencies suffered a tragic fate after the war as a result of distrust and intrigues of the Yugoslav Communist Party and the Yugoslav intelligence services.

Chapter Notes

Abbreviations and Codes for Chapter Notes and Bibliography

A Force—Organization to facilitate the escape of Allied prisoners of war behind enemy lines

ACRU—Air Crew Rescue Unit

AFHQ—Allied Force Headquarters for operations in the western Mediterranean

BAF—Balkan Air Force

CCS—Combined Chiefs of Staff (British-American)

CLN—Committee of National Liberation Italy (*Comitato di liberazione nazionale*)

CLNG—Committee of National Liberation Venezia Giulia (*Comitato di liberazione nazionale Giuliano*)

COI—Coordination of Information (precursor of the OSS)

FIS—Foreign Information Service

FNB—Foreign Nationalities Branch

FO—Foreign Office

Force 133—Cover name for SOE Middle East

FRUS—Foreign Relations of the United States

G-2—Army Intelligence

HQ—Headquarter(s)

IAMM—Independent American Military Mission

ISLD—Inter-Services Liaison Department

JCS—Joint Chiefs of Staff

JPO-SS—Slovenian Section of the Yugoslav Auxiliary Committee (*Jugoslovanski pomožni odbor-slovenska sekcija*)

KP—Communist Party (*Komunistična partija*)

Chapter Notes

MACMIS—Maclean's Mission

Massingham—SOE mission in Africa covering Italy

MEDTO—Mediterranean Theatre of Operations

METO—Middle East Theater of Operations

MID—Military Intelligence Division

MI6 (also SIS)—Military Intelligence 6, Secret (Special) Intelligence Service

MI9—Military Intelligence 9, Combined Services Detailed Interrogation Centre, Escape and Evasion Service

NATO—North African Theater of Operations

NKOJ—National Committee of National Liberation of Yugoslavia (*Nacionalni komite narodne osvoboditve Jugoslavije*)

NKVD—People's Commissariat for Internal Affairs (*Narodnyi Kommissariat Gosudarstvennoi Bezopastnosti*)

ÖFF—Austrian Liberation Front (*Österreichische Freiheits Front*)

ONI—Office of Naval Intelligence

OSS—Office of Strategic Services

OSS/MO—OSS / Moral Operations Branch

OSS/R&A (also R&A)—Research and Analysis

OSS/SI—OSS / Secret Intelligence, also Information Branch

OSS/SICE—OSS / Secret Intelligence Central Europe

OSS/SO—OSS / Special Operations Branch

OWI—Office of War Information

OZNA—Department of National Security (*Organizacija za zaščito naroda*)

POW—Prisoner-of-war

PWB—Psychological Warfare Branch

PWE—Political Warfare Executive

RAF—Royal Air Force

RG—Records Group

SACMED—Supreme Allied Commander Mediterranean

SBS—Special Bari Service

SCI—Special Counter-Intelligence

SCU 6—Cover for Massingham mission, also known as the British Inter Services Signal Unit

SIS—Secret Intelligence Service (*Servizio informazioni segrete*)

SOE—Special Operations Executive

SOM—Special Operations Mediterranean

SPOC—Special Projects Operations Center

UDBA—State Security Department (*Uprava državne bezbednosti*), also known as the UDV (*Uprava državne varnosti*)

Ultra—British code name for intelligence gathered by decrypting German wireless communications enciphered on the Enigma machine during the Second World War

USAFIME—United States Army Forces Middle East

Preface

1. Ford 1992.
2. Cave Brown 1976.
3. Harris Smith 1972.
4. Smith 1983.
5. Pirker 2010.
6. Jakub 1999.
7. O'Donnell 2004.
8. Chalou (ed.) 1992.
9. Lindsay 1998.
10. Makdauel 2015.
11. Seitz 1953.
12. Kloman 2005.
13. Pešić 2004.
14. Pavlović 1998.

Chapter 1

1. O'Donnell 2004, pp. xiv–xvi.
2. Smith 1983, pp. 50–51.
3. The National Archives, London, Kew (TNA) Foreign Office (FO) 371/26966, Addressed to Sofia no. 6, My Telegram no. 4, 18 January 1941.
1942; Pavlović 1998, p. 9; Roberts 1973, p. 12.
4. Pavlović 1998, pp. 10–12.
5. Biber 1996, p. 42.
6. TNA PREM 4/25/5, Donovan's Report, pp. 1–6.
7. Loewenheim et al. 1975, p. 133.
8. Tasovac 1999, pp. 55–163.
9. Tasovac 1999, pp. 156–157.
10. Klemenčič 1987, p. 143.
11. Klemenčič 1987, p. 146.
12. Keegan 2005, pp. 155–156.
13. Since 1942 they were called the Yugoslav Army in Fatherland.
14. Harris Smith 2005, pp. 118–119.
15. Klemenčič 1987, p. 146
16. Loewenheim et al. 1975, p. 498.
17. Terzić 2008, pp. 120–132.
18. Čepić 2014, pp. 11–12. German harsh reprisals in Serbia against the civilians were the key element to understand why the Mihailovic forces halted their military operations in November 1941. But they remained anti-Axis oriented untile the end of the war.

Chapter 2

1. TNA HS 8/115, Record of discussion regarding collaboration between British and United States SOE, 26 June 1943; TNA HS 8/115, Summary of agreement between British SOE and American SO, 8 September 1942, pp. 1–9; D. Biber: Neuspeh neke misije: Ameriški podpolkovnik OSS Robert McDowell v štabu Draže Mihajlovića leta 1944, Borec, Vol. 41, No. 10–11, 1989 (hereinafter: Biber: Neuspeh), p. 1066.
2. TNA WO 204/1160, Extract from a letter from Lord Moyne to Field Marshal Sir John Dill, 29 June 1943; HS 5/150, G/A1/415, no date.
3. NARA, RG 226, E 144, B 87, F 938, SOE/OSS Collaboration in the Middle East, 28 July 1943; E 99, B 55, F 5, August 1943, n.d.; Lindsay: Ognji v noči, p. 47.
4. TNA HS 5/150, Minutes of meeting between OSS and SOE, 29 September 1943, pp.1–2.
5. TNA HS 8/7, OSS in the Balkans, 16 November 1943.
6. NARA, M 1642, Rol l18, Memorandum to Joint Warfare Committee, 1 December 1942.
7. NARA, RG 226, E 190, B 125, F 637, Interesting Facts about the Development of OSS, Bari, no date, p. 5; TNA HS 3/57, SOE/OSS Relation in North Africa, 27

September 1943; E 144, B 87, F 938, Historical Report, Operations of OSS Based on Middle East, 31 July 1944; Bajc 2006, p. 68; Smith 1983, pp. 179–180.

8. The cover name for SOE Middle East was also Force 133.

9. NARA, M 1642, Roll 2, OSS Activities in the North African Theater Based on Algiers, no date, p. 19.

10. TNA HS 7/283, SOE/OSS in the Middle East, June 1943, p. 177.

11. NARA, RG 226, E 99, B 54, F 2, History of OSS-Cairo, no date, pp. 1–12.

12. Pavlović 1998, p. 134.

13. NARA, RG 226, E 190, B 72, F 15, Organization of American Intelligence in Guerrilla-Controlled Yugoslavia, 15 July 1943.

14. NARA, RG 226, E 99, B 55, F 1, 14 July 1943.

15. NARA, RG 226, E 99, B 36, F 8, Establishment of Operations and Intelligence Net in Yugoslavia, 7 August 1944, pp. 1–6; E 99, B 55, F 1, Mocarski to Macfarland, no date.

16. NARA, RG 226, E 154, B 19, F 254, Yugoslav Section SI in Bari, Italy-from 30 October 1943 to 12 July 1944, pp. 1–34.

17. NARA, RG 226, E 99, B 35, F 7, Cables, 30 August 1944; E 190, B 72, F 12, Cairo/Bari Relationship, 25 March 1944.

18. NARA, RG 226, E 99, B 135, F 210, OSS Contact with Tito via Italy, no date.

19. NARA, RG 226, E 99, B 135, F 210, OSS, SO Shipping Operation, Italy-Yugoslavia, no date, p. 13.

20. Ford 1992, pp. 24, 26.

21. NARA, RG 226, E 190, B 125, F 637, Interesting Facts about the Development of OSS, Bari, no date, p. 5.

22. NARA, RG 226, E 99, B 135, F 210, OSS Contact with Tito via Italy; E 99, B 135, F 210, Josip Smodlaka, no date.

23. NARA, RG 226, E 99, B 135, F 210, Base at Vis, no date, p. 15; E 165, B 9, F 84, Supply Difficulties Being Encountered by This Section, no date, p. 1; E 165, B 9, F 84, Major F. N. Arnoldy, HQ SBS, Bari, 23 May 1944.

24. NARA, RG 226, E 190, B 125, F 637, Interesting Facts about Development of OSS, Bari, no date, pp. 2–4, Ford 1992, p. 28.

25. NARA, RG 226, E 144, B 96, F 15,

SO Operations in Yugoslavia, 8 January 1944.

26. NARA, M 1642, Roll 2, Appendix F, OSS Activities in the Middle East—Central African Theater Based on Cairo, p. 27.

27. NARA, RG 226, E 190, B 125, F 637, Interesting Facts about the Development of the OSS, Bari, from 18 March to 1 May, 1945, pp. 1–13; Pavlović 1998, pp. 156–159; Ford 1992, pp. 28–29.

28. NARA, RG 226, E 154, B 14, F 190, Intelligence Officer and Chief, SI, SBS, 23 June 1944.

29. NARA, RG 226, E 154, B 19, F 256, Major Arnoldy to Director OSS Donovan, 28 August 1944; Biber 2006, p. 339; E 154, B 19, F 255, Personal History, no date; E 154, B 23, F 317, Yugoslav Reaction to Marshal Alexander's Statement, no date.

30. For more details on the Yugoslav Royal Guard Battalion: Torkar 2014; DREŠČek 2004.

31. NARA, RG 226, E 154, B 15, F 200, Joining Instruction for no. 4 Parachute Training School, CMF, no date; RG 226, E 99, B 43, F 214, Training, no date, pp. 2–5.

32. NARA, RG 226, E 99, B 29, F 210, Semi-Monthly Training Report, 30 November 1944.

33. NARA, RG 226, E 99, B 29, F 5, Monthly Training Report, 14 December 1944.

34. NARA, RG 226, E 154, B 15, F 200, Organization of Training of the Yugoslav Section SI, Advance Base Bari, Italy, 11 February 1944.

35. NARA, RG 226, E 154, B 6, F 99, Report for the Week 30 January to 5 February, no date.

Chapter 3

1. Ford 1992, p. 4.
2. Ford 1992, p. 21
3. Biber 1989, p. 1067; Ford 1992, pp. 3–5.
4. Ford 1992, pp. 51, 53.
5. NARA, M 1642, Roll 185, Report of Walter Mansfield, pp. 3–5.
6. NARA, RG 226, E 144, B 97, F 1019, Seitz to OSS, 25 October 1943.
7. NARA, RG 226, E 99, F 5, B 55, November 1943.

8. ACRU was independent American unit under the command of Mediterranean Allied Air Force (MAAF) and attached to the Fifteenth Air Force in attempt to separate it from the intelligence-gathering and special-operations functions of OSS.

9. For more details on the Halyard Mission (known as Operation Air Bridge): NARA, RG 226, E 154, B 25, F 357, Report on Halyard Mission, ACRU, 10 January 1945, pp. 1–9; E 99, B 42, F 8, Report by 1st Lt. George S. Musulin on the Activities of the Halyard Mission in Connection with the Evacuation of Airmen from Mihailovich (Chetnik) Territory between 5 July 1944 and 27 August, pp. 1–5; Freeman 2009.

10. NARA, M 1642, Roll 185, Air Rescue Unit, 18 August 1944; Ford 1992, pp. 100–101, 109.

11. For more details on the Ranger mission: NARA, RG 226, E 99, B 42, F 8, Yugoslavia-An Examination of Yugoslav Nationalism, 23 November 1944; E 99, B 34, F 174, Mihailovich's Field Report 1944, 10 December 1944; Biber 1989; Tomasevich 1975; Ford 1992.

12. NARA, RG 226, E 139, B 273, F 3992, General Information Yugoslavia, 30 June 1944; RG 226, E 136, B 21, F 219, Donovan-Glavin, 19 September 1944; M 1642, Roll 185, Air Rescue Unit, 18 August 1944; O'Donnell 2005, pp. 96–99; Kimbal 1986, p. 80; Biber 1989, pp. 1069–1070; Ford 1992, pp. 114–133.

Chapter 4

1. More on Captain Melvin Benson's activity at the Supreme Headquarters of the Yugoslav Partisans can be found in his final reports: NARA, RG 226, E 154, B 25, F 359, Final Report Capt. Melvin O. Benson, 22 June 1944, pp. 1–42; M 1642, Roll 85, Report of Liaison with Tito and Operations in Yugoslavia, Captain M. G. Benson, 28 January 1945, pp. 1–30.

2. Ford 1992, p. 4.

3. Ford 1992, pp. 17,19.

4. Ford 1992, pp. 33–35.

5. Ford 1992, pp. 76–77.

6. Sulzberger 1969, pp. 244–245.

7. TNA FO 178/31, Location state of BMM to JANL personnel in the field, 12 September 1944, pp.1–6; Ford 1992, p. 61.

8. NARA, RG 226, E 190, B 660, F 985, Selvig Report, no date; Ford 1992, pp, 151.

9. NARA, RG 226, E 154, B 25, F 354, Reedwood mission, no date; Ford 1992, pp. 157, 158.

10. Ford 1992, pp. 79–80.

11. NARA, RG 226, E 190, B 116, Holt Green to Paul West, 1 February 1944; Ford 1992, p. 138.

12. NARA, RG 226, E 146, B 63, F 859, Weil to Richard Sudgeit, 21 April 1944; Roberts 1973, pp. 205, 212–213; Horvat 2006, p. 79.

13. Ford 1992, pp. 139, 155.

14. TNA FO 178/31, Location state of BMM to JANL personnel in the field, 12 September 1944, pp.1–6; Ford 1992, pp. 139, 172.

15. TNA FO 178/31, Location state of BMM to JANL personnel in the field, 12 September 1944, pp.1–6; Ford 1992, pp. 143–144.

16. Ford 1992, p. 144.

17. Ford 1992, p. 152.

18. John Hamilton was the allias of the Hollywood actor Sterling Walter Hayden.

19. NARA, RG 226, E 224, B 308 and 320, F "Hayden, Sterling W.," catalog. archives.gov/id/2175283; Ford 1992, p. 157.

20. TNA FO 178/31, Location state of BMM to JANL personnel in the field, 12 September 1944, pp.1–6; NARA, RG 226, E92, F231, F2.

21. TNA CAB 122/1595, Control of SOE/OSS Operations in the Balkans, 17 February 1944, pp. 1–2.

22. FRUS 1966, pp. 1369–1370.

23. NARA, RG 226, E 154, B 69, F 176, Robert Joyce to John Toulmin, 25 August 1944; M 1642, Roll 85, Memorandum of Information for the Joint U.S. Chiefs of Staff, March 1945; RG 226, E 154, B 25, F 352, Activities of the American Military Mission, from 9 April to 15 April 1945.

24. Harris Smith 2005, pp. 121–150; Klemenčič 1987, p. 154.

25. NARA, RG 226, E 99, B 43, F 4, The Independent American Military Mission to Marshal Tito, March 1945, pp. 1–2; E 139, B 273, F 3992, Independent American Military Mission to Marshall Tito, 11 August 1944.

26. NARA, RG 226. E 133, B 273, F 3992, From Gen. Donovan to Col. Huntington, no date, pp. 1–2; Bajc 2006, p. 212.

27. Ford 1992, pp. 161–162.

28. NARA, RG 226, E 99, B 34, F 3, Mediterranean Theater of Operations, December 1944; E 154, B 24, F 330, Independent American Military Mission to Marshal Tito-Final Report of Colonel Ellery C. Huntington, Jr., 27 December 1944, p. 11.

29. NARA, RG 226, E 99, B 43, F 4, Activities of the American Military Mission, 9 October 1944–15 April 1945, pp. 1–6; Klemenčič 1987, pp. 156–157; ; Ford 1992, p 160.

30. NARA, RG 226, E 154, B 25, F 351, OZNA-Tito's Secret Police, no date, pp. 1–5; RG 226, E 99, B 43, F 4, The Independent American Military Mission to Marshal Tito, March 1945, pp. 1–2; RG 226, E 190, B 89, F 26, Activities of the American Military Mission, 9 October 1944–15 April 1945.

31. In March 1945, Tito's National Liberation Army was renamed the Yugoslav Army.

32. NARA, RG 226, E 154, B 22, F 301, Memorandum to U.S. Ambassador to Yugoslavia, 15 May 1945, pp. 1–2: RG 226, E 90, B 6, F 68, Lindsay Belgrade #1365 to Glavin and Maddox, 13 May 1945.

33. NARA, RG 226, E 190, B 167, F 1199, Status of OSS Missions in Yugoslavia, 21 May 1945.

34. NARA, RG 226, E 154, B 22, F 306, Memorandum, American Military Mission to Marshal Tito, 15 May 1945; RG 226, E 190, B 167, F 1199, Attachment of OSS Unit with II Corps, Trieste, 24 May 1945.

35. Biber 2006, p. 330.

36. NARA, RG 226, E 154, B 22, F 301, Slovene Student Group-2nd Training Period, 25 September 1943.

37. NARA, RG 226, E 154, B 22, F 301, Alum Amazon Operations, October 9th, 1943.

38. NARA, RG 226, E 108 B, B 35, F 318, Yugoslav Section, no date.

39. The Slovenian Home Guard units (Sln. *Domobranci*, Germ. *Slowenische Landwehr*) were Slovenian anti-communist and quisling units that operated under the SS as the Police units.

40. Archive of the Republic of Slovenia, Ljubljana (AS) 1851, t.e. 53/II, a.e. 1627, Glavni štab Slovenije, Brzojavke zavezniških misij l. 1943, American Alum Mission, prevod brzojavk ameriške misije, 4 December 1944; West 1992, p. 145; Cave Brown 1976, p. 273.

41. AS 1851, t.e. 53/II, a.e. 1627, Glavni štab Slovenije, Brzojavke zavezniških misij l. 1943, American Alum Mission, prevod brzojavk ameriške misije, 4 December 1944; t.e. 67/I, a.e. 1807, Podatki o slovenskih članih amerikanskih misij.

42. AS 1851, t.e. 24/II, a.e. 1022, Telegrami anglo-ameriške misije v Sloveniji (okt. 1943–jan. 1944), American mission (Amerikanska misija).

43. Biber 1991, p. 100; Biber 2006, p. 331; NARA, RG 226. E 99, B 43, F 214, History of SI Branch, no date; RG 226, E 146, B 205, F 2870, Report on Field Conditions in Slovenia (Yugoslavia), 28 November 1944; RG 226, E 154, B 22, F 301, A Digest from Reports of the Alum Team at the Partisan HQ, no date; RG 226, E 190, B 72, F 13, Letter to Lt. Comdr. McBaine, 16 December 1943; AS 1851, t.e. 67/I, a.e. 1807, American Missions, March–April 1944.

44. NARA, RG 226, E 99, B 43, F 214, History of SI Branch, no date; RG 226, E 99, B 37, F 3, The Activities of the Alum Mission behind the Enemy Lines for the 15th USAAF, no date, p. 16.

45. Biber 2006, p. 337.

46. NARA, RG 226, E 154, B 22, F 301, Yugoslavia-Psychological-Political Warfare and Partisan Culture in Slovenia, 26 August 1944, pp. 1–11; TNA WO 204/9672 A, Psychological-Political Warfare and Partisan Culture in Slovenia, 26 August 1944.

47. Biber 2006, p. 333.

48. Biber 2006, p. 336.

49. NARA, RG 226, E 154, B 22, F 301, Political Appraisal of Slovenia, 14 August 1944, pp. 1–25; TNA WO 204/9672 A, Political Appraisal of Slovenia, 14 August 1944, pp. 1–23; TNA WO 204/9672 A, Psychological-Political Warfare and Partisan Culture in Slovenia, 26 August 1944; RG 226, E 154, B 22, F 301, Military Sit-

uation in Slovenia, 22 August 1944, pp. 1–15.

50. RG 226, E 154, B 22, F 301, How to Do SI Job in Slovenia, 16 August 1944, pp. 1–5.

51. RG 226, E 154, B 22, F 301, A Digest from Reports of the Alum Team at the Slovene Partisan HQ, pp. 1–2; RG 226, E154, B 22, F 301, to Lieutenant Desich, 2 October 1944.

52. Česnik 2007.

53. Lindsay 1998, pp. 58–60.

54. NARA, RG 226, E 154, B 22, F 301, Alum Team, no date; RG 226, E 146, B 205, F 2870, Report on Field Conditions by Captain George S. Wuchinich, 30 November 1944; D. DeBardeleben to Chief SI, November 30th, 1944; RG 226, E 154, B 22, F 301, A Digest from Reports of the Alum Team at the Slovene Partisan HQ, pp. 1–3.

55. NARA, RG 226, E 154, B 19, F 263, Yugoslav Personalities, no date; Lindsay 1998, pp. 58–60.

56. For more on Desich's operation: NARA, RG 226, E 190, B 89, F 26, Supplementary Report of Lt. Desich (Alum Team), Appendix A, 12 June 1945.

57. NARA, RG 226, E 154, B 22, F 301, to Lieutenant Desich, Chief of the Intelligence Service of the American Army (OSS-SI), 2 October 1944; RG 226, E 154, B 19, F 263, Yugoslav Personalities, no date.

58. AS 1851, t.e. 24/I, a.e. 1014, Reports of the Federal Officer with the Federal Missions (April 1945) Poročila zveznega oficirja z zavezniškimi misijami (april 1945), Vrhovnom štabu NOV i PO Jugoslavije, 30 September 1944, p. 2; NARA, M 1642, Roll 85, List of Personnel in Yugoslavia, October 16th, 1944, 12 December 1944; AS 1851, t.e. 24/I, Vrhovnom štabu NOV i PO Jugoslavije, 30 November 1944, p. 2.

59. AS 1851, t.e. 67/I, a.e. 1807, Ameriške misije, May–September 1944.

60. AS 1851, t.e. 67/I, Dopisi z zavezniško misijo (januar 1945), a.e. 1808, por. G. B. Desich, January 1945.

61. NARA, RG 226, E 99, B 31, F 5, Progress Report of Yugoslavia Section, SI, for the Period 1 February to 15 February, 16 March 1945; RG 226, E 136, B 31, F 317, From Alum via Caserta to Cox, 11 February 1945.

62. RG 226, E 154, B 22, F 301, Alum, 2. Report: Political Appraisal of Slovenia, 14 August 1944, pp. 9, 23–24.

63. NARA, RG 226, E 136, B 37, F 417, From Florence to Relay, 3 June 1945; RG 226, E 190, B 89, F 26, Supplementary Report of Lt. Desich (Alum Team), Appendix A, 12 June 1945; Biber 1992, p. 133.

64. AS 1851, t.e. 24/II, a.e. 1023, Člani zavezniških vojnih misij v Sloveniji (1943–1945), kartoteka članov zavezniških vojnih misij v Sloveniji, 1943–1945; NARA, RG 226, E 154, B 22, F 301, SI Yugoslavia, Operations File, no date.

65. Lindsay 1998, p. 61.

66. Lindsay 1998, p. 122.

67. Jevnikar 2000b, pp. 203–205; Lindsay 1998, p. 61.

68. NARA, RG 226, E 154, B 22, F 301, Replacement of Personnel at Alum Met, 17 July 1944.

69. AS 1851, t.e. 24/I, a.e. 1014, Poročilo zveznega oficirja z zavezniškimi misijami (april 1945), Seznam osebja britanske in ameriške misije na ozemlju Slovenije, November 1944, p. 4; NARA, RG 226, E 154, B 23, F 319, Mission to Northern Slovenia, 18 April 1944, pp. 1–3.

70. For more on MI 9 and Lindsay: Foot and Langley 1979, p. 205.

71. NARA, RG 226, E190, B 167, F 1212, Recommendation for Award, 23 May 1945; TNA WO 202/457, Cuckold Mission, 17 July 1944

72. Lindsay 1998, p. 56.

73. NARA, RG 226, E 154, B 23, F 319, MO Operations in Slovenia, 4 April 1944, pp. 1–4; Lindsay 1998, pp. 55–56.

74. NARA, RG 226, E 154, B 23, F 319, Moral Operations in Slovenia, 4 April 1944.

75. NARA, RG 226, E 144, B 79, F7 90, Attached Report, 5 April 1944, pp. 1–4; RG 226, E 154, B 23, F 319, MO Operations Slovenia, 4 April 1944.

76. NARA, RG 226, E 99, B 31, F 5, Report of Major Franklin A. Lindsay, 13 January 1945, pp. 1–22; the report is published in Slovenian together with remarks by Tone Ferenc (1983b, pp. 84–98).

77. For more on the Bearskin and Ratweek operations: Bajc 2008.

78. NARA, RG 226, E 154, B 21, F 292,

Cuckold Mission Difficulties, 26 October 1944; Lindsay 1998, p. 213.
79. Lindsay 1998, p. 193.
80. NARA, RG 226, E 99, B 31, F 5, Report of Major Franklin A. Lindsay, 13 January 1945, pp. 17–19.
81. NARA, RG 226, E 99, B 31, F 5, Report of Major Franklin A. Lindsay, 13 January 1945, p. 18.
82. AS 1931, 301–88/ZA, t.e. 742, Ameriška vojna misija pri GŠS, Lindsay Franklin A, III181739, p. 1.
83. Lindsay 1998, p. 145.
84. Lindsay 1998, p. 255.
85. AS 1931, 301–88/ZA, t.e. 742, Ameriška vojna misija pri GŠS, Seznam članov ameriške vojne misije pri GŠS.
86. NARA, RG 226, E 136, B 29, F 209, from Goodwin to Suker, 27 September 1944.
87. NARA, RG 226, E 136, B 29, F 209, from Goodwin to Suker, 27 September 1944.
88. AS 1851, t.e. 24/I, a.e. 1011, Poročila zveznega oficirja z zavezniškimi misijami (April 1945), Vrhovnom štabu NOV i PO, p. 4.
89. AS 1851, t.e. 24/I, a.e. 1011, Poročila zveznega oficirja z zavezniškimi misijami (April 1945), Vrhovnom štabu NOV i PO, p. 4.
90. NARA, M 1642, Roll 102, Flotsam Mission, pp. 12–13.
91. NARA, RG 226, E 99, B 31, F 5, Progress Report of Yugoslavia Section, SI, for the Period 1 February to 15 February, 16 March 1945; RG 226, E 154, B 25, F 356, Final Report of Mulberry Team, March 1944-March 1945.
92. NARA, RG 226, E 154, B 25, F 343, Report of Flotsam Mission, Final report, no date.
93. Captain John Blatnik (1911–1991), an American Slovenian, had parents from Dobindol and Gorenje Sušice near Novo Mesto. He was a child of Slovenian immigrants, born in the mining town of Chisholm, Minnesota. Before the war, he was a member of the Minnesota Senate, and a member of the Congress after the war.
94. AS 1931, 301–88/ZA, t.e. 742, Ameriška vojna misija pri GŠS), Blatnik, II18172.

95. Biber 1988e; also in: NARA, RG 226, E 154, B 25, F 348, Report of Captain John Blatnik on His Duty Tour in Yugoslavia (Croatia and Slovenia), during the Period August 1944-September 1944 and November 1944- May 1945.
96. Biber 1998e, p. 200
97. NARA, RG 226, E 154, B 22, F 306, Intelligence Cables Received from Field Agents during the Period 1 August to 15 December 1944.
98. Biber 1998e, p. 203.
99. Biber 1998e, p. 209.
100. Biber 1998e, pp. 208–209.
101. Biber 1998e, pp. 210–211.
102. NARA, RG 226, E 136, B 22, F 229, Arrow no. 2778, 18 January 1945.
103. AS 1851, t.e. 67/I, archival unit 1808, February 1945, March 1945, Gospodu kapetanu Blatniku.
104. Xa MAS was a special military unit of the Italian Navy. After 8 September 1943, it remained faithful to Mussolini and the Italian Social Republic (RSI). The unit received its name from the Italian light torpedo boat MAS.
105. AS 1851, t.e. 67/I, archival unit 1808, February 1945, March 1945, Gospodu kapetanu Blatniku.
106. NARA, RG 226, E 139, B 38, F 249, Arrow no. 89, 1 January 1945; Bajc 2006, pp. 327, 359.
107. NARA, RG 226, E 154, B 25, F 332, Intelligence Report, 18 April 1945.
108. NARA, RG 226, E 139, B 38, F 245, Arrow no. 87, May 1st, 1945; RG 226, E 136, B 22, F 229, 17 January 1945. Biber 1995, p. 263.
109. Biber 1992, p. 132; Bajc 2006, p. 327.
110. This was an Italian intelligence service that crossed over to the Anglo-American side after the capitulation of Italy. According to certain information, Lago's mission was also sent by ISLD, but under the name Patriot.
111. NARA, RG 331, E British-U.S. Zone, B 872, F 59, Oreste Lago for Blatnik, 30 July 1945; Bajc 2006, pp. 204–206.
112. Biber 1992, p. 134. For more: Pirjevec 2009.
113. In the American archival documents he is mentioned under the name

Michael Hollinger (born 30 August 1919 in Chicago, who came to study in Yugoslavia in 1936). More on Hollinger in: NARA, RG 226, E 154, B 25, F 367, Michael Hollinger; E 190, B 168, F 121, Michael Hollinger, 4 March 1945; Dornik Šubelj 2006, pp. 81–92.

114. AS 1931, 301–88/ZA, t.e. 742, Ameriška vojna misija pri GŠS, Rekonstrukcija ameriških misij in "comandusov") III181812; NARA, RG 226, E 154, B 25, F 367, Michael Hollinger, no date; E 190, B 168, F 121, Michael Hollinger, 4 March 1945.

115. NARA, RG 226, E 154, B 25, F 367, Michael Hollinger, no date.

116. AS 1931, 301–88/ZA, t.e. 742, Ameriška vojna misija pri GŠS, Rekonstrukcija ameriške misije iz dobe NOB, Blatnik John-poročilo, III0014790.

117. The region forms the western part of Yugoslavia, bordering the Italian region of Friuli-Venezia Giulia. It stretches from the Adriatic Sea in the south to the Julian Alps in the north. The Slovenian Littoral comprises two traditional provinces: Gorizia and Slovenian Istria.

118. Bajc 2006, p. 107.

119. AS 1851, t.e. 20/I, Glavnemu štabu NOV in PO Slovenije in obveščevalnemu oddelku pri Gl. Štabu, 19 May 1944.

120. NARA, RG 226, E 99, B 35, F 581, Theater Officer Puch Review, 2 September 1944; RG 226, E 154, B 21, F 293, E. Q. Daddario-It. Branch SI to James Goodwin: Team Date Activities with Partisans and Chetniks, 2 August 1944, pp. 1–3; E 133, B 64, F 553, Confirmation of Parachute Training Taken by Valerio Melchiori, ASN 31795408,5 September 1945; Bajc 2006, pp. 106–107.

121. Moretti 1973.

122. Bajc 2006, p. 109.

123. AS 1851, t.e. 20/I, Poročilo prve ameriške grupe G3 Brindisi, no date.

124. Bajc 2006, pp. 114–115.

125. NARA, RG 226, E 190, B 159, F 1106, Humar Dusan, no date; Bajc 2006, p. 112.

126. NARA, RG 226, E 154, B 22, F 306, Arthur Cox, Acting Chief, Y Desk-HQ 2677th Regt. OSS (Prov.) APO 512, U.S. Army for Col. Huntington: Intelligence Cables Received from Field Agents during the Period 1 August to 15 December, 20 December 1944; E 136, B 37, F 417, Cox for J-3 Pfeiffer (no. 149), April 1945; Maddox for J-3 Pfeiffer (nos. 158 and 159), 28 and 29 April 1945; Cox for J-3 Pfeiffer (no. 163), 1 May 1945.

Chapter 5

1. NARA, RG 226, E 154, B 14, File F 185, Project Austrian Desk SI, 2 March 1944, pp. 1–3; For more on the OSS and the infiltration of other OSS missions to Austria: Biber 2003, pp. 419–420; Bajc 2006, pp. 117–121.

2. Biber 1981, pp. 537–538.

3. Lindsay 1998, pp. 184–187. For more on Hesketh-Prichard's death: Linasi 2004, pp. 112–114.

4. NARA, RG 226, E 190, B 97, F 125, to Bari from Kollender, 12 August 1944; RG 226, E 154, B 25, F 360, Tunic Project, no date.

5. Gorjan 2003, p. 158.

6. AS 1931, 301–88/ZA, t.e. 742, Ameriška vojna misija pri GŠS, Rekonstrukcija ameriške misije iz dobe NOB).

7. NARA, RG 226, E 154, B 25, F 365, Tunic Project, no date, pp. 1–3.

8. NARA, RG 226, E 190, B 118, F 435, Orchid Operation, 30 December 1944; RG 226, E 154, B 18, F 246, Progress Report for Period 1 August-15 August 1944, 14 August 1944; AS 1851, t.e. 24/I, a.e. 1014, Poročila zveznega oficirja zavezniškimi misijami (April 1945) Vrhovnom štabu NOV I PO Jugoslavije, pp. 5, 8; AS 1851, t.e. 24/II, a.e. 1023, Člani zavezniških vojnih misij v Sloveniji, 1943–1945, Kartoteka članov zavezniških vojnih misij v Sloveniji, 1943–1945.

9. NARA, RG 226, E 124, B 28, F 220, Report on Orchid Team, 19 January 1945, p. 2.

10. NARA, RG 226, E 190, B 118, F 435, Orchid Operation, 30 December 1944; RG 226, E 154, B 18, F 246, Progress Report for Period 1 August-15 August 1944, 14 August 1944.

11. NARA, RG 226, E 124, B 28, F 220, Report on Orchid Team, 19 January 1945, pp. 2–13; Lindsay 1998, p. 196.

12. AS 1851, t.e. 21/III, a.e. 893,

Politična poročila štaba 4. operativne cone, 19 October 1944; Ferenc 1983a.

13. NARA, RG 226, E 124, B 28, F 220, Report of Lieutenant Robert Quinn, 4 February 1945, p. 2; RG 226, E 154, B 18, F 246, Progress Report of Labor Desk, 15 October 1944; Biber 2003, pp. 419–420; RG 226, 136, B 34, F 378, Orchid to Chapin, Mosk, 2 October 1944.

14. NARA, RG 226, E 124, B 28, F 220, Report of Lieutenant Robert Quinn, 4 February 1945, pp. 1–3.

15. NARA, RG 226, E 136, B 27, F 283, from Orchid to Mosk, 29 November 1944; RG 226, E 154, B 18, F 246, Operations, 15 January 1945.

16. Biber 2003, p. 422; Lindsay 1983, p. 203; Gorjan 2003, p. 142.

17. NARA, RG 226, E136, B 20, F 206, from Fisher to Chapin, Mosk and McCulloch, Bari, December 22nd, 1944; E 136, B 27, F 283, from Orchid to Mosk, 18 December 1944; AS 1851, t.e. 24/II, a.e. 1023, Člani zavezniških vojnih misij v Sloveniji, Kartoteka članov zavezniških vojnih misij v Sloveniji, 1943–1945.

18. AS 1931, 301–103/ZA, t.e. 610, Koroški odred-obveščevalni center. The reports of two OSS agents were published by Linasi (2004, pp. 112–114); NARA, RG 226, E 190, B 118, F 435, Operations, 15 January 1945; Linasi 2010, p. 296.

19. NARA, RG 226, E 99, B 34, F 6, Mediterranean Theater of Operations, December 1944; E 99, B 33, F 4, Monthly Report for May 1945, 31 May 1945.

20. NARA, RG 226, E 190, B 118, F 435, Operations, no date; E 154, B 18, F 246, Orchid Team Operations, no date; RG 226, E 124, B 28, F 220, Report on Orchid Team Operations, 25 January 1945, pp. 1–13.

21. NARA, RG 226, E 124, B 28, F 220, Report of Lieutenant Robert Quinn, 4 February 1945, pp. 1–3; Ferenc 1983a.

22. NARA, RG 226, E 124, B 28, F 220, Report on Orchid Team, 25 February 1945, p. 3.

23. NARA, RG 226, E 124, B 28, F 220, Report of Captain Fisher, 8 October 1944, pp. 1–2.

24. NARA, RG 226, E 124, B 28, F 220, Report of Captain Fisher, 8 October 1944, p. 3.

25. NARA, RG 226, E 136, B 20, F 206, from Fisher to Chapin, Suker, Cox, 1 December 1944.

26. NARA, M 1642, Roll 46, Captain Charles Fisher, 22 August 1945; E 136, B 20, F 206, from Fisher to Chapin, 1 December 1944; AS 1851, t.e. 24/II, a.e. 1023, Člani zavezniških vojnih misij v Sloveniji, Kartoteka članov zavezniških vojnih misij v Sloveniji, 1943–1945; Linasi 2010, p. 297.

27. NARA, M 1642, Roll 46, Letter to Mrs. Fisher, 25 September 1945.

28. NARA, RG 226, E136, B 31, F 317, 3 March 1945.

29. AS 1931, 301–88/ZA, t.e. 742, Ameriška vojna misija pri GŠS, problem "Hollywood-SBS."

30. AS 1851, t.e. 24/II, a.e. 1023, Člani zavezniških vojnih misij v Sloveniji, Kartoteka članov zavezniških vojnih misij v Sloveniji, 1943–1945.

31. NARA, RG 226, E 133, B 64, F 534, Maple-Grady Mission, 4 June 1945.

32. Gorjan 2003, pp. 147–149.

33. NARA, RG 226, E 139, B 38, F 255, Grady to HMC, May 24th, 1945.

34. Biber 1992, pp. 134–135; NARA, M 1642, Roll 46, Maple-Grady Mission, 31 May 1945; RG 226, E 190, B 118, F 435, Report from Capt. Fisher, no date; E 133, B 64, F 534, Maple, Mansion, 4 June 1945; RG 226, E 124, B 28, F 220, Report from Bob Perry, pp. 1–7; Gorjan 2003, pp. 147–150; RG 226, E 99, B 34, F 6, Mediterranean Theater of Operations, January 1945; RG 226, E 99, B 33, F 4, Monthly Report for May 1945, 3 May 1945.

35. NARA, RG 226, E 99, B 32, F 1, Progress Report, German-Austrian Section, 16–28 February 1945, p. 1.

36. NARA, RG 226, E 99, B 33, F 4, Monthly Report for May 1945, 31 May 1945, p. 3; E 99, B 32, F 1, Progress Report, German-Austrian Section, 16–28 February 1945, pp. 1–2; RG 226, E 124, B 28, F 220, Report on Operation Dania, 20 May 1945.

37. NARA, RG 226, E 124, B 28, F 220, Dania Project, pp. 16–21.

38. NARA, RG 226, E 124, B 28, F 220, Dania Project, p. 23.

39. More about Greenup mission: Pirker 2019.

40. NARA, RG 226, E 124, B 28, F 220, Dania Project, pp. 16–21.

41. NARA, RG 226, E 124, B 28, F 220, Report on Operation Dania, 20 May 1945, p. 23.
42. NARA, RG 226, E 190, B 127, F 676; RG 226, E 99, B 34, F 6, Mediterranean Theater of Operations, January 1945.
43. NARA, RG 226, E 99, B 33, F 3, Semi-Monthly Report of G-4 Section for the Period 16–30 April 1945, 30 April 1945, p. 1.
44. Lindsay 1998, pp. 192–193.
45. Lindsay 1998, pp. 198–199.
46. Linasi 2004, pp. 114–115.
47. For more on the Dillon Mission: NARA, RG 226, E 99, B 32, F 1, Dillon Ground Panel, 28 February 1945.
48. NARA, RG 226, E 108 B, B 64, F 311, German-Austrian Section, no date, p. 3.

Chapter 6

1. Tito 1982, p. 213.
2. Biber 1984c, p. 324.
3. Jenkins 1996, pp. 50–53.
4. NARA, RG 226, E 99, B 34, F 7, MEDTO OG's on Vis, 11 April-12 May 1944; Jenkins 1996, pp. 53–56.
5. NARA, RG 226, E 99, B 35, F 581, Theater Officer Pouch Review, 2 September 1944; E 99, B 26, F 1, Operational Groups, Report for Period 1–31 July 1944, p. 2.
6. TNA, WO 204/577, Commando Raid on Solta, 24 April 1944; NARA, RG 226, E 144, B 68, F 598, Report no. 16, 1 April 1944; M 1642, Roll 2, OSS Activities in the North African Theater Based in Algiers, p. 23; E 99, B 34, F 3, Mediterranean Theater of Operations, December 1944, p. 23; Drešček 2004.
7. NARA, RG 226, E 99, B 36, F 3, Progress Report, 1 May to15 June 1944; Dear 2002, pp. 168–169.
8. NARA, RG 226, E 144, B 68, F 598, Report no. 16, 1 April 1944; E 144, B 68, F 591, Report on Operation Flounced, 13 June 1944; E 144, B 68, F 591, Operation against Mljet, Report on Operation Flounced, 23 May 1944; E 144, B 68, F 599A, 26 June 1944; E 99, B 53, F 4, 11 February 1944; E 99, B 40, F 8, Report on Operation "Theorem," 26 June 1944, pp. 1–3.

Chapter 7

1. Bajc 2000b, p. 133; Klemenčič 1987, p. 166.
2. NARA, RG 226, E 154, B 5, F 85, Interview with Dr. Smodlaka, 2 February 1945.
3. Biber 1996, p. 43.
4. NARA, RG 226, E 100, B 101, Memorandum for Col. Donovan, 20 January 1945; Biber 1995, p. 264.
5. NARA, FNB, INT-30YU-1083 to 1092, 1, Basic Military and Political Situation in Yugoslavia, 17 August 1943.
6. NARA, FNB INT-30YU-1377 to 1386, DeWitt C. Poole, Memorandum for General Donovan, 6 May 1944.
7. Biber 2000, p. 231.
8. NARA, RG 226, E 469, F 3, Received from McBaine, 10 August 1943.
9. NARA, RG 226, E 144, B 97, F 1017, Yugoslavia, Dr. Ivan Čok, no date; E 10 8A, B 26, 20 February 1946, Leading Yugoslav Personalities in Venezia Julia, no date.
10. NARA, RG 226, E 99, B 5, F 1, Introduction, The SI Branch of OSS/ME, no date; RG 226, E 106, B 11, F 55, Emigree Yugoslav Personalities, 17 May 1943; Biber 2000, pp. 232–234.
11. NARA, RG 226, E 210, B 467, Dr. Ivan M. Cok (Tchock), 13 August 1943, pp. 1–2; RG 226, E 154, B 19, F 261, Dr. I. Čok, 5 February 1944.
12. Biber 2000, pp. 232–234.
13. Biber 2000, pp. 232–234.
14. NARA, RG 226, E 154, B 19, F 261, Dr. Tchok's Statement, pp. 1–2.
15. Klemenčič 1987, p. 161; for more on Adamic: Stanonik 1981; Žitnik Serafin 1992.
16. Klemenčič 1987, p. 184.
17. NARA, RG 226, E 106, B 10, F 52, Adamic's Letter to President Roosevelt, 3 February 1942; President Roosevelt's Letter, 3 March 1942.
18. Biber 1988b, p. 68; Klemenčič 1987, p. 224.
19. NARA, RG 226, E 192, B 191, F 17, Inside Yugoslavia by Louis Adamic, 18 December 1942; RG 226, E 92, B 253, F 31, Letter from Captain Murray I. Gurfein to LTC Duke, 27 February 1943; Biber 1988b, pp. 676–692.
20. NARA, RG 226, E 92, B 269, F

30, Letter to Brigadier Donovan, 5 April 1943.

21. Stanonik 1981, pp. 375–376; Arnež 2002, pp. 376–380.

22. NARA, RG 226, E 210, B 469, F 1, From McBaine to Shepardson, 15 September 1943; INT-30YU-674, Memorandum of Conversation with Father Zakrajšek, February 9th, 1943, pp. 1–4; D. Friš 1995, p. 174.

23. NARA, RG 226, E 92, B 515, F 25, Interview with Louis Adamic, 18 February 1944.

24. NARA, RG 226, E 106, F 52, Adamic to Roosevelt, 3 February 1942; E 154, B 19, F 262, Letter to Mr. President, 3 February 1944.

25. Rahten 2009, pp. 108–109.

26. Biber 1995, pp. 263–264.

27. NARA, RG 226, E 106, B 11, F 55, Emigree Yugoslav Personalities, 17 May 1943; Biber 1988b, pp. 676–692.

28. NARA, RG 226, E 92, B 529, The Slovenes and the Partisans, 17 April 1944, pp. 1–13.

29. TNA HS 7/875, Cairo, 2 January 1942; Bajc 2002b, p. 235; NARA, RG 226, E 154, B 15, F 200, Yugoslav Section, SI Personnel, no date, p. 2.

30. NARA, RG 226, E 106, B 15, F 62, Slovenes, Year 1943; RG 226, E 154, B 14, F 190, Section Personnel, pp. 1–3; NARA, RG 226, E 154, B 19, F 263,17 March 1944, from Arnoldy to Močarski.

31. NARA, RG 226, E 106, B 15, F 62, Slovenes, Year 1943; RG 226, E 154, B 19, F 260, Reports on Slovenia by Lt. Bratina, 9 November 1944; RG 226, E 92, B 177, F 1; Sheet "C," pp. 1–2; Žitnik Serafin and Glušič 1999, p. 414; for more on Kobal and his interwar activities: Kobal 1975; Moškon Mešl 2005, pp. 125–154; Žitnik Serafin 1992, pp. 80–92.

32. Kobal 1975, p. 242.

33. Kobal 1975, p. 243.

Chapter 8

1. Vodušek Starič 2002, pp. 350–351. On enemy intelligence service operations in the fight against the resistance movement in Slovenia: Guštin 2009, pp. 24–25.

2. Biber 2005, p. 147.

3. NARA, RG 226, E 125, B 12, F 192, Memorandum, 10 November 1944; Biber 2005, p. 147.

4. Biber 2005, pp. 147, 150.

5. Vauhnik 1972, p. 179.

Chapter 9

1. Smith 1983, p. 190.

2. Biber 1992, p. 127.

3. Peterson 1996, p. 147.

4. Peterson 1996, p. 166.

5. Peterson 1996, p. 177.

Chapter 10

1. Biber 1979a, pp. 145–146.

2. AS 1931, 301–86/ZA, t.e. 742, Angleška vojna misija pri GŠS, Kratek elaborat članov angleških misij in njihovih zvez, p. 113.

3. AS 1931, 301–86/ZA, t.e. 742, Angleška vojna misija pri GŠS, "Inteligens servis!" 11 February 1945, p. 1.

4. AS 1931, 301–86/ZA, t.e. 742, Angleška vojna misija pri GŠS, "Intelligens servis!" 11 February 1945, pp. 1–2.

5. AS 1931, 301–86/ZA, t.e. 742, Angleška vojna misija pri GŠS, "Intelligens servis!" 11 February 1945, p. 3.

6. AS 1931, 301–86/ZA, t.e. 742, Angleška vojna misija pri GŠS, "Intelligens servis!" 11 February 1945, p. 6.

7. AS 1931,301–88/ZA,t.e.742,Ameriška vojna misija pri GŠS, Rekonstrukcija ameriške misije iz dobe NOB), III0019790, p. 1. The meaning of "Be-ga" is unknown.

8. AS 1931,301–2/ZA,t.e.697,OZNA za Jugoslavijo, Poverjeništvo narodne obrambe NKOJ, 10 September 1944, pp. 3–4.

Chapter 11

1. Biber 1996, pp. 47–54; NARA, RG 226, E 92, B 239, F 19, Slovene Underground Newspapers, c. 1943; RG 226, E 92, B 279, F 9, Yugoslav Exiled Officials and the Partisans, 27 August 1943, pp. 1–5.

2. Pleterski 1998.
3. Biber 1995, p. 261.
4. Biber 1995, pp. 263–264.
5. Rahten 2009, pp. 99–100.
6. Kimbal 1986, p. 133.
7. NARA, RG 226, E 144, B 79, F 790, Slovenes under Italy, Prof. Rudolf, pp. 1–2.
8. Biber 1992, pp. 130–131.
9. Biber 2005, pp. 147, 150.
10. Biber 1995, p. 264.
11. Pirjevec 2007, pp. 287–289.
12. NARA, RG 226, E 146, B 64, F 876, Territorial Aspirations of Partisan Yugoslavia, 24 September 1944.
13. Pirjevec 2007, p. 284.
14. Biber 1992, pp. 126–127.
15. Biber 1995, p. 264.
16. Pirjevec 2007, p. 296.
17. NARA, RG 226, E 190, B 167, F 1200, Venezia Giulia, Istria and Southern Austria, 27 April 1945, pp. 1–3.
18. NARA, RG 226, E 190, B 167, F 1199, Attachment of OSS Unit with II Corps, Trieste, 24 May 1945; RG 226, E 99, B 32, F 3, City Units for North Italy, 10 March 1945; Bajc 2009, p. 299.
19. Biber 1992, p. 133.
20. NARA, M 1642, Roll 85, British-Yugoslav Agreements on Occupation of Fiume and Port of Trieste, 3 May 1945; RG 226, E 190, B 167, F 1199, Partisan Actions Pertaining to OSS Intelligence Missions in Yugoslavia, 14 May 945; Biber 1980, p. 440.
21. Biber 1978, p. 476.
22. NARA, RG 226, E 154, B 53, F 909, Immediate Disposition of SO Personnel in Yugoslavia, 11 October 1944, pp. 1–3.
23. TNA, 121/602/178; Pirjevec 2007, p. 312; Biber 1980, p. 439.

Conclusion

1. Ford 1992, pp. 180, 181.
2. NARA, RG 226, E 154, B 23, F 319, Cuckold Mission, no date.

Bibliography
and Primary Sources

Primary Source Abbreviations

AS—Archive of the Republic of Slovenia, Ljubljana

AS 1851—Archive of the Republic of Slovenia, General Headquarters of the National Liberation Army and Partisan Detachments of Slovenia

AS 1931—Archive of the Republic of Slovenia, ex-Archive of the Ministry of Interior Affairs, collection of the Department of National Security (OZNA) Reco US military mission at the General Headquarters; British military mission at the General Headquarters.

NARA—National Archives and Records Administration, College Park, MD; Washington, D.C.

NARA, FNB INT-30YU—National Archives and Records Administration, Foreign Nationalities Branch, collection of microfiches about Yugoslavia

NARA, M 1642—National Archives and Records Administration, Washington's Director's Office, microfilm collection of General William O'Donovan

NARA, RG 226—National Archives and Records Administration, Office of Strategic Service (OSS)

NARA, RG 331—National Archives and Records Administration, Allied Force Headquarters (AFHQ)

PAK—Koper Regional Archive, collection SI PAK KP 834. 2, SI PAK 834. 5, SI PAK 648 (copies of documents from NARA)

TNA—The National Archives, London, Kew

TNA CAB—The National Archives, Cabinet Office

TNA FO—The National Archives, Foreign Office

TNA FO 371—The National Archives, Foreign Office, General Correspondence: Political

TNA FO 898—The National Archives, Foreign Office, Political Warfare Executive, PWE

Bibliography and Primary Sources

TNA HS—The National Archives, Special Operations Executive

TNA HS 3—The National Archives, Special Operations Executive, Africa and Middle East

TNA HS 5—The National Archives, Special Operations Executive, Balkans

TNA HS 6—The National Archives, Special Operations Executive, Western Europe

TNA HS 7—The National Archives, Special Operations Executive, War Diaries, Histories

TNA HS 8—The National Archives, Special Operations Executive, Records of the leadership of the SOE

TNA KV—The National Archives, Records of the Security Service

TNA PREM—The National Archives, Prime Minister's Office

TNA WO—The National Archives, War Office

TNA WO 202—The National Archives, War Office, War of 1939 to 1945, Military Headquarters Papers: Military Missions

TNA WO 204—The National Archives, War Office, War of 1939 to 1945, Military Headquarters Papers: Allied Force Headquarters

Bibliography

Adamic, Louis. 1946. *Dinner in the White House.* New York: Harper.

Alsop, Stewart, and Thomas Braden. 1946. *Sub Rosa: The OSS and American Espionage.* New York: Reynal and Hitchcock.

Armstrong, Hamilton Fish. 1951. *Tito and Goliath.* New York: Macmillan.

Arnež, John A. 2002. *SLS, Slovenska ljudska stranka, Slovenian People's Party: 1941–1945.* Washington: Studia Slovenica.

Bailey, Roderick. 2001. *Target: Italy: The Secret War Against Mussolini 1940–1943.* London: Faber&Faber.

Baily, Ronald H., et al. 1978. *Partisans and Guerrillas.* Alexandria, VA: Time-Life Books.

Bajc, Gorazd. 2000a. Historiografija 1985–2000 o Julijski krajini med svetovnima vojnama. *Prispevki za novejšo zgodovino* 40(1): 331–366.

Bajc, Gorazd. 2000b. *Zapletena razmerja, Ivan Marija Čok v mreži primorske usode.* Koper: Društvo TIGR Primorske.

Bajc, Gorazd. 2002a. Collaboration between Slovenes from the Primorska Region, the Special Operations Executive and the Inter-Services Liaison Department after the Occupation of Yugoslavia. *Annales, Series Historia et Sociologia* 12(2): 363–384.

Bajc, Gorazd. 2002b. *Iz nevidnega na plan, Slovenski primorski liberalni narodnjaki v emigraciji med drugo svetovno vojno in ozadje britanskih misij v Sloveniji* (= *Knjižnica Annales* 30). Koper: Zgodovinsko društvo za južno Primorsko—Znanstvenoraziskovalno središče Republike Slovenije.

Bajc, Gorazd. 2004. Italijanske misije v Furlaniji (1944–1945) v dokumentih Special Operations Executive. *Acta Histriae* 12(2): 147–168.

Bajc, Gorazd. 2005a. Misije Special Operations Executive med italijanskimi partizani v Furlaniji in Karniji (1944–1945) ter njihova percepcija problema jugoslovansko-italijanske razmejitve. *Prispevki za novejšo zgodovino* 45(1): 115–130.

Bajc, Gorazd. 2005b. Pregled britanskih obveščevalnih služb ter njihovih misij, podmisij in operacij med partizani na Primorskem, v Furlaniji in v Karniji (1943–1945). In *Vojna in mir na Primorskem, Od kapitulacije Italije leta 1953 do Londonskega memoranduma leta 1954*, ed. Jože Pirjevec, Gorazd Bajc, and Borut Klabjan, 151–164. Koper: Založba Annales.

Bajc, Gorazd. 2006a. Načrti Special Operations Executive za sabotaže proti nemškim železniškim komunikacijam na Slovenskem od pomladi 1943 do poletja 1944. *Prispevki za novejšo zgodovino* 46(1): 341–349.

Bajc, Gorazd. 2006b. *Operacija Julijska krajina*. Koper: Založba Annales.

Bajc, Gorazd. 2008. Anglo-Američani in sabotaže slovenskih partizanov na južni železnici. *Acta Histriae* 16(3): 343–358.

Bajc, Gorazd. 2009. Gli anglo-americani e le "foibe." In *Foibe, Una storia d'Italia*, ed. Jože Pirjevec, 295–316. Turin: Einaudi.

Bank, Aaron. 1986. *From OSS to Green Berets: The Birth of Special Forces*. Novato: Presidio Press.

Barker, Elisabeth. 1980. *Churchill in Eden v vojni*. Zagreb: Globus.

Barker, Elisabeth. 1982. L'opzione istriana: obiettivi politici e militari della Gran Bretagna in Adriatico (1943–1944). *Qualestoria* 10(1): 3–44.

Barker, Thomas Mack. 1991. *Socialni revolucionarji in tajni agenti, Koroški slovenski partizani in britanska tajna služba*. Ljubljana: Mladinska knjiga.

Biber, Dušan. 1978. Britansko-jugoslovanski nesporazumi okrog Koroške 1944–1945. *Zgodovinski časopis* 32(4): 475–489.

Biber, Dušan. 1979a. Jugoslovanska in britanska politika o Koroškem vprašanju 1941–1945. *Zgodovinski časopis* 32(1): 127–143.

Biber, Dušan. 1979b. Zavezniške misije in obveščevalne službe v NOB. In *Zaščita narodnoosvobodilnega boja*, 140–149. Ljubljana: Republiški sekretariat za notranje zadeve SR Slovenije.

Biber, Dušan. 1980. Britanska in ameriška politika o italijansko–jugoslovanski meji v drugi svetovni vojni. *Zgodovinski časopis* 34(4): 431–441.

Biber, Dušan. 1981. *Tito-Churchill, Strogo tajno*. Zagreb: Globus.

Biber, Dušan. 1983. Pojdem na Štajersko, gledat kaj delajo. *Borec* 35(2): 82–83.

Biber, Dušan. 1984a. Britanske misije o slovenskih etničnih mejah, *Borec* 36(10): 574–575.

Biber, Dušan. 1984b. Le missioni alleate nel Litorale Sloveno (1943–1945), Problemi di storia della Resistenza in Friuli. In *Resistenza e questione nazionale*, ed. Elena Agarossi, 303–319. Udine: Del Bianco.

Biber, Dušan. 1984c. Novi britanski vojaški dokumenti o Titu. *Borec* 36(5): 321–335.

Biber, Dušan. 1988a. Jugoslovanski partizani in Britanci v letu 1944. *Prispevki za zgodovino delavskega gibanja* 25(1–2): 77–93.

Biber, Dušan. 1988b. Louis Adamič v arhivih OSS. *Borec* 40(10): 675–692.

Biber, Dušan. 1988c. "Strogo poverljivo..." (1939–1941): iz zaupnih in strogo zaupnih ukazov kraljevske jugoslovanske vojske. *Borec* 40(11): 1107–1118.

Biber, Dušan. 1988d. Zavezniške misije v Slovenskem primorju. *Borec* 35(8–9): 501–511.

Biber, Dušan. 1988e. Poročilo o službovanju v Jugoslaviji (na Hrvaškem in v Sloveniji), od avgusta 1944 do septembra 1944 in od novembra 1944 do maja 1945. *Borec* 40(2): 199–211.

Biber, Dušan. 1989. Neuspeh neke misije, Ameriški podpolkovnik OSS Robert Mcdowell v štabu Draže Mihajlovića leta 1944. *Borec* 41(10–11): 1065–1091.

Biber, Dušan. 1991. Zavezniške in sovjetske misije ter obveščevalne službe v NOB. *Borec* 43(1–3): 77–138.

Biber, Dušan. 1992. Mednarodni zapleti ob koncu druge svetovne vojne (Ocene in poročila ameriških obveščevalcev, OSS). *Prispevki za novejšo zgodovino* 32 (1–2): 125–137.

Biber, Dušan. 1995. Federalna državnost Slovenije v zavezniških dokumentih do maja 1945. In *Slovenci in država*, 261–266. Ljubljana: Slovenska akademija znanosti in umetnosti.

Biber, Dušan. 1996. OSS o Jugoslaviji—vojna do iztrebljanja. *Prispevki za novejšo zgodovino* 36(1–2): 41–55.

Bibliography and Primary Sources

Biber, Dušan. 1997a. Pastir brez črede. Dr. Ivan Šubašić in OSS Shepherd Project. *Prispevki za novejšo zgodovino* 37(2): 383–398.

Biber, Dušan. 1997b. Utrinki iz arhiva SOE. *Mikužev zbornik*, 145–154. Ljubljana: Oddelek za zgodovino Filozofske fakultete.

Biber, Dušan. 2000. Dr. Ivan Marija Čok kot uslužbenec OSS. *Prispevki za novejšo zgodovino* 15(1): 231–238.

Biber, Dušan. 2001. NOB Slovenije v zavezniških dokumentih, Odpor 1941. In *Zbornik s posveta o 60. letnici Osvobodilne fronte slovenskega naroda*, 213–218. Ljubljana: Borec.

Biber, Dušan. 2003. Ameriške misije, slovenski partizani in prodor na sever. In *Zbornik Janka Pleterskega*, 417–425. Ljubljana: ZRC SAZU.

Biber, Dušan. 2005. Velika Slovenija—Združene države Evrope? In *Vojna in mir na Primorskem: od kapitulacije Italije leta 1953 do Londonskega memoranduma leta 1954*, 147–150. Koper: Založba Annales.

Biber, Dušan. 2006. Poveljnik ameriške obveščevalne misije ALUM o Sloveniji 1943–1944. *Prispevki za novejšo zgodovino* 46(1): 329–340.

Carlisle, Rodney. 2003. *The Complete Idiot's Guide to Spies and Espionage*. New York: Alpha Books.

Cave Brown, Anthony. 1976. *The Secret War Report of the OSS*. New York: Berkley Publishing Corporation.

Cave Brown, Anthony. 1982. *The Last Hero: Wild Bill Donovan*. New York: Times Books.

Čepić, Zdenko. 2014. The Character of World War II, Yugoslav Liberation Struggle and the Alliance. In *Together: Combat Comradeship between the Slovenian Partisans and the Allies*, 11–12. Ljubljana: ZZNOB.

Chalou, George C. 1992. *The Secrets War: The Office of Strategic Services in World War II*. Washington, D.C.: National Archives and Records Administration.

Constantinides, George C. 1983. *Intelligence and Espionage: An Analytical Bibliography*. Boulder, CO: Westview Press.

Corson, William R. 1977. *The Armies of Ignorance: The Rise of the American Intelligence Empire*. New York: Dial Press.

Corvo, Max. 1990. *The OSS in Italy, 1942–1945: A Personal Memoir*. New York: Praeger.

Davidson, Basil. 1946. *Partisan Picture*. London: Bedford Books.

Davies, Philip H. 2005. *MI6 and the Machinery of Spying*. London: Frank Cass.

Deakin, Frederick William Dampier. 1976. *Gora trdnjava*. Ljubljana: DZS.

Dear, Ian. 2002. *Sabotage and Subversion: The SOE and OSS at War*. London: Cassel Military Paperbacks

Djilas, Milovan. 1973. *Memoir of a Revolutionary*. New York: Harcourt, Brace, Jovanovich.

Dobrila, Pavel. 1973. Prvi stik slovenskih partizanov z vojsko Velike Britanije. *Prispevki za zgodovino delavskega gibanja* 13(1–2): 185–209.

Dornik Šubelj, Ljuba. 1999. *Oddelek za zaščito naroda za Slovenijo*. Ljubljana: Arhiv Republike Slovenije.

Dornik Šubelj, Ljuba. 2006. Fieldingova misija v zapisih OZNE, *Prispevki za novejšo zgodovino* 46(2): 81–92.

Dulles, Allen. 1947. *Germany's Underground*. New York: Macmillan.

Dulles, Allen. 1963. *The Craft of Intelligence*. New York: Harper and Row.

Dulles, Allen. 1966. *The Secret Surrender*. New York: Harper and Row.

Dunlop, Richard. 1982. *Donovan: America's Master Spy*. Chicago: Rand McNally.

Dwyer, John B. 1998. *Commandos from the Sea: The History of Amphibious Special Warfare in World War II and the Korean War*. Boulder, CO: Paladin Press.

Earle, John. 2005. *The Price of Patriotism: SOE and MI6 in the Italian–Slovene Borderlands During World War II*. Lewes, UK: Guild.

Enciklopedija druge svetovne vojne 1939–1945. 1982. Ljubljana: Založba Borec.

Feis, Herbert. 1968. *Churchill, Roosevelt, Stalin, vojna, ki so jo vodili in mir, ki so ga krojili*. Ljubljana: Borec.

Bibliography and Primary Sources

Ferenc, Tone. 1977. *Akcije organizacije TIGR v Avstriji in Italiji spomladi 1940.* Ljubljana: Borec.

Ferenc, Tone. 1983a. Opombe k poročilu Franklina Lindsaya. *Borec* 35(2): 112.

Ferenc, Tone. 1983b. Poročilo Franklina A. Lindsaya o misiji na Štajerskem 1944. leta, *Borec* 35(2): 99–114.

Ferenc, Tone. 2002. *Dies irae, Četniki, vaški stražarji in njihova usoda jeseni 1943.* Ljubljana: Modrijan.

Ferenc, Tone, and Milan Ževart. 1982. *Enciklopedija druge svetovne vojne 1939–1945.* Ljubljana: Borec.

Foot, Michael Richard Daniel. 1999. *SOE, Special Operations Executive 1940–1946.* London: Pimlico.

Foot, Michael Richard Daniel, and James Maydon Langley. 1979. *MI 9, The British Secret Service that Fostered Escape and Evasion, 1939–1945 and Its American Counterpart.* London: M. W. Books.

Ford, Corey. 1970. *Donovan of OSS.* Boston: Little, Brown.

Ford, Kirk, Jr. 1992. *OSS and the Yugoslav Resistance, 1943–1945.* College Station, TX: Texas A&M University Press.

Freeman, Gregory A. 2009. *The Forgotten 500: The Untold Story of the Men Who Risked All for the Greatest Rescue Mission of the World War.* New York: New American Library.

Friš, Darko. 1995. *Korespondenca Kazimirja Zakrajška, O.F.M. (1928–1958).* Ljubljana: Arhivsko društvo Slovenije.

Friš, Darko. 2001. Ameriški Slovenci v leto 1941. *Prispevki za novejšo zgodovino* 41(2): 267–279.

FRUS 1961. *Foreign Relation of the United States: 1943, The Conferences at Cairo and Tehran.* Washington, D.C.: Department of State.

FRUS 1964. *Foreign Relation of the United States: 1944,* vol. 2, *Europe.* Washington, D.C.: Department of State.

FRUS 1966. *Foreign Relation of the United States: 1944,* vol. 4, *Europe.* Washington, D.C.: Department of State.

Godeša, Bojan. 1995. *Kdor ni z nami, je proti nam, Slovenski izobraženci med okupatorji, Osvobodilno fronto in protirevolucionarnim taborom.* Ljubljana: Cankarjeva založba.

Gorjan, Bojan. 2003. *Zavezniške misije na Koroškem in Štajerskem 1944–1945, operacija Avstrija.* Koper: Lipa.

Guštin, Damijan. 2005. Sodelovanje Slovencev v zavezniških vojskah ter NOV in POJ zunaj Slovenije. In *Slovenska novejša zgodovina,* ed. Neven Borak et al., 738–740. Ljubljana: Mladinska knjiga.

Guštin, Damijan. 2009. Obveščevalne službe okupatorjev v boju z odporniškim gibanjem: Slovenija 1941–1945. In *Mednarodni znanstveni sestanek "Tajno stoletje"— obveščevalne in varnostne službe ter protiterorizem v 20. stoletju,* 24–25. Koper: Znanstveno-raziskovalno središče.

Harris Smith, Richard. 2005. *OSS: The Secret History of America's First Central Intelligence Agency.* Guilford, UK: The Lyons Press.

Hinsley, Francis Harry. 1994. *British Intelligence in the Second World War.* London: Her Majesty's Stationery Office.

Horvat, Mitja. 2006. *Delovanje diverzantsko obveščevalnih služb SOE in OSS v Jugoslaviji med drugo svetovno vojno,* Bachelor's thesis. Ljubljana, FDV.

Huot, Louis. 1965. *Puške za Tita.* Ljubljana: Borec.

Hymoff, Edward. 1972. *The OSS In World War II.* New York: Ballantine.

Icardi, Aldo. 1956. *American Master Spy.* New York: University Books.

Jakub, Jay. 1999. *Spies and Saboteurs: Anglo-American Collaboration and Rivalry in Human Intelligence Collection and Special Operations, 1940–45.* New York: Palgrave MacMillan.

Jenkins, William G. 1996. *Commando Subaltern at Wars: Royal Marine Operations in Yugoslavia and Italy, 1944–1945.* Mechanicsburg, PA: Greenhill Books.

Bibliography and Primary Sources

Jevnikar, Ivo. 2000a. Iz italijanskega taborišča med padalce OSS I: zgodba Marjana Česnika. *Mladika* 44(7/8): 173–175.

Jevnikar, Ivo. 2000b. Iz italijanskega taborišča med padalce OSS II: zgodba Marjana Česnika. *Mladika* 44(9): 203–205.

Jones, William. 1962. *Dvanajst mesecev s Titovimi partizani.* Ljubljana: Borec.

Kacin-Wohinz, Milica, and Jože Pirjevec. 2000. *Zgodovina Slovencev v Italiji 1866–2000.* Ljubljana: Nova revija.

Keegan, John. 2004. *Intelligence in War: Knowledge of the Enemy from Napoleon to al-Qaeda.* London: Pimlico.

Keegan, John. 2005. *The Second World War.* London: Penguin Books.

Kent, Sherman. 1951. *Strategic Intelligence for American World Policy.* Princeton, NJ: Princeton University Press.

Kimbal, Warren F. (ed.). 1986. *Churchill and Roosevelt: The Complete Correspondence,* vol. 3. Princeton, NJ: Princeton University Press.

Klanjšček, Zdravko. 1999. *Deveti korpus slovenske narodnoosvobodilne vojske 1943–1945.* Ljubljana: Društvo piscev zgodovine NOB Slovenije.

Klemenčič, Matjaž. 1987. *Ameriški Slovenci in NOB v Jugoslaviji, naseljevanje, zemljepisna razprostranjenost in odnos ameriških Slovencev do stare države od sredine 19. stoletja do konca druge svetovne vojne.* Maribor: Obzorja.

Klemenčič, Matjaž. 1997. Načrti za spreminjanje meja, ustvarjanje novih državnih tvorb in meddržavnih povezav v vzhodni srednji Evropi, politika ZDA ter ameriških Slovencev med drugo svetovno vojno. *Prispevki za novejšo zgodovino* 37(2): 399–412.

Kloman, Erasmus H. 2005. *Assignment Algiers: With the OSS in the Mediterranean Theater.* Annapolis, MD: Naval Institute Press.

Kobal, Andrej. 1975. *Svetovni popotnik pripoveduje,* vol. 1. Gorizia: Goriška Mohorjeva družba.

Kristen, Samo. 2000. *Meje in misije, Dileme slovensko–hrvaške razmejitve v Istri v vojaškem, političnem, diplomatskem in obveščevalnem metežu II. svetovne vojne.* Ljubljana: Društvo 2000 / Inštitut za narodnostna vprašanja.

LaFeber, Walter. 1996. *The American Age: United States Foreign Policy at Home and Abroad 1750 to the Present.* New York: W. W. Norton & Company.

Laurie, Clayton D. 1996. *The Propaganda Warriors: America's Crusade against Nazi Germany.* Lawrence, KS: University Press of Kansas.

Linasi, Marjan. 2004. Še o zavezniških misijah ali kako in zakaj je moral umreti britanski major Cahusac. *Zgodovinski časopis* 57(1–2): 99–116.

Linasi, Marjan. 2010. *Koroški partizani: protinacistični odpor na dvojezičnem Koroškem v okviru slovenske Osvobodilne fronte.* Klagenfurt: Mohorjeva družba.

Lindsay, Franklin. 1983. *Beacons in the Night: With the OSS and Tito's Partisans in Wartime Yugoslavia.* Stanford, CA: Stanford University Press.

Lindsay, Franklin. 1998. *Ognji v noči: z OSS in Titovimi partizani v medvojni Jugoslaviji.* Ljubljana: Zveza združenj borcev in udeležencev NOB.

Liptak, Eugene. 2009. *Office of Strategic Services 1942–1945: The World War II Origins of the CIA.* New York: Osprey Publishing.

Loewenheim, Francis L., Harold D. Langley, and Manfred Jonas, eds. 1975. *Roosevelt and Churchill: Their Secret Wartime Correspondence.* London: Barril and Jenkins.

Mackenzie, William. 2002. *The Secret History of SOE: The Special Operations Executive 1940–1945.* London: St Ermin's Press.

Maclean, Fitzroy. 1957. *Tito, the Man Who Defied Hitler.* New York: Ballantine Books.

Maclean, Fitzroy. 1965. *Eastern Approaches.* London: Four Square Books.

Makdauel, Robert. 2015. *Streljanje istorije: ključna uloga Srba u drugom svetskom ratu.* Beograd: RAD.

Mattingly, Robert E. 1989. *Herringbone Cloak—GI Dagger: Marines of the OSS.* Washington, D.C.: History and Museums Division Headquarters, U.S. Marine Corps.

Menčak, Franc. 1999. Med padalci ameriške službe OSS. *Mladika* 3(10): 241–245.

Bibliography and Primary Sources

Messenger, Charles. 1985. *Commandos: The Definitive History of Commando Operations in the Second World War.* London: William Kimber & Co. Ltd.

Mlakar, Boris. 2003. *Slovensko domobranstvo 1943–1945, Ustanovitev, organizacija, idejno ozadje.* Ljubljana: Slovenska matica.

Moretti, Aldo. 1973. Le missioni militari alleate e italiane nel periodo della resistenza in Friuli. *Storia Contemporanea in Friuli* 3(4): 81–118.

Moškon Mešl, Mojca. 2005. *Politično delovanje Andreja Kobala v ZDA.* Master's thesis. Ljubljana: University of Ljubljana.

Nećak, Dušan. 1972. Pisarna za zasedeno ozemlje. *Kronika* 20(2): 101–106.

Nećak, Dušan. 1991. Jugoslovanska begunska vlada in problem meja na Slovenskem (1941). In *Slovenski upor 1941, Osvobodilna fronta slovenskega naroda pred pol stoletja,* ed. Ferdo Gestrin, Bogo Grafenauer, and Janko Pleterski, 201–213. Ljubljana: Slovenska akademija znanosti in umetnosti.

O'Donnell, Patrick K. 2004. *Operatives, Spies and Saboteurs: The Unknown Story of the Men and Women of World War II's OSS.* New York: Free Press.

Pavlović, Vojislav G. 1998. *Od monarhije do republike: SAD in Jugoslavija (1941–1945).* Belgrade: Clio.

Persico, Joseph E. 1979. *Piercing the Reich: The Penetration of Nazi Germany by American Secret Agents during World War II.* New York: Viking Press.

Persico, Joseph E. 2001. *Roosevelt's Secret War, FDR and World War II Espionage.* New York: Random House.

Pešić, D. Miodrag. 2004. *Misija Haljrad: spasavanje američkih pilota od strane četnika generala Draže Mihailovića u Drugom svetskom ratu.* Belgrade: Pogledi.

Peterson, Neal H., ed. 1996. *From Hitler's Doorstep: The Wartime Intelligence Reports of Allen Dulles, 1942–1945.* University Park, PA: The Pennsylvania State University Press.

Philby, Kim. 1968. *My Silent War.* New York: Grove Press.

Piekalkiewicz, Janusz. 1973. *Secret Agents, Spies, and Saboteurs.* New York: William Morrow.

Piekalkiewicz, Janusz. 1973. *Vohuni, agenti, vojaki, Za kulisami druge svetovne vojne.* Ljubljana: Cankarjeva založba.

Pirjevec, Jože. 1995. *Jugoslavija 1918–1992, Nastanek, razvoj ter razpad Karadjordjevićeve in Titove Jugoslavije.* Koper: Lipa.

Pirjevec, Jože. 2000. Britanska tajna organizacija na Slovenskem (1940–1941). *Prispevki za novejšo zgodovino* 40(1): 323–330.

Pirjevec, Jože. 2007. *"Trst je naš!": boj Slovencev za morje (1848–1954).* Ljubljana: Nova revija.

Pirjevec, Jože. 2009. *Foibe: Una storia d'Italia.* Turin: Einaudi.

Pirjevec, Jože, et al. 2005. *Vojna in mir na Primorskem. Od kapitulacije Italije leta 1943 do Londonskega memoranduma leta 1954.* Koper: Založba Annales.

Pirker, Peter. 2010. *Gegen das "Dritte Reich": Sabotage und transnationaler Widerstand in Österreich und Slowenien 1938–1940.* Klagenfurt: Kitab.

Pirker, Peter. 2013. SOE Agents in Austria: Persecution, Post-War Integration and Memory. *Zgodovinski časopis* 67(1/2): 202–227.

Pirker, Peter. 2019. *Codename Brooklyn: Jüdische Agenten im Feindesland. Die Operation Greenup 1945.* Innsbruck: Tyrolia.

Pleterski, Janko. 1998. Predlog za ohranitev rapalske meje in delitev Slovenije. *Acta Histriae* 6(6): 326–328.

Polmar, Norman, and Allen Thomas Benton. 2004. *Spy Book, The Encyclopedia of Espionage,* 2nd ed. New York: Random House.

Rahten, Andrej. 2009. *Izidor Cankar: diplomat dveh Jugoslavij.* Mengeš: Center za evropsko prihodnost and Ljubljana: Znanstvenoraziskovalni center Slovenske akademije znanosti in umetnosti.

Repe, Božo. 1988. *Mimo odprtih vrat, Izbrani dokumenti o dejavnosti okupatorjevih sodelavcev na Slovenskem.* Ljubljana: Borec.

Bibliography and Primary Sources

Rigden, Denis. 2001. *SOE Syllabus: Lessons in Ungentlemanly Warfare World War II*. London: Public Record Office.

Ritchie, Sebastian. 2004. *Our Man in Yugoslavia. The Story of a Secret Service Operative*. London: Frank Cass.

Roberts, Walter A. 1973. *Tito, Mihailovich and the Allies*. New Brunswick, NJ: Rutgers University Press.

Roosevelt, Kermit. 1976. *The War Report of the OSS*. New York: Walker.

Sacquety, Troy James. 2007. The OSS. *Veritas: Journal of Army Special Operations History* 3(4): 34–51.

Schmidt, Amy. 2002. Hrvatska i zapadni saveznici. *Časopis za suvremenu povijest* 34(1): 71–91.

Schmidt, Amy. 2005. Vladko Maček i Hrvatska seljačka stranka: prizori iz izbjeglištva. *Časopis za suvremenu povijest* 37(2): 407–422.

Seitz, Albert. 1953. *Hoax or Hero?* Ohio: Columbus.

Šepić, Dragovan. 1983. *Vlada Ivana Šubašića*. Zagreb: Globus.

Smith, Bradley F. 1983. *The Shadow Warriors: OSS and the Origins of CIA*. New York: Basic Books.

Stafford, David. 2000a. *Roosevelt & Churchill: Men of Secrets*. London: Abacus.

Stafford, David. 2000b. *Secret Agent, The True Story of the Special Operations Executive*. London: BBC.

Stanonik, Janez. 1981. *Louis Adamič, simpozij, symposium*. Ljubljana: Univerza v Ljubljani.

Stewart, Richard W. 2005. *American Military History: The United States Army in a Global Era*, vol. 2. Washington, D.C.: US Army Center of Military History.

Sulzberger, Cyrus Leo. 1969. *A Long Row of Candles*. New York: Macmillan.

Tasovac, Ivo. 1999. *American Foreign Policy and Yugoslavia 1939–1941*. College Station, TX: Texas A&M University Press.

Terzić, Milan. 2008. American-Yugoslav Relations in the Second World War (1941–1945). In *125 Years of Diplomatic Relations between the USA and Serbia*, ed. Ljubinka Trgovčević, 120–132. Belgrade: Faculty of Political Sciences.

Tito [Josip Broz]. 1982. *Sabrana djela*, vol. 23. Belgrade: Komunist.

Tomasevich, Jozo. 1975. *War and Revolution in Yugoslavia, 1941–1945, The Chetniks*. Stanford: Stanford University Press.

Torkar, Blaž. 2012. *Prikriti odpor: ameriška obveščevalna služba na Slovenskem med drugo svetovno vojno.* Celovec: Mohorjeva.

Torkar, Blaž. 2014. Slovenci in Jugoslovanski kraljevi gardni bataljon. *Prispevki za novejšo zgodovino* 54(1): 144–157.

Troha, Nevenka. 1999. *Komu Trst: Slovenci in Italijani med dvema državama*. Ljubljana: Modrijan.

Vauhnik, Vladimir. 1972. *Nevidna fronta*. Foreword by Makso Šnuderl. Ljubljana: Delo.

Vodušek Starič, Jerca. 2002. *Slovenski špijoni v SOE: 1938–1942*. Ljubljana: author.

West, Nigel. 1992. *Secret War: The Story of SOE, Britain's Wartime Sabotage Organization*. London: Hodder & Stoughton.

Žitnik Serafin, Janja. 1982. *Louis Adamič in sodobniki: 1948–1951*, Ljubljana: Slovenska akademija znanosti in umetnosti.

Žitnik Serafin, Janja, and Helga Glušič (eds.). 1999. *Slovenska izseljenska književnost 2, Severna Amerika*. Ljubljana: Rokus.

Oral Sources

Česnik, Marijan. 2007. Marijan Česnik, 1919–2011, wireless operator, interpreter and a member of OSS missions Arkansas in Alum at Slovenian Partisan headquarters. Oral report (interview).

Drešček, Janko. 2004. Janko Drešček, 1921–2009, member of the Yugoslav Royal Guard Battalion and British commandos. Oral report (interview).

Index

Index

Index

183

Index

Index